Questions *and* Answers

D1205399

Questions *and* Answers

Intellectual Foundations of Judaism

JACOB NEUSNER

© 2005 by Hendrickson Publishers, Inc.
P. O. Box 3473
Peabody, Massachusetts 01961-3473

ISBN 1-56563-865-4

Printed in the United States of America

First Printing — November 2005

Cover Art: Menorah with 7 branches. Joseph Assarfati, Cervera Bible. 1299. Cervera, Spain. Ms. 72, f. 316v. Location: Biblioteca Nacional, Lisbon, Portugal.

Photo Credit: Giraudon / Art Resource, NY. Used with permission.

Library of Congress Cataloging-in-Publication Data

Neusner, Jacob, 1932–
    Questions and answers : intellectual foundations of Judaism / Jacob Neusner.
        p. cm.
    Includes indexes.
    ISBN 1-56563-865-4 (alk. paper)
    1. Rabbinical literature—History and criticism. 2. Judaism—History.
3. Jews—History. 4. Judaism—Doctrines. I. Title.
    BM496.5.N48165 2005
    296.1'206—dc22
                                        2005023160

For
Dick and Sue Rader
Oklahoma Baptist University
Shawnee, Oklahoma
Who, together with their colleagues and students, inspired this book

TABLE OF CONTENTS

Part 4. The Sources of Rabbinic Judaism:
Lore (Aggadah)

Part 6. Halakah and the Theology of Rabbinic Judaism: How Does the Law Embody the Torah's Narrative Theology?

Part 7. Social Doctrines of Rabbinic Judaism: Family, Gender, Virtue, and Work

Part 8. Rabbinic Judaism and Christianity: Points of Intersection of Two Coordinate Scriptural Systems

ACKNOWLEDGMENTS

William S. Green

Mayer Gruber

Ithamar Gruenwald

Douglas Knight

John Kutsko

A. J. Levine

INTRODUCTION

Two world religions emerged from antiquity. Each one in its way realized a universal vision of humanity in God's image, after God's likeness. Both spoke of a Messiah, a kingdom of priests, and a holy nation. Both held as God's word the holy Scriptures of ancient Israel. They shared fundamental theological and ethical teachings, beginning with the Golden Rule: "You shall love your neighbor as yourself." (Lev 19:18b)

The other one is rabbinic Judaism.

Everybody knows about Christianity. A great many people want to know more about the other, and for them, I wrote this book. I aim at affording access to rabbinic Judaism in its own integrity and categories, as much as possible illustrated by its own authentic and authoritative texts, in English.

Two religions from one Scripture

What makes the two religious traditions comparable? Christianity in its orthodox, catholic statement and Judaism as constructed by the rabbinic sages intersect in the Hebrew Scriptures of ancient Israel. They represent comparable, but conflicting, responses to the same Scriptures. What I set forth is how to understand another religious language, besides that of Christianity, which emerges from ancient Israelite Scripture. That religious language forms the idiom of rabbinic Judaism in its own terms. At the end, I address questions concerning rabbinic Judaism as it intersects with Christianity. But even answering questions of particular interest to students of the New Testament, I focus on rabbinic Judaism, its classical sources and perspective. I do not pretend to be a scholar of the New Testament, only a student of scholars of that subject.

Knowing about rabbinic Judaism is important for Christianity because it provides a context for comparison and contrast. It affords perspective on both religious systems. That is captured in the questions, *How else* serve the God made known in ancient Israelite Scripture? What other way to tell the next chapter in Scripture's story? How otherwise to read Scripture, than "our" way? In place of the Bible of Christianity, the Old and New Testaments, rabbinic Judaism points to the Torah, written and oral. By "the Torah," or teaching, rabbinic Judaism means the written revelation (Christianity's Old Testament) as interpreted by oral tradition written down by the rabbinic sages of the first six centuries C.E.[1]

Christianity first read forward from apocalyptic and prophetic passages of the Old Testament to the New. It then also read backward from the New Testament to the Old, finding the meaning of the ancient Scriptures in the person of Jesus Christ set forth in the new ones. Rabbinic Judaism first read backward from the oral tradition to the written, finding validation for the one in the other. It then also read forward from what it called the written Torah to the oral Torah, grounding tradition in Scripture, continuing the story of Israel that Scripture told about the holy people. Rabbinic Judaism found the meaning of the ancient Scriptures to be realized in Israel's enduring life of sanctification now aimed at salvation in the end of days. It insisted that holy Israel, God's people, defined as those that know God and accept his dominion, continued to embody and carry forward the narrative of the Torah.

Today Jews and Christians concur that Judaism is the religion of the Old Testament. That is both true and untrue. Judaism rests on the Hebrew Scriptures, but the Torah encompasses more than those Scriptures. And, for its part, Christianity is no less the religion of the Old Testament. (That is so even though some Christians may not see a close tie between the Hebrew Scriptures and their beliefs about Jesus or the Christian ethic.) But Christianity finds the Scriptures' realization in the New. Each heir to Scripture gains perspective in the encounter with the common heritage as framed by the other.

Judaism benefits the student of the New Testament

Why then should New Testament learning find place for the rabbinic writings of the same formative age? Beginning students in introductory courses in New Testament and early Christianity frequently ask

---

[1] C.E. = the Common Era, equivalent to A.D.

the questions addressed here because they take up writings that presuppose knowledge of the ancient Scriptures and traditions. Jesus taught what he understood to be the Torah, at numerous points going over ground shared with rabbinic tradition. The Gospels were written by people who revered the Torah. The Evangelists and the apostle Paul took for granted that God had revealed his will to Moses at Mount Sinai and that the record of that revelation set the stage for the advent of Jesus Christ, defined his mission, explained his message.

Not all Christians concurred. Gnostic Christians rejected the Hebrew Scriptures and the God who made himself known in them. Gnostic Christianity can be studied without constant reference to Israelite Scriptures and others' reading of them. But orthodox, catholic Christianity cannot. That is because in the fullness of its formation, normative Christianity would make a critical component of its statement in the Bible, the Old and New Testaments joined. And because of that conjunction there is scarcely a line of the New Testament that one can fully and exhaustively understand without knowledge of the heritage of ancient Israel. In that setting rabbinic Judaism affords access to the context in which competing Israelites received and realized that heritage. It supplies not only facts that clarify passages in the Gospels and writings of Paul, but perspective. And it does so systematically, so that the two religious traditions, the Christian and the rabbinic-Judaic, may be compared as wholes, each in its entirety, to one another.

But I focus not on rabbinic Judaism through the ages but only upon aspects that interest New Testament studies. I address the frequently asked questions about rabbinic Judaism most likely to confront New Testament students as they seek a context for the life and teachings of Jesus, his disciples and apostles: What options in understanding the life of Jesus were available to Christians? Why did they reject some of those options? And why did other Jews exercise them? Here I spell out simple answers to basic questions of fact. I spell out what the competing system—the other Judaism, the one that began in the same time as, and endured for more than 2,000 years in competition with, Christianity—looked like when fully realized in its own earliest writings beyond Scripture.

Traits of rabbinic Judaism that enrich New Testament study

Students must immediately ask, do the rabbinic documents of the first six centuries actually tell us about the Judaism that Jesus practiced?

Are we really able to find handbooks of first century Judaism when we open the Mishnah, ca. 200 C.E., the Tosefta, ca. 300 C.E., the Talmud of the Land of Israel, ca. 400 C.E., the Talmud of Babylonia, ca. 600 C.E., and the Midrash-compilations of Scriptural exegesis produced by the rabbinic sages from ca. 250 to ca. 600 C.E.? Surely we cannot take for granted that writings completed 200 to 600 years later can routinely attest to facts and conceptions of the time of Jesus, centuries earlier!

The Gospels alone tell us about the shape of knowledge that informs them. They guide. They form the best test for defining the world of Judaism in which they took shape. They take for granted facts of normative behavior and belief: law and theology. How then does the much later Rabbinic canon contribute, if we cannot look into the Mishnah and Talmuds and Midrash for a handbook of Judaism in Jesus's time?

First, facts of the Gospels and Paul's letters and the rabbinic writings intersect. When we find that numerous legal and theological passages of the canon of rabbinic Judaism address these same facts, we see how the two readings of the Torah compete and gain perspective on both. True, that is not in time, synchronically. Rather, it is in logic. The two approaches appeal to the same received revelation, each in accord with its own system and logic.

What we learn when we see how Christian and Judaic writings deal with the same facts of shared Scripture is how, in a concrete way, each applies its distinctive, basic approach. At that point in common each realizes a certain logic that in its view the shared Scripture sustains. One example serves. The Christian approach to the Sabbath—"the son of Man is Lord of the Sabbath"—contrasts with the Rabbinic Judaic approach to the Sabbath, which emphasizes that one is *required* to save life even through violating the sanctity of the Sabbath. Talking about the same matter, each finds its distinctive message, and we may contrast the two systems. So too comparison is illuminating. Each reading of the common Scripture finds the point of the commandments in the same verse, Lev 19:18, as we have already noticed. So they concur on purpose and proportion, and that is so even though the Rabbinic reading surfaces in a document that came to closure much later than the Gospel's reading.

That is why, though not synchronic, each approach to Scripture's imperatives represents an option exercised by a body of people who thought they, uniquely, constituted the true Israel of which Scripture spoke, to which the Torah was entrusted. And therefore exercises of comparison and contrast prove illuminating. To compare whole systems of thought with one another, we show how one basic logic intersects with the other at transactions of Scripture common to them both. To answer questions of religion, theology, and culture, rabbinic Judaism provides a massive analogue for the purpose of comparison and contrast that religious and theological study requires: context above all else.[2]

In that setting, we turn to our frequently asked questions. My job is to get things straight and make them clear. I will do my best to clarify important traits of rabbinic Judaism that enrich the study of the New Testament and enhance appreciation for its message in its own language and context.

The impetus to write this work

It was when giving the Schusterman Lecture at Oklahoma Baptist University, Shawnee, Oklahoma, that I began thinking about what questions newcomers to New Testament studies were asking themselves about Judaism. Faced with intellectually rigorous Southern Baptist students, whose counterparts in Roman Catholic universities, at Brigham Young University for the Church of Jesus Christ of Latter Day Saints ("Mormons"), and at countless Protestant colleges and seminaries I had been meeting over decades, I decided to write this book. I did so by recollecting frequently asked questions out of forty years of lecturing and adding a few questions I wished that people *would* ask. I submitted my frequently asked questions to colleagues who teach New Testament and Judaism and benefited from their counsel.

---

[2] Jacob Neusner, *Rabbinic Literature and the New Testament: What We Cannot Show, We Do Not Know* (Philadelphia: Trinity Press International, 1993); idem, *Children of the Flesh, Children of the Promise: An Argument with Paul about Judaism as an Ethnic Religion* (Cleveland: Pilgrim Press, 1995); Jacob Neusner and Bruce D. Chilton, *Christianity and Judaism: The Formative Categories* (3 vols.; Philadelphia: Trinity Press International, 1995–1997); idem, *The Intellectual Foundations of Christian and Jewish Discourse: The Philosophy of Religious Argument.* (London: Routledge, 1997 [E-book edition, London: Taylor and Francis, 2001]); idem, *Judaeo-Christian Debates: God, Kingdom, Messiah* (Minneapolis: Fortress Press, 1998); idem, *Judaism in the New Testament: Practices and Beliefs* (London: Routledge, 1995 [E-book edition, London: Taylor and Francis, 2001]); idem, *Types of Authority in Formative Christianity and Judaism: Institutional, Charismatic, and Intellectual* (London: Routledge, 1999 [E-book edition, London: Taylor and Francis, 2001]); idem, *Comparing Spiritualities: Formative Christianity and Judaism on Finding Life and Meeting Death* (Harrisburg: Trinity Press International, 2000); Jacob Neusner and Bruce D. Chilton, eds., *The Brother of Jesus: James the Just and his Mission* (Louisville: Westminster John Knox Press, 2001); Jacob Neusner, Bruce D. Chilton, and Craig A. Evans, eds., *The Missing Jesus: Rabbinic Judaism and the New Testament* (Leiden: E. J. Brill, 2003).

The dedication to two principals of my OBU encounter is because Dick and Sue Rader have found in the holy Scriptures of ancient Israel solace and significance for their suffering; from them I have learned about our shared sense of Scripture.

The use of gender language in this work

A note on gender language and tense. Where I speak in my own voice, I use gender-neutral language. Where I represent rabbinic Judaism, I generally preserve its use of "man" and "his." In the classical writings set forth here, Adam/Man commonly means Adam and Eve. It is rare that Man refers to males only. In these pages, God produces "his."

Also, to describe rabbinic Judaism in its formative age, corresponding to the initial period in the history of Christianity, I use the past tense throughout, for example, rabbinic Judaism maintained . . . believed . . . taught . . . But as a matter of fact, rabbinic Judaism is a living religion, practiced in both its classical formulations, in accord with the theology and law described in these pages, and its modern and contemporary extensions and revisions. At Section 46 we briefly consider the continuation of rabbinic Judaism into our own age.

ABBREVIATIONS

a.k.a.	also known as
b.	*ben,* son
B.C.E.	before the Common Era
ca.	*circa,* about, approximately
C.E.	Common Era
cf.	*confer,* compare
e.g.	*exempli gratia,* for example
Exod	Exodus
Gen	Genesis
i.e.	*id est,* that is
Jer	Jeremiah
Lev	Leviticus
m.	Mishnah
Num	Numbers
p(p).	page(s)
repr.	reprinted
RSV	Revised Standard Version
Song	Song of Songs
vol(s).	volume(s)

PART 1

DEFINING RABBINIC JUDAISM

1. EARLY STAGES OF JUDAISM

What was Judaism in the early centuries of the Common Era?

Judaism, like Christianity, was a religion: a supernaturally-grounded set of beliefs (worldview) and practices (way of life) that defined the life of a given, elect group (holy people, church). Then by "religion" we mean an account of the God-given way of life and the worldview of a determinate social entity: a shared culture grounded in a concept of the holy. In accord with this definition, a religion speaks for not only an "I" but a "we." It is not only the report of an individual's convictions but a systematic account of the way of life of a social group.

Once we stress the social foundations of the religions, Judaism and Christianity, we realize that different groups formed and realized different conceptions of conviction and conduct within those broader groups, different Judaisms or Christianities. That is because diverse groups took shape, each with its way of life and worldview attributed to origin in God's revelation. These groups intersect at some points, e.g., sharing elements of Scripture in common. But they also diverge.

In Christianity we know of orthodox, catholic Christianity, based on Scripture and tradition and realized in the Bible, and also of Gnostic Christianity, groups that rejected the Old Testament and the knowledge of God made known in it. Within orthodox, catholic Christianity, moreover, were diverse Church-communities, for example, the Armenian or the Ethiopian. Christianity came to expression in Aramaic and Syriac, Greek and Latin, Armenian and Coptic, and many other languages, each with its distinctive corpus of holy books as well as Scripture held in common. In Judaism we know of distinct communities of Judaism formed by (1) rabbinic Jews, (2) the community represented by the Dead Sea Scrolls, (3) the community in Egypt documented through papyri from Elephantine, and diverse others. So we must speak of not a single, unitary, monolithic Judaism or Christianity, but Judaisms and Christianities, species of the genus, Judaism, Christianity, respectively.

As soon as we do, we must ask what traits characterize all Judaisms and no other religious systems, distinguishing (any) Christianity from (any) Judaism. A Judaism—any Judaism—was uniquely formed by a worldview, a theory of the social group, and a way of life, defined as follows: (1) A Judaism was a religious system that regarded the Torah as the complete, exhaustive account of God's will; it privileged the Hebrew Scriptures of ancient Israel and within those Scriptures the Torah, i.e., the Pentateuch or Five Books of Moses (Genesis, Exodus, Leviticus, Numbers, and Deuteronomy). (2) A Judaism was a religious system the members of which regarded themselves as uniquely the Israel of which the ancient Scriptures spoke. (3) A Judaism was a religious system the members of which regarded themselves as uniquely subject to God's imperative to carry out the religious obligations contained within the Hebrew Scriptures.

Among the Judaic religious systems of ancient times, the writings of which come down to us, would all qualify? Take the Dead Sea Library, for a test. If the library stands for a determinate community of Israel, as many maintain, then that community certainly (1) privileged the Hebrew Scriptures and among them the Torah of Moses; that community (2) regarded itself as not only Israel but the only Israel; and that community most certainly did (3) observe and keep the commandments of Scripture. The same test validates the claims of communities that are represented by other Judaic writings, besides the Dead Sea Scrolls or those of rabbinic Judaism, to qualify as Judaisms, however much they differ from one another.

Does a Christianity (a "Christian religious system") qualify as a Judaism? It depends upon the particular system, assessed by the criteria just now set forth. Rejecting the Hebrew Scriptures entirely, as the Gnostic Christians did, would serve as a disqualifying fact. Not privileging the Pentateuch would form a negative indicator. Rejecting some, though not all, of the divine imperatives of Scripture would exclude orthodox, catholic Christianity from Pentecost forward. But Jesus and Paul and generations of Christians thought of themselves as part of Israel.

Jesus revered and taught the Torah. He affirmed the uniqueness and election of Israel and regarded his teachings and followers as embodying the Scripture's story. And he kept the commandments. As to Paul, the following captures his view of matters: "But this I admit to you, that according to the Way, which they call a sect, I worship the God of our fathers, believing everything laid down by the law [Torah] or written in the prophets" (Acts 24:14 RSV). On all three indicative matters, to be sure, Jesus and Paul set forth a particular viewpoint and message, which distinguished their view of Israel, its way of life and worldview, from that of other Judaic systems. But that commonplace fact is what requires us to establish the base indicators that we have identified, and by those indicators, the communities formed around Jesus and Paul and James and Peter qualify, with variations, as Judaisms.

What was the relationship between Judaism and ancient Israel?

Judaism—every Judaism—insisted that it continued the life and traditions of ancient Israel. Every Judaism invoked the covenant between God and the founders of the extended family of Israel, Abraham and Sarah's descendants. Each one affirmed the revelation at Sinai that turned the family into a holy people. It staked its claim to truth upon that continuity, regarding its teachings as set forth in the Scriptures of ancient Israel or an extension of those Scriptures.

That continuity represented more than a verbal justification through proof texts drawn from the ancient Scripture for the Judaic system of the day. In fact, there was a historical-theological claim: the Israel of Scripture continued in the Israel of the later times, and the stories of Scripture pertained to that same living Israel.

Judaism, the religion, called itself "the Torah," meaning, the teaching revealed by God to Moses at Sinai, and it defined the Jews—in secular terms sometime an ethnic group and sometime a nation—as the "Israel" about which the Torah spoke.

Then "Israel" encompassed those who told about themselves the stories of the Israelite Scriptures, who took personally those narratives, and who saw the group of which they were part as the continuation, after the flesh and after the spirit, of Israel at Sinai.

2. RABBINIC JUDAISM

What is rabbinic Judaism?

Rabbinic Judaism is the Judaic religious system defined by the belief that at Sinai God revealed the Torah to Moses in two media, writing and memory. Thus it is the Judaism of the dual Torah, written and oral.

The "written Torah" refers to the Hebrew Scriptures of ancient Israel: meaning the Torah, Genesis through Deuteronomy; the Prophets, Isaiah, Jeremiah, Ezekiel, and the Twelve Minor Prophets; and the Writings, Proverbs, Psalms, Job, Chronicles, the Five Scrolls, and so on. The oral or memorized Torah, unique to rabbinic Judaism, was transmitted from master to disciple, from God to Moses, Moses to Aaron, Aaron to Joshua, and so on down, until it was ultimately recorded in the documents produced by the rabbinic sages of the first six centuries C.E. These compilations then claim to preserve the originally-oral tradition.

The Mishnah states in tractate *Avot* 1:1A–B: "Moses received Torah at Sinai and handed it on to Joshua, Joshua to elders, and elders to prophets. And prophets handed it on to the men of the great assembly." The documents in which the rabbinic sages in the chain of tradition from Sinai wrote down the originally oral tradition were the Mishnah (200 C.E.), Tosefta (250 C.E.), two Talmuds (400, 600 C.E.), and Midrash-compilations (250–600 C.E.), which we shall meet later on (cf. Sections 9–17).

Rabbinic Judaism then forms a type of Judaism, not a period in the history of Judaism. It is called "rabbinic," because its official writings were produced by, and constantly cite, sages who bear the honorific title "rabbi" meaning "my lord."[1] Only rabbinic Judaism called Moses "our rabbi." Rabbinic Judaism sometimes is called "Talmudic Judaism," after the Talmud, the commentary to the Mishnah that forms the principal

---

[1] That title applied not only to the authorities of rabbinic Judaism, but also was used as a gesture of respect for other masters of the Torah of Moses at Sinai.

authoritative document of that same Judaism. It is furthermore called "normative Judaism," because, over time, it alone defined the official norms, setting forth "Judaism" pure and simple without further qualification. In these pages we deal with the formative age of that singular Judaic religious system, hence, also, "formative Judaism." But among these names, "rabbinic Judaism" is the most familiar.

How did rabbinic Judaism regard the other Judaic systems and other Jews of antiquity?

Rabbinic Judaism completely ignored other Judaic systems of its time and place. But it explicitly found a place in its salvific plan for most other Jews as essential to "all Israel," whether or not they obeyed the Torah as the rabbinic sages taught it. So the system was at the same time exclusive, as all systems are, and inclusive, making place for nearly all Jews, whether conforming or not, within its account of who and what is "Israel."

Relying only on the rabbinic writings we could not reconstruct the presence of any other system, only of Israelites who did not fully carry out the Torah. True, there were dissenters, but they knew the Torah perfectly well, even though they rejected it in their invincible ignorance. This is how the rabbinic writings characterize "the Minim":

> The books of the Evangelists and the books of the *minim* they do not save from a fire {on the Sabbath day, when it is prohibited to handle fire}. But they are allowed to burn where they are, they and {even} the references to the Divine Name {ordinarily to be protected from destruction} which are in them.

> R. Yosé the Galilean says, "On ordinary days, one cuts out the references to the Divine Name which are in them and stores them away, and the rest burns."

> Said R. Tarfon, "May I bury my sons, if such things come into my hands and I do not burn them, and even the references to the Divine Name which are in them.

> And if someone was running after me, I should go into a temple of idolatry, but I should not go into their houses [of worship].

> For idolators do not recognize the Divinity in denying him, but these recognize the Divinity and deny him.

> And about them Scripture states, *Behind the door and the doorpost you have set up your symbol [for deserting me, you have uncovered your bed]* (Is. 57:8)."

Said R. Ishmael, "Now if to bring peace between a man and his wife, the Omnipresent declared that a scroll written in a state of sanctification should be blotted out by water, the books of the *minim*, which bring enmity between Israel and their Father who is in heaven, all the more so should be blotted out, they and the references to the Divine Name in them.

And concerning them has Scripture stated, *Do I not hate them that hate thee, O Lord? And do I not loathe them that rise up against thee? I hate them with perfect hatred, I count them my enemies* (Ps. 139:21–22)."

Tosefta *Shabbat* 13:5A–J[2]

While not all passages of the rabbinic writings mean by "Minim" Christians (of some sort), this one surely does. Then the point is, the beliefs of the Christians, clearly of Israelite origin ("these recognize . . . and deny") simply reject the truth of the Torah. They have no system of their own.

In regard to the less-than-perfectly-conforming Jews rabbinic Judaism took an inclusive position. They too inherit the world to come, are restored to the Garden of Eden in the general resurrection of the dead. They atoned for sin by death and would inherit the world to come within all Israel. So nearly all Jews formed part of that Israel that is comprised by those who will overcome death, rise from the grave, and regain Eden.

This encompaning policy is expressed in the opening two lines of the famous passage of the Mishnah that announces, all Israelites with few exceptions possess a portion in the world to come (for the exceptions, see below pp. 12–13).

All Israelites have a share in the world to come, as it is said, *your people also shall be all righteous, they shall inherit the land forever; the branch of my planting, the work of my hands, that I may be glorified* (Is. 60:21).

Mishnah *Sanhedrin* 10:1A–B

How did another Judaic system, besides the rabbinic one, regard other Jews of antiquity?

What is the view of a competing Judaic system? A glance at the attitude toward the rest of Israel set forth in the Dead Sea library is instructive. By "Israel" the library of Qumran meant "us"—and no one else. By "us" they indicated simply "Israel," or "the true Israel." That is why the group organized itself as a replication of "all Israel," as they read

---

[2] Brackets originally found in the block quotes are retained. Text found within braces contain the author's additional comments.

about "Israel" in those passages of Scripture that impressed them. They structured their group, in Geza Vermes's language, "so that it corresponded faithfully to that of Israel itself, dividing it into priests and laity, the priests being described as the 'sons of Zadok'—Zadok was High Priest in David's time—and the laity grouped after the biblical model into twelve tribes."[3]

One detail tells us how this group implicitly conceived of itself as the whole of "Israel." It is that the group lived apart from the Temple in Jerusalem and had its liturgical life worked out in utter isolation from the central rites. They had their own calendar, which differed from the one people take for granted and which was observed in general, for their calendar was reckoned not by the moon but by the sun. This completely different method yielded different dates for the holy days and effectively marked the group as utterly out of touch with other Jews. Rabbinic Judaism, by contrast, legislated for the entirety of the Jews, all of them conceived as integral to its "Israel."

---

[3] Geza Vermes, *The Dead Sea Scrolls: Qumran in Perspective* (London: Collins, 1977), 88.

3. JEWS WITHIN RABBINIC JUDAISM

———◆———

Who was, and who was not, a Jew by the definition of rabbinic Judaism?

By the law of rabbinic Judaism, the child of a Jewish mother, even if the father was a gentile, was a Jew. Caste status—priest, Levite, Israelite, and so on—followed that of the father. At issue was marrying within the Israelite community, as made explicit by the law. There were ten castes, with restrictions on marrying from caste to caste as indicated:

> Ten castes came up from Babylonia [in the return to Zion]: (1) priests, (2) Levites, (3) Israelites, (4) impaired priests, (5) converts, and (6) freed slaves, (7) *mamzers*, (8) *Netins,* (9) "silenced ones" [*shetuqi*], and (10) foundlings.
>
> Priests, Levites, and Israelites are permitted to marry among one another.
>
> Levites, Israelites, impaired priests, converts, and freed slaves are permitted to marry among one another.
>
> Converts, freed slaves, *mamzers, Netins,* "silenced ones," and foundlings are permitted to marry among one another.
>
> And what are "silenced ones"?
>
> Any who knows the identity of his mother but does not know the identity of his father.
>
> And foundlings?
>
> Any who was discovered in the market and knows neither his father nor his mother.
>
> Mishnah *Qiddushin* 4:1–2D

Levites were Temple singers and assisted in various rites. Israelites in this context means all those validly born into Israel who have no standing in the Temple. Impaired priests are the offspring of a union prohibited to the priesthood by the Torah, e.g., a priest who married a divorcée. Mamzers are the children of parents who can never legally wed, e.g., a brother and a sister. Netins are descendants of Temple servants of ancient Israelite times. Silenced ones and foundlings are defined in context. All of these form the castes of Israel, meaning, in secular language, they qualified as Jews.

Was Jesus a Jew by the definition of Judaism? Was Paul a Jew?

By any definition Jesus and Paul, Peter, James, Stephen, Matthew, Mary, Joseph, among the entire family and community of nascent Christianity—all belonged to Israel the holy people. None at any point in his or her life thought otherwise.

Did the rite of circumcision mean that one was a Jew, and would its absence disqualify?

An Israelite male was born into Israel, as was a female, and that identification was indelible from the womb. Circumcision was required of all males, home-born and converts. But it did not mark a male as an Israelite, birth did. An Israelite by birth who could or did not undergo the rite of circumcision remained a perfectly valid Israelite. Circumcision marked entry into the covenant of Abraham, as we shall see at Section 37.

The rite of circumcision by itself did not transform a Gentile into an Israelite. This is expressed indirectly at Mishnah-tractate *Nedarim* 3:11G–I as follows:

> [If he said,] "*Qonam* [meaning, forbidden to me as is a sacrifice on God's altar in the Temple of Jerusalem] if I derive benefit from the uncircumcised," [thus, if he said, "I am forbidden to derive benefit from uncircumcised males"], he is permitted [to derive benefit] from uncircumcised Israelites but prohibited [from deriving benefit] from circumcised gentiles.

> "*Qonam* if I derive benefit from the circumcised"—he is prohibited [to derive benefit] from uncircumcised Israelites and permitted [to derive benefit] from circumcised gentiles.

For the word "uncircumcised" is used only as a name for gentiles, as it is written, *For all the nations are uncircumcised, and the whole house of Israel is uncircumcised at heart* (Jer. 9:26).

Here is a clear statement of the law of rabbinic Judaism that an Israelite who was not circumcised was a perfectly valid Israelite for all intents and purposes, and a Gentile who was circumcised remained a Gentile.

Could someone stop being a Jew? What caused one to no longer be regarded as part of the group? In other words, did rabbinic Judaism practice some form of "excommunication"?

Once born an Israelite, one could never stop being an Israelite, no matter what he or she did, affirmed, or denied. An Israelite who apostatized could be shunned by the community. But if he or she wanted to return to the community of Israel, the apostate could do so without a rite of reversion; rabbinic Judaism in its formative age never made provision for such, since it held, "An Israelite who sins remains an Israelite."

What about excommunication (Hebrew: *nidui*)? A judicial penalty for maintaining the social order, "excommunication" represented separation from the community, for example, for a period of time for refusing to obey the authority of a rabbinic sage. It was a form of banishment or ostracism. It did not remove the banished person from belonging to Israel. Nothing could.

Why in rabbinic Judaism did belonging to Israel matter?

As we saw above from Mishnah *Sanhedrin* 10:1A–B (see p. 8), the status of being an Israelite mattered, because Israelites were destined to eternal life, meaning, at the end of days they would rise from the grave, stand in judgment, and enter into the world to come, which was Eden restored. Here is how the Mishnah-law states matters explicitly:

All Israelites have a share in the world to come, as it is said, *your people also shall be all righteous, they shall inherit the land forever; the branch of my planting, the work of my hands, that I may be glorified* (Is. 60:21).

And these are the ones who have no portion in the world to come:

(1) He who says, the resurrection of the dead is a teaching which does not derive from the Torah, (2) and the Torah does not come from Heaven; and (3) an Epicurean {hedonist}

R. Aquiba says, "Also: He who reads in heretical books,

"and he who whispers over a wound and says, *I will put none of the diseases upon you which I have put on the Egyptians, for I am the Lord who heals you* (Ex. 15:26)."

Abba Saul says, "Also: He who pronounces the divine Name as it is spelled out."

Mishnah Sanhedrin 10:1A–G

First, it is clear that all Israelites, with the stated exceptions, inherit the world to come, no matter what. When they die, they attain atonement for their sins committed in life. When they are raised from the dead, they then are righteous and return to Eden. The exceptions are self-designated: one does not get what one rejects: resurrection as a teaching of the Torah, the God-given status of the Torah, and the life lived wholly in worldly pleasure, with no thought to eternity.

Second, reversing the predicate and the subject yields, "All those who have a share in the world to come are Israelites." That encompasses all who acknowledge the kingdom of Heaven and accept the yoke of the Torah; they alone know and love God. If all Israelites have a share in the world to come, then all those who have a share in the world to come belong to Israel. (The status of Gentiles does not figure here. They are those who rejected the Torah of Sinai. We deal with Gentiles at Section 22, in the setting of theology.)

Why is the system so inclusive, and how come sinners are promised resurrection? Mishnah-tractate *Sanhedrin* 6:2B is explicit that the sinner or criminal who confesses has a share in the world to come. That is because the confession transforms the death into an act of atonement for sin. Then the sin is removed, and the way to resurrection lies open:

. . . whoever confesses has a share in the world to come.

For so we find concerning Achan, to whom Joshua said *My son, I pray you, give glory to the Lord, the God of Israel, and confess to him, [and tell me now what you have done: hide it not from me.] And Achan answered Joshua and said, Truly have I sinned against the Lord, the God of Israel, and thus and thus I have done* (Josh. 7:19[7:20]).

And how do we know that his confession achieved atonement for him? For it is said, *And Joshua said, Why have you troubled us? The Lord will trouble you this day* (Josh. 7:25)—*This day* the Lord will trouble you, but you will not be troubled in the world to come.

Thus through his death, Achan atoned for his sin and qualified for life eternal. Then in the law of rabbinic Judaism death is a medium for removing sin and reconciling the sinner with God (cf. Section 27). That is why nearly every Israelite who dies will rise from the grave to eternal life.

4. THE PLACE OF THE TEMPLE

What was the Temple?

The Temple was a building in Jerusalem set aside for offerings and prayer. The written Torah in the books of Exodus, Leviticus, Numbers, and Deuteronomy provided for worship of God through the provision of animal sacrifices, the blood of the offerings securing atonement when tossed on the altar of unhewn stone. Certain parts of the animal were burned up, with the scent of the smoke reaching heaven. Offerings of grain and wine, the Land's best produce, also were required. The book of Deuteronomy declared that all offerings were to be presented at "the place that I shall choose," understood to mean, Jerusalem's Temple.

That building, held to be God's abode on earth, was erected by King David's son, King Solomon, in the tenth century B.C.E. and stood until 586 B.C.E., when it was destroyed and the people were exiled by the Babylonians. It was restored three generations later, in ca. 530 B.C.E., when the Persian king of kings, Cyrus (whose original kingdom was located in the general area of present-day Iran), took power over the Land of Israel and restored to the Land those exiles who wished to return. The second Temple stood from 530 B.C.E. to 70 C.E.

But it was not a grand edifice. The full restoration took place in ca. 450 B.C.E., the time of Ezra the Scribe and Nehemiah, the Jewish ruler assigned to Jerusalem by the Persians. That second building, greatly improved by King Herod before the turn of the first century C.E., stood until 70 C.E., when it was destroyed by the Romans at the climax of a war fought by Jewish zealots against Roman rule in the Land of Israel. The established pattern of exile and return—586 followed by 530—then was tested once more. Three generations after 70, in ca. 132–135 C.E., an effort to restore the Temple led by the Jewish general, Bar Kokhba, failed, and the Romans forbade Jews even from entering Jerusalem. They furthermore ploughed over the Temple mount and built a pagan temple there.

The definitive end of efforts to restore the animal sacrifices in the Jerusalem Temple came in 360 C.E., after two generations of Christian emperors of Rome (from Constantine, who legalized Christianity in 312). Then a pagan emperor, Julian, came to the throne. In order to embarrass Christianity, which had pointed to the destruction of the Jerusalem Temple as a mark of God's rejection of Israel for denying Christ, he permitted the Jews to rebuild the Jerusalem Temple. But he died in battle before the work had progressed very far.

Does Judaism still practice animal sacrifice, and what media of atonement persist with the Temple in ruins?

From the time of the emperor Julian to the present, Jews have prayed for the advent of the Messiah, who would restore the people of Israel to the Land of Israel, and the Temple and its offerings to Jerusalem. From 70 to the present, in place of animal sacrifices, Judaic worship took the form of prayer, Torah-study, and acts of loving-kindness, which take priority as the medium of atonement:

> One time [after the destruction of the Temple] Rabban Yohanan ben Zakkai was going forth from Jerusalem, with R. Joshua following after him. He saw the house of the sanctuary lying in ruins.
>
> R. Joshua said, "Woe is us for this place which lies in ruins, the place in which the sins of Israel used to come to atonement."
>
> He said to him, "My son, do not be distressed. We have another mode of atonement, which is like [atonement through sacrifice], and what is that? It is deeds of loving kindness.
>
> "For so it is said, 'For I desire mercy and not sacrifice, [and the knowledge of God rather than burnt offerings] (Hos. 6:6).'"
>
> *The Fathers According to Rabbi Nathan* IV:v.2

Contemporary Orthodox Judaism prays for the restoration of the Temple and its offerings. Conservative, Reform, and Reconstructionist Judaisms regard animal sacrifice as a concluded phase in the history of Judaism.

What happened in the Temple?

Sacrifices were of two kinds, public and individual. Individuals would present sin offerings in expiation of violations of the Torah inadvertently committed. Public sacrifices in behalf of all Israel were presented morning and at twilight as well. These were paid for by a half-shekel offering taken from all male Israelites, and atoned for the sin of corporate Israel, as distinct from that of individuals. To make that payment possible, money changers were required to provide the necessary service of changing foreign coinage into that which served in the Temple:

> Once they {the tables of money-changers} were set up in the Temple {to collect the Temple tax}, they began to exact pledges [from those who had not yet paid the tax in specie].

> Mishnah *Sheqalim* 1:3C

Overturning the tables and driving the money changers out, as Jesus is said to have done in John 2:14–16, made it impossible for individuals to join in the corporate atonement. What made the participation of all Israelites critical was to secure for the corporate community atonement for its public sin, beginning with the Golden Calf in the time of Moses and Aaron at Mount Sinai:

> They exact pledges from Israelites for their *sheqels,* so that the public offerings might be made of their [funds].

> This is like a man who got a sore on his foot, and the doctor had to force it and cut off his flesh so as to heal him. Thus did the Holy One, blessed be he, exact a pledge from Israelites for the payment of their *sheqels,* so that the public offerings might be made of their [funds].

> For public offerings appease and effect atonement between Israel and their father in heaven.

> Likewise we find of the heave-offering of *sheqels* which the Israelites paid in the wilderness, as it is said, *And you shall take the atonement money from the people of Israel [and shall appoint it for the service of the tent of meeting; that it may bring the people of Israel to remembrance before the Lord, so as to make atonement for yourselves]* (Ex. 30:16).

> Tosefta *Sheqalim* 1:6B–E

In addition to the public offerings morning and twilight, there were votive offerings presented by individuals through the day. On the three pilgrim festivals, Passover, Pentecost, and Tabernacles (Section 35), festal offerings were presented by Israelites from various parts of the Land and overseas as well. So the Temple was a principal focus of Judaic religious life. Public prayer also was recited, and the Torah was declaimed on occasion as well (Section 7).

Why was the Temple important in rabbinic Judaism?

In the law and theology of rabbinic Judaism, the Temple of Jerusalem was the place at which God and holy Israel meet. That is the highest point on earth, where God receives His share of the natural gifts of the Holy Land—meat, grain, wine, and olive oil—and where through the presentation of these gifts, the Israelite fulfills his obligations to God, inclusive of atoning for sin. Concomitantly, prayers are to be recited in the direction of the Temple. For instance:

> If he was travelling in a ship or on a raft, he should direct his heart towards the Chamber of the Holy of Holies.
>
> Mishnah *Berakhot* 4:6

The priority of the Land of Israel over all other lands, and Jerusalem over all other places, and the Temple over the rest of Jerusalem, is expressed in this language:

> Those who are outside the Land turn toward the Land of Israel, . . . Those who are in the Land of Israel turn toward Jerusalem, . . . Those who are in Jerusalem turn toward the Temple, . . . Those who are in the Temple turn toward the Chamber of the Holy of Holies and pray, . . . It turns out that those standing in the north face south, those in the south face north, those in the east face west, and those in the west face east. Thus all Israel turn out to be praying toward one place.
>
> Tosefta *Berakhot* 3:15A, C; 16A, C. E–F

Why was the Temple so central to rabbinic Judaism? This question is answered in the exposition of the statement that one of the three pillars of the world is the Temple service:

> Simeon the Righteous was one of the last survivors of the great assembly. He would say: "On three things does the world stand: (1) On the Torah, (2) and on the Temple service, (3) and on deeds of loving kindness."
>
> Mishnah *Avot* 1:2

". . . on the Temple service": how so?

> So long as the Temple service of the house of the sanctuary went on, the world was blessed for its inhabitants and rain came down in the proper time. For it is said, "To love the Lord your God and to serve him with all your heart and with all your soul that I will provide the rain of your land in its season, the former rain and the latter rain . . . and I will provide grass in your fields for your cattle" (Deut. 11:13–14).

But when the Temple service of the house of the sanctuary ceased to go on, the world was not blessed for its inhabitants, and rain did not come down in the proper time,

as it is said, "Take heed to yourselves lest your heart be deceived . . . and he shut up the heaven so that there shall be no rain" (Deut. 11:16–17).

The Fathers According to Rabbi Nathan IV:iv.1

The Temple and its sacrificial service therefore forms the foundations for the natural world in which Israel and humanity thrived.

5. THE PLACE OF THE SYNAGOGUE

———◦◦◦———

In the definition of rabbinic Judaism what was a synagogue?

By "synagogue" diverse systems meant different things. How did rabbinic Judaism define the matter in its own context? To know the answer, we start with the simple question, where does Israel meet God?

Viewed as a whole, the law of rabbinic Judaism identifies two locations for the encounter of God and Israel: the altar of the Temple of Jerusalem at the center, and the households and villages arrayed round about. The field or orchard in the Land of Israel, subject as they are to divine commandments, present occasions for the encounter with God; e.g., in the division of the crop between the Israelite proprietor and God's designated surrogates, the priests and the poor. The household provides for meeting with God at mealtime, as another example. Archaeology has turned up buildings devoted to Israelite public gatherings, and in those erected at certain periods the presence of a niche in the wall is generally interpreted to mean that Scrolls of the Torah were located there. Hence such buildings are classified as synagogues, meaning, places for public worship, prayer, and assembly.

But so, in the law of rabbinic Judaism, was the Temple. The Temple was a center not only of sacrificial offerings but also of prayer. Integral to the rites was the recitation of the Shema ("Hear, O Israel, the Lord our God, the Lord is one") and associated blessings:

> The superintendent said to them {the priests}, "Say one blessing."
>
> They said a blessing, pronounced the Ten Commandments, the Shema [Hear O Israel (Dt. 6:4–9)], *And it shall come to pass if you shall hearken* (Dt. 11:13–21), and *And the Lord spoke to Moses* (Num. 15:37–41).
>
> They blessed the people with three blessings: *True and sure, Abodah,* and the blessing of priests.

Mishnah *Tamid* 5:1A–C

The upshot is, prayer—public or personal—in no way is linked by the law of rabbinic Judaism to the synagogue in particular.

And that leads us to ask, where and how does the law find for the synagogue a singular, if not unique, place in its structure and system? Since sages explicitly state that study of the Torah may take place anywhere, and since not only votive but obligatory prayer is offered wherever one is located at the time (excepting inappropriate places such as privies), what is left for the synagogue as a location, or, more to the point, the synagogue as an occasion for meeting God? The answer of the law of the Torah is, the synagogue represents the occasion at which ten or more Israelite males assemble *to provide for the declamation of the Torah to Israel* (embodied in the quorum). The synagogue then takes place anywhere Israel assembles for hearing the Torah declaimed. What is required, even then, is the quorum and the Torah-scroll, not a building consecrated for that purpose.

I cannot overemphasize the limited role assigned to the synagogue building even when a quorum assembles. Among fewer than ten (1) One does not conduct the recitation of the Shema; (2) one does not pass before the ark to lead public worship; (3) one does not raise his hands in the priestly benediction; (4) one does not read in the Torah; (5) one does not conclude from a Prophet; (6) one does not stop and sit after attending a funeral; (7) one does not recite the blessing for mourners; or (8) consolations for mourners; or (9) the groom's blessing; and (10) one does not invite people to say the grace after a meal in God's name (Mishnah-tractate *Megillah* 4:3). Of the items on the list, some may be performed in private by an individual, e.g., (1) and (10); the others are conducted only within the required quorum. Some of the items on the list—the funeral cortège, for instance—clearly do not involve a particular contained space, a synagogue building, others may. But, we realize, since a quorum may assemble in any suitable space, a synagogue finds its definition in terms not of space but of circumstance. While the synagogue is embodied in the quorum, not in the building, once the building is sanctified, it is deemed holier than a contained (or open) space that has not been sanctified.

How is the synagogue defined by the law of Judaism?

So the synagogue finds its definition in its function; it is *not* a place to which Israelites go to meet God, as the Temple is. Rather, it is utopian in the simplest sense: anywhere where ten Israelite males conduct a specified activity, the declamation of the Torah. Then the function of the synagogue is carried out, and that is without regard to the location of the Israelites or the character of the space, if any, that contains them. Now, as a matter of fact, that is explicitly *not* the case when we define the two other venues where Israel and God meet, the Temple and the household living in the "Land of Israel," extending to the village, that is, the household in the land of Israel possessed of a plot of land in the "Land."[4]

To state matters negatively, the Temple cannot be defined as the place where ten Israelites come together to kill a cow. The household in possession of land in the Land of Israel cannot be set forth as a location where ten Israelites produce crops, only a plot of ground owned by an Israelite in the Land of Israel that produces crops. The Temple is locative in that it can only be where it is and nowhere else, in Jerusalem, on the Temple Mount. And, in positive terms, it is there and only there that the activities characteristic of the Temple can be carried out. Israelites may say their prayers anywhere, may gather to hear the Torah declaimed in any location. But to slaughter an animal designated for God, to collect its blood and toss the blood upon a stone altar, to burn up parts (or all) of the animal as an offering made by fire to God—these activities can take place only in one place.

A specific ruling embodies the entire theological message. In its scale of priorities, the synagogue ranks low, well below a Torah-scroll:

> Townsfolk who sold (1) a street of a town {square may} buy with its proceeds a synagogue. [If they sold] (2) a synagogue, they {may} buy an ark {with its proceeds}. [If they sold] (3) an ark, they {may} buy {Torah} wrappings {with its proceeds}. [If they sold] (4) {Torah} wrappings, they {may} buy scrolls [of the prophets or writings] {with its proceeds}. [If they sold] (5) scrolls, they {may} buy a Torah {with its proceeds}.
>
> But if they sold (5) a Torah scroll, they should not buy scrolls {with its proceeds}. [If they sold] (4) scrolls, they should not buy {Torah} wrappings. If they sold (3) {Torah} wrappings, they should not buy an ark. [If they sold] (2) an ark, they should not buy a synagogue. [If they sold] (1) a synagogue, they should not buy a street.
>
> Mishnah *Megillah* 3:1A–J

In the synagogue Israel encounters the publicly-declaimed Torah, and, in the words that are proclaimed, Israel hears God. In that one aspect, the synagogue actualizes the Kingdom of God, not as a place but as an event.

---

[4] We have placed "Land of Israel" and "Land" in quotes to assist the reader to understand these as specific theological terms. This is a theological term used commonly in this book and throughout Judaism.

6. AUTHORITIES IN RABBINIC JUDAISM

Who were the authorities in rabbinic Judaism?

Rabbinic Judaism recognized the rabbinic sage as the highest authority in the holy people of Israel. He was qualified as an authority by mastery of the Torah, knowledge attained through discipleship, in a chain of tradition extending backward to Sinai. But that authority was not institutionalized in a political organization exercising more than moral authority.

The law of rabbinic Judaism designated two institutions to exercise political authority, the king and the high priest. We should immediately remind ourselves that at the time of the Mishnah, the first document after Scripture of rabbinic Judaism, in 200 C.E., there was neither a Temple and high priesthood nor a monarchy to govern the Israelite people. So this account of authority concerned itself with the age of restoration, when the Temple would be rebuilt and the Israelite monarchy in the Davidic house restored.

In the hierarchy of authority, involving high priest, king, and sage, who took priority? As between the high priest and the king, the more important was the king, who was above the law:

> A high priest judges, and [others] judge him; gives testimony, and [others] give testimony about him;
>
> Mishnah *Sanhedrin* 2:1A–B

> The king does not judge, and [others] do not judge him; does not give testimony, and [others] do not give testimony about him;
>
> Mishnah *Sanhedrin* 2:2A–B

But the highest authority of all was the sage, who takes priority over the king and the high priest, by reason of his mastery of the Torah:

A sage takes precedence over a king.

[For if] a sage dies, we have none who is like him, {while} [if] a king dies, any Israelite is suitable to mount the throne.

Tosefta *Horayot* 2:8

What about the high priest? In the hierarchy of the genealogical castes, with the priest at the top, the freed slave at the bottom, the mastery of the Torah disrupts the normal pecking order established by genealogy:

A priest takes precedence over a Levite, a Levite over an Israelite, an Israelite over a *mamzer,* a *mamzer* over a *Netin* {Temple factotum}, a *Netin* over a proselyte, a proselyte over a freed slave.

Under what circumstances? When all of them are equivalent.

But if the *mamzer* {an illegitimate person, whose parents cannot legally marry, e.g., the offspring of incest or of adultery} was a disciple of a sage and a high priest was an *am haares* {ignorant person}, the *mamzer* who is a disciple of a sage takes precedence over a high priest who is an *am haares* {ignorant person}.

Mishnah *Horayot* 3:8

To a society concerned with genealogy, where status was determined by lineage, it would be difficult to express in a more radical way the priority of the Torah in qualifying a person as an authority. Stating that a disciple of a sage who was a Mamzer, excluded from the normal marriage castes, took priority over the high priest, who stood at the pinnacle of the social order, delivers a stunning message.

What was a priest?

In rabbinic Judaism the priest, or *kohen* in Hebrew, was a descendant of Aaron and attained his position through valid genealogy. He was in charge of the sacrificial service to the Lord. Aaron, brother of Moses, was consecrated as the first Israelite priest, and from him all Israelite priests trace their origin via the male line. Scripture holds that the priests are the tribe of Levi, one of the Israelite tribes. The Levites had no land assigned to them in the Land of Israel; they were counted separately in the census; they were supported by a tithe of the crop of the Land. The Levites were chosen for God's service by reason of their loyalty when others strayed. This is the picture of Leviticus chapters 8–10. Priests were sanctified and had to keep purity laws and were restricted in whom they might marry; they could not contract corpse uncleanness except for near of kin. They also taught Torah-instruction to the people, administered the Temple, and maintained its facilities.

What was a rabbi?

A rabbi was a master of the Torah. The rabbi functioned in the Jewish community in ancient times as judge and administrator. But he lived in a society in some ways quite separate from that of Jewry as a whole. The rabbinical academy was, first, a law school. As stated, some of its graduates served as judges and administrators of the law. The rabbinical school was by no means merely a center for legal study, however. It was, like the Christian monastery, the locus for a peculiar kind of religious living. Only one of its functions concerned those parts of the Torah to be applied in everyday life through the judiciary. In ancient, medieval, and modern times these activities and institutions remained remarkably stable.

The school, or *yeshiva* (literally, session), was a council of Judaism, a holy community. In it men learned to live a holy life, to become saints. When they left, sages continued to live by the discipline of the school. They invested great efforts in teaching that discipline by example and precept to ordinary folk. Through the school, rabbinic Judaism transformed the Jewish people into its vision of the true replica of Mosaic revelation. The schools, like other holy communities, imposed their own particular rituals intended in the first instance for the disciples and masters. Later, it was hoped, all Jews would conform to those rituals and so join the circle of master and disciples. As with study, the schools' discipline transformed other ordinary, natural actions, gestures, and functions into rituals—the rituals of "being a rabbi."

What was the basis of the authority of a priest and of a rabbi?

The priest/*kohen* was qualified for his task and authority through genealogy, descent from Aaron; the rabbi through mastery of the Torah learned in discipleship.

Did rabbinic Judaism have priests or honor the priesthood?

Some rabbinic sages originated in the priestly caste and were qualified to do what priests do. They could receive the priestly rations, tithes, and offerings assigned to the priesthood by the Torah. But their status in the rabbinical estate was determined by their mastery of the Torah.

While criticizing the conduct of certain high priests, rabbinic Judaism honored the priesthood, believed in its mission, and placed a high value on the sacrificial offerings to atone Israel's sin, both corporate and personal. That is why, when the Temple was destroyed, rabbinic Judaism mourned for the lost holy place and instituted prayers for its restoration.

Did rabbis perform miracles and were they expected to?

While rabbinic sages are represented as miracle workers, it was their knowledge of the Torah that validated their teaching, and not their capacity to perform miracles. That is expressed in a famous story about a wonder-worker, Honi the Circle-Drawer (a title explained in the story at hand), and how the sages disapproved of his exercise of his wonder-working power:

> On account of every sort of public trouble (may it not happen) do they sound the *shofar* {ram's horn, to awake Heaven to Israel's plight, in commemoration of Abraham's binding of Isaac, Genesis 22},
>
> except for an excess of rain.
>
> [The story is told:] They said to Honi the circle drawer, "Pray for rain."
>
> He said to them, "Go and take in the clay ovens used for Passover, so that they not soften {in the rain which is coming}."
>
> He prayed, but it did not rain.
>
> What did he do?
>
> He drew a circle and stood in the middle of it and said before Him, "Lord of the world! Your children have turned to me, for before you I am like a member of the family. I swear by your great name—I'm simply not moving from here until you take pity on your children!"
>
> It began to rain drop by drop.
>
> He said, "This is not what I wanted, but rain for filling up cisterns, pits, and caverns."

It began to rain violently.

He said, "This is not what I wanted, but rain of good will, blessing, and graciousness."

Now it rained the right way, until the Israelites had to flee from Jerusalem up to the Temple Mount because of the rain.

Now they came and said to him, "Just as you prayed for it to rain, now pray for it to go away."

He said to them, "Go, see whether the stone of the strayers {those who stray} is disappeared {under water}."

Simeon b. Shatah said to him, "If you were not Honi, I should decree a ban of excommunication against you. But what am I going to do to you? For you importune before the Omnipresent, so he does what you want, like a son who importunes his father, so he does what he wants.

"Concerning you Scripture says, *Let you father and you mother be glad, and let her that bore you rejoice*" (Prov. 23:25).

Mishnah Ta'anit 3:8

Simeon b. Shetah's comment is taken to represent the view of rabbinic Judaism that wonder-working is recognized but not deemed the highest form of Heavenly validation. But stories are told of Heaven's answers to sages' prayers and of miracles done for them.

Was Jesus a rabbi?

The Gospels represent Jesus in many ways, and one of them is as a teacher of the Torah in the manner of a rabbinical sage, disciple of John the Baptist. He expounded the Torah when it was declaimed in the synagogue. He appeared like Moses on the Mountain. So by the formal criteria of rabbinic Judaism, in the Gospels' account he certainly qualified as a rabbinical sage. But by the normative criteria of the Torah, written mediated by oral, of rabbinic Judaism he did not. No normative rabbinical sage could use the language, "You have heard it said, but I say to you . . ."

7. PRAYER IN RABBINIC JUDAISM

Where did prayer take place?

People take for granted that synagogues, like churches, are built to accommodate the faithful at prayer. But rabbinic Judaism did not regard the synagogue as the sole or the principal location of public worship. God's service was carried on in the Temple sacrifices, where prayer also was said (cf. Section 5). Prayers, obligatory and votive, could be recited in fields at work, in the home, on a ship, wherever worshipping Israelites were located. What was required for public worship was not a particular location but a quorum of Israelite males (Hebrew: *minyan*), and such a quorum for its part also could assemble anywhere. (Indeed, in contemporary Judaism activities of worship take place in the home, for example, the ceremonial meal for Passover, the rite of circumcision, or a marriage ceremony.) *When* a quorum for worship takes place, then God is present. *Where* that happens makes no difference.

Were there other media of prayer besides worship?

Prayer defined as "communication between the faithful community and God" took place when Israelites addressed God and when God spoke to them. Israel addressed God through prayers, both obligatory and votive, and they received God's words in the Torah as an occasion for God to speak to them. Obligatory prayers include the declaration of God's unity (Shema) and The Prayer (a silent composition of praise and petition), which we meet at Section 8.

Votive prayers were blessings said in response to receiving a blessing from God. For example, when one ate food, a blessing was to be recited, as set forth in the following:

What blessing does one recite over produce?

Over fruit of a tree one says, "{Blessed are you, O Lord, our God, King of the Universe} Creator of the fruit of the tree,"

except for wine.

For over wine one says, "{Blessed are you, Lord our God, king of the universe} Creator of the fruit of the vine."

And over produce of the earth, one says, "{Blessed are you, Lord our God, king of the universe}. Creator of fruit of the ground,"

except for loaves [of bread].

For over the loaf he says, "{Blessed are you, Lord our God, king of the universe} Who brings forth bread from the earth,"

And over greens he says, "{Blessed are you, Lord our God, king of the universe}, Creator of the fruit of the ground."

Mishnah Berakhot 6:1A–H

But enjoying the gifts of God through nature does not present the only occasion for reciting a blessing. Any exceptional event provokes gratitude to Heaven or acceptance of God's beneficent rule:

One who sees a place in which miracles were performed for Israel says, "Blessed is he who performed miracles for our fathers in this place."

[One who sees] a place from which idolatry was uprooted says, "Blessed is he who uprooted idolatry from our land."

Mishnah Berakhot 9:1

For meteors, earth tremors, lightning, thunder, and the winds, one says, "Blessed is he whose power and might fill the world."

For mountains, hills, seas, rivers, and deserts, he says, "Blessed is the maker of [all of] creation . . ."

For the rains and for good tidings, he says, "Blessed is he who is good and does good."

And for bad tidings he says, "Blessed is the true judge."

Mishnah Berakhot 9:2A–B, E–F

If he built a new house, or bought new clothes he says, "Blessed . . . who kept us alive [and brought us to this occasion]."

One [who] recites over evil the blessing [used] for good, or [who recites] over good [the blessing used] for evil

[or] one who cries out about the past—

lo, this is a vain prayer.

How so? If one's wife was pregnant and he said {prayed}, "May it be thy will that she give birth to a male"—lo, this is a vain prayer.

If he was coming along the road and heard a noise of crying in the city and he said, "May it be thy will that those [who are crying] are not members of my household"—lo, this is a vain prayer.

Mishnah Berakhot 9:3

We see that the life of prayer is continuous. The moment of prayer comes when it will. The rabbinic sages reckoned that a pious person would recite upwards of a hundred blessings a day, living a life spent in thanks to God.

How did "study of the Torah" qualify as prayer?

Study of the Torah formed the foundation of piety in rabbinic Judaism. "An ignorant person cannot be pious," tractate *Avot* maintained. In the Torah the Israelite confronted God's word in God's own wording. But in the ordinary sense of prayer as encounter with God's own presence, did study of the Torah qualify as prayer? That question is answered in so many words in the following:

Rabbi Halafta of Kefar Hananiah says, "Among ten who sit and work hard on Torah-study the Presence comes to rest, as it is said, 'God stands in the congregation of God' (Ps. 82:1) {and 'congregation' involves ten persons}.

"And how do we know that the same is so even of five? For it is said, 'And he has founded his vault upon the earth' (Amos 9:6).

"And how do we know that this is so even of three? Since it is said, *And he judges among the judges* {a court being made up of three judges} (Ps. 82:1).

And how do we know that this is so even of two? Because it is said, *Then they that feared the Lord spoke with one another, and the Lord hearkened and heard* (Mal. 3:16).

And how do we know that this is so even of one? Since it is said, *In every place where I record my name I will come to you and I will bless you* (Ex. 20:24) {and it is in the Torah that God has recorded His name}."

Mishnah Avot 3:6

God is present when Israel takes up study of the Torah. That is so because the Torah's words contain the record of God's self-manifestation to humanity at Sinai. It is the permanent account of the encounter with God that the prophets of Scripture and the sages of the Mishnah, Talmud, and Midrash record. In study of the Torah, Israelites return to Sinai and replicate the encounter and make it their own.

What was at stake in study of the Torah?

At stake in study of the Torah is humanity's access to God, and this is stated explicitly in the following account of the plot of Ahaz to wipe out Israel:

> "And it came to pass in the days of Ahaz" (Is. 7:1).
>
> What was the misfortune that took place at that time?
>
> The Syrians on the east and the Philistines on the west [devour Israel with open mouth]" (Is. 9:12).
>
> The matter [the position of Israel] may be compared to a king who handed over his son to a tutor, who hated [the son]. The tutor thought, "If I kill him now, I shall turn out to be liable to the death penalty before the king. So what I'll do is take away his wet nurse, and he will die on his own."
>
> So thought Ahaz, "If there are no kids, there will be no he-goats. If there are no he-goats, there will be no flock. If there is no flock, there will be no shepherd. If there is no shepherd, there will be no world."
>
> So did Ahaz plan, "If there are no children, there will be no disciples; if there are no disciples, there will be no sages; if there are no sages, there will be no Torah; if there is no Torah, there will be no synagogues and schools; if there are no synagogues and schools, then the Holy One, blessed be he, will not allow his Presence to come to rest in the world."
>
> What did he do? He went and locked the synagogues and schools.
>
> That is in line with the following verse of Scripture: "Bind up the testimony, seal the Torah [teaching] among my disciples" (Is. 8:16).

Leviticus Rabbah XI:vii.3A–H

The letters that yield in Hebrew the English, "it came to pass," can be rearranged to produce "woe," with the result that, sages maintain, the formula "and it came to pass" introduces a tale of woe. That accounts for the question at hand. The plan of Ahaz then carries us to our point of interest: why does Talmud Torah set forth the way to God through learning? Here the point is explicit: children produce disciples, disciples define sages—no one is a teacher without students, no one is a student without teachers. Sages then carry forward Torah-study. Without Torah there are no synagogues and schools, and, when God's presence comes to rest in the world, it is in synagogues and schools.

Do rabbinic Judaism and Christianity meet at prayer? How does Matthew 6:9–10 compare with the Qaddish?

When Jesus instructs his disciples in prayer, he cites the wording of the qaddish-prayer, which is central to obligatory worship in Judaism, and which sanctifies God's name and pleads for the coming of God's kingdom:

> Our father who art in heaven
>
> Sanctified be your name
>
> Your kingdom come
>
> Your will be done
>
> On earth as it is in heaven

Matt 6:9–10

> Magnified and *sanctified be the name of God* in the world he created according to his will.
>
> *May his kingdom come* in your lives and in your days and in the life of the whole house of Israel, quickly and soon.

Qaddish-prayer

The Lord's Prayer and Qaddish intersect at two points: (1) sanctification of God's name, and (2) petition that God will establish his rule on earth as in heaven. Both liturgies position the worshippers at the threshold of the kingdom of God. There rabbinic Judaism and Christianity meet at prayer.

8. THE CELEBRATION OF GOD

What was the creed of rabbinic Judaism?

Rabbinic Judaism in the first six centuries produced no official creed, because it had no counterpart to the structure of authorities—bishops in charge of districts, not just priests of individual churches—that made possible church councils in Christianity. But normative beliefs did establish themselves. These took the form of prayers, in which the faithful community declared its beliefs, and chief among them was the Shema, "Hear . . . ," after the opening word of the rite. The creed declares the proclamation of the Unity of God, "Hear, O Israel, the Lord our God, the Lord is one," which, fully articulated, declares the principal theological convictions of Judaism concerning creation, revelation, and redemption. The one, only, unique God is celebrated for creating the world, revealing the Torah, and redeeming Israel in the end of days.

The Shema was recited morning and night, in the Temple and in the synagogue, at home and in public. While many centuries would pass before Judaism had adopted fixed wordings for the prayers, the Shema is attested to the formative age by the Mishnah itself. In the following statement, we find that in addition to reciting the Shema, blessings before and after are specified. One concerns itself with God's activity in nature—sunrise, sunset—and the other with God's giving the Torah, a sign of his everlasting love of holy Israel. The blessing afterward concerns God's redemption of Israel at the Red Sea and points to his future redemption of Israel at the end of days:

> In the morning one recites two blessings before it [the *Shema*] and one after it. [The two before are "Who Creates Light" and "Everlasting Love." The one after is "True and Certain."]

And in the evening, two before it and two after it. [The two before are, "Who Causes Evening to Pass," and "Everlasting Love." The two after are, "True and Certain," and "Lie Us Down in Peace."]

Mishnah Berakhot 1:4A–B

The exact wording of the blessings before and after the declaration of the faith in the Shema was not finalized for many centuries, but the theme, and the theological proposition, clearly had come to definition by the time of the closure of the Mishnah in ca. 200 C.E.

How was God celebrated in Creation?

The recital of the Shema is introduced by a celebration of God as Creator of the world. In the morning, one says,

Praised are You, O Lord our God, King of the universe.

You fix the cycles of light and darkness;

You ordain the order of all creation

You cause light to shine over the earth;

Your radiant mercy is upon its inhabitants.

In Your goodness the work of creation

Is continually renewed day by day. . . .

O cause a new light to shine on Zion;

May we all soon be worthy to behold its radiance.

Praised are You, O Lord, Creator of the heavenly bodies.[5]

The corresponding prayer in the evening refers to the setting of the sun:

Praised are You. . . .

Your command brings on the dusk of evening.

Your wisdom opens the gates of heaven to a new day.

---

[5] *Weekday Prayer Book,* ed. by the Rabbinical Assembly of American Prayerbook Committee, Rabbi Jules Harlow, Secretary (New York: Rabbinical Assembly, 1962), 42.

With understanding You order the cycles of time;

Your will determines the succession of seasons;

You order the stars in their heavenly courses.

You create day, and You create night,

Rolling away light before darkness. . . .

Praised are You, O Lord, for the evening dusk.

Morning and evening the faithful Israelite responds to the natural order of the world with thanks and praise of God who created the world and who actively guides the daily events of nature. Whatever happens in nature gives testimony to the sovereignty of the Creator. And that testimony is not in unnatural disasters, but in the most ordinary events: sunrise and sunset. These, especially, evoke the religious response to set the stage for what follows.

How in revelation?

For the faithful Israelite God is not merely Creator, but purposeful Creator. The works of creation serve to justify and to testify to the Torah, the revelation of Sinai. The Torah is the mark not merely of divine sovereignty, but of divine grace and love, source of life here and now and in eternity. So goes the second blessing:

Deep is Your love for us, O Lord our God;

Bounteous is Your compassion and tenderness.

You taught our fathers the laws of life,

And they trusted in You, Father and king,

For their sake be gracious to us, and teach us,

That we may learn Your laws and trust in You.

Father, merciful Father, have compassion upon us:

Endow us with discernment and understanding.

Grant us the will to study Your the Torah,

To heed its words and to teach its precepts. . . .

Enlighten our eyes in Your the Torah,

Open our hearts to Your commandments. . . .

Unite our thoughts with singleness of purpose

To hold You in reverence and in love. . . .

You have drawn us close to You;

We praise You and thank You in truth.

With love do we thankfully proclaim Your unity.

And praise You who chose Your people Israel in love.[6]

Here is the way in which revelation takes concrete and specific form in the Judaic tradition: God, the Creator, revealed his will for creation through the Torah, given to Israel his people. The Torah contains the "laws of life."

The Shema: The unity of God

In the Shema, the Torah—revelation—leads Jews to enunciate the chief teaching of revelation:

Hear, O Israel, the Lord Our God, the Lord is One.

This declaration represents accepting the yoke of the Kingdom of God upon oneself. It is the moment at which the Israelite enters the Kingdom of God and accepts God's rule.

What about the details? A benediction follows:

Blessed be the Name of his glorious Kingdom forever and ever.

This declaration represents accepting the yoke of the commandments, the resolve to carry out religious obligations of commission and omission. So in reciting the Shema, the Israelite enters the kingdom of God and accepts God's rule on earth, in everyday life, through the commandments.

This proclamation, by which the pious person enters the dominion of God and in attitude and action accepts God's rule, is followed by three Scriptural passages. The first is Deut 6:5–9:

---

[6] Ibid., 45–56.

You shall love the Lord your God with all your heart, with all your soul, with all your might.

And further, one must diligently teach one's children these words and talk of them everywhere and always, and place them on one's forehead, doorposts, and gates.

The second set of verses of Scripture is Deut 11:13–21, which emphasizes that if Jews keep the commandments, they will enjoy worldly blessings; if they do not, they will be punished and disappear from the good land God gives them.

The third is Num 15:37–41, the commandment to wear fringes on the corners of one's garments. The fringes are today attached to the prayer shawl worn at morning services by Conservative and Reform Jews, and worn on a separate undergarment for that purpose by Orthodox Jews, and they remind the faithful Israelite of *all* the commandments of the Lord.

How in redemption?

In the end of the declaration of the creed, the final unit of the Shema, it is the theme of God, not as Creator or Revealer, but God as Redeemer, that concludes the twice-daily drama:

You are our King and our father's King,

Our redeemer and our father's redeemer.

You are our creator. . . .

You have ever been our redeemer and deliverer

There can be no God but You. . . .

You, O Lord our God, rescued us from Egypt;

You redeemed us from the house of bondage. . . .

You split apart the waters of the Red Sea,

The faithful you rescued, the wicked drowned. . . .

Then Your beloved sang hymns of thanksgiving. . . .

They acclaimed the King, God on high,

Great and awesome source of all blessings,

The ever-living God, exalted in his majesty.

He humbles the proud and raises the lowly;

He helps the needy and answers His people's call. . . .

Then Moses and all the children of Israel

Sang with great joy this song to the Lord:

Who is like You O Lord among the mighty?

Who is like You, so glorious in holiness?

So wondrous your deeds, so worthy of praise!

The redeemed sang a new song to You;

They sang in chorus at the shore of the sea,

Acclaiming Your sovereignty with thanksgiving:

The Lord shall reign for ever and ever.

Rock of Israel, arise to Israel's defense!

Fulfill Your promise to deliver Judah and Israel.

Our redeemer is the Holy One of Israel,

The Lord of hosts is His name.

Praised are You, O Lord, redeemer of Israel.[7]

Redemption is both in the past and in the future. That God not only creates but also redeems is attested by the redemption from Egyptian bondage. The congregation repeats the exultant song of Moses and the people at the Red Sea, not as scholars making a learned allusion, but as participants in a narrative drama, one that concerns the story of the salvation of old and of time to come. Then the people turn to the future and ask that Israel once more be redeemed.

---

[7] Ibid., 50–52.

PART 2

THE SOURCES OF RABBINIC JUDAISM: SCRIPTURE AND MIDRASH

9. RABBINIC JUDAISM AND THE HEBREW SCRIPTURES

What is Midrash?

"Midrash" is the Hebrew word for exegesis of Scripture and it is also applied to the collection of such exegeses. The word derives from the Hebrew verbal root, "to inquire." The word Midrash as commonly used today bears three meanings.

First is the sense of Midrash as the explanation, by Judaic interpreters, of the meaning of individual verses of Scripture. The result of the interpretation of a verse of Scripture is called a Midrash-exegesis.

Second, the result of the interpretation of Scripture is collected in Midrash-compilations or a Midrash-document. The various Midrash-compilations exhibit distinctive traits. Seen individually and also as a group, they are connected, intersect at a few places but not over the greater part of their scope. These Midrash-compilations as a whole are compilations of Midrash, but they are not individual compilations, but rather each is a freestanding composition. These documents emerge as sharply differentiated from one another and clearly defined, each through its distinctive viewpoint, particular polemic, and formal and aesthetic qualities.

Third, the process of interpretation, for instance, the principles which guide the interpreter, is called Midrash-method. There are three types of interpretation of Scripture characteristic of rabbinic Midrash-compilations.

What are Midrash Halakah and Midrash Aggadah?

Midrash Halakah, the exegesis of Scripture for legal purposes, was the exegesis of legal, or Halakic, passages of Scripture. It is contained in *Sifra, Sifré to Numbers,* and *Sifré to Deuteronomy,* as well as in the two Talmuds (Sections 12, 13). Midrash Aggadah, the reading of Scripture for

narrative and theological purposes, was the exegesis of the narrative, prophetic, wisdom, and exhortatory passages of Scripture. It is contained
in *Genesis Rabbah, Leviticus Rabbah,* and the other *Rabbah* Midrash-
compilations (Sections 15–17). In addition, both Talmuds contain ample
selections of Midrash Aggadah.

What defines the particular approach to Scripture of rabbinic Judaism?

Can we characterize the modes of reading the written Torah in
these components of the oral Torah? Midrash-hermeneutics, that is, approaches to the systematic interpretation of Scripture, yielded three kinds
of readings of the written Torah in the oral: (1) Midrash-as-paraphrase,
(2) Midrash-as-prophecy, and (3) Midrash-as-parable or allegorical
reading of Scripture.

In the first of these, the exegete would paraphrase Scripture, imposing fresh meanings by the word choices or even by adding additional
phrases or sentences and so revising the meaning of the received text. This
I call Midrash-as-paraphrase because the fresh meaning is imputed by
obliterating the character of the original text and rendering or translating
it in a new sense. The barrier between the text and the comment here
is obscured and the commentator joins in the composing of the text.
Midrash-as-paraphrase may also include fresh materials, but these are
presented as if they formed an integral part of the original text. In the other
two modes of Midrash, the boundary between text and imputed meaning
is always clearly marked. *Sifra* and the two *Sifrés* operate along these lines.

In the second, the exegete would ask Scripture to explain meanings of events near at hand, and Scripture would serve as a means of
prophetic reading of the contemporary world. Midrash-as-prophecy
produces the identification of a biblical statement or event with a contemporary happening. Here the scriptural verse or text retains its particularity, being kept distinct from the commentary or exegesis. But in its
substance, as against its form, Midrash-as-prophecy treats the historical
life of ancient Israel and the contemporary times of the exegete as essentially the same, reading the former as a prefiguring of the latter. Through
Midrash-as-prophecy, therefore, Scripture addresses contemporary times
as a guide to what is happening even now—and, more to the point, what
is going to happen in the near future. *Genesis Rabbah* and *Leviticus
Rabbah* work on the problems of history.

In the third type of Midrash as process, which for the sake of convenience I call Midrash-as-parable, though the categories of allegory or

metaphor also pertain, the exegete reads Scripture in terms other than those in which the scriptural writer speaks. Scripture, for instance, may tell the story of love of man and woman as in the Song of Songs, but Judaic and Christian exegetes heard the song as addressing the love between God and Israel or the love between God and the church. Scripture in Genesis speaks of the family of Abraham, Isaac, and Jacob, while in *Genesis Rabbah* the great Judaic sages read the history of the children of Israel, down to the present time.

What was the view of the Hebrew Scriptures set forth by rabbinic Judaism in its Midrash-compilations?

Reading one thing in terms of something else, the builders of the Midrash-documents systematically adopted for themselves the reality of the Scripture, its history and doctrines. They transformed that history from a sequence of onetime events, leading from one place to some other, into an ever-present mythic world. No longer was there one Moses, one David, one set of happenings of a distinctive and never-to-be-repeated character. Now whatever happened of which the thinkers propose to take account must enter and be absorbed into that established and ubiquitous pattern and structure founded in Scripture. It is not that biblical history repeats itself. Rather, biblical history no longer constitutes history as a story of things that happened once, long ago, and pointed to some one moment in the future. Rather it becomes an account of things that happen every day—the source for knowledge of the governing patterns of life.

Midrash shows us how the sages of the dual Torah mediated between God's word and their own world, equally and reciprocally invoking the one as a metaphor for the other. They learned from Scripture about what it meant for humanity to be "in our image, after our likeness," and they learned in the difficult world in which they lived how life in God's image of humanity, as Scripture set forth that image, was to be not only endured but lived in full holiness. It was to be the godly life on earth, life as the imitation of God. That theological conviction of the dual Torah frames a theology of culture, one that constantly refers to Scripture in the interpretation of everyday life, and to everyday life in the interpretation of Scripture. Such a theology of culture invokes both the eternal and continuing truths of Scripture and also the ephemeral but urgent considerations of the here and the now. Midrash then forms that bridge, defines that metaphor, holds in the balance those two worlds of the here and now and the always. It reads the one in the light of the other, imparting one meaning to both, drawing each toward the plane of the other. Midrash reads the everyday as the metaphor against which the eternal is to be read, and the eternal as the metaphor against which the everyday is to be reenacted.

There is a constant interplay, an ongoing interchange, between everyday affairs and the word of God in the Torah—Scripture. What we see reminds us of what Scripture says—and what Scripture says informs our understanding of the things we see and do in everyday life. And the deep structure of human existence, framed by Scripture and formed out of God's will as spelled out in the Torah, forms the foundation of our everyday life. Here and now, in the life of the hour, we can and do know God. So everyday life forms a commentary on revealed Scripture—on the Torah—and Scripture, the Torah, provides a commentary on everyday life. Life flows in both directions. Rabbinic Midrash forms the medium for the exchange.

What was rabbinic Judaism's view of the Dead Sea Scrolls? Of the New Testament?

The Midrash Aggadah and Midrash Halakah of rabbinic Judaism interpreted Scripture within the framework of its overriding theological system (Section 2) and did not acknowledge the writings of any other Judaism in the first six centuries C.E. It therefore took no view of the Dead Sea Scrolls or of the New Testament. The Midrash-exegesis of those systems took a different view of Scripture. Each one interpreted even the same verses of Scripture in its own distinctive way.

Random points of intersection take on meaning when we compare systems, beginning with systems of Midrash-exegesis. Comparing the Midrash-exegesis of rabbinic Judaism with that of earliest Christianity or the Dead Sea library or Philo of Alexandria captures the difference between and among the distinct systems, all of them based on the same Scripture. That affords a deep perspective on the entire group of religious systems built upon ancient Israelite Scripture.

Was the Hebrew Bible an "Old Testament" in rabbinic Judaism?

The rabbinic writings constantly refer back to the Hebrew Scriptures, citing them as proof texts for important propositions much as do the Gospels. Consequently, the Hebrew Scriptures function within rabbinic Judaism much as they do in the form of the "Old Testament" within Christianity. So the equation is commonly assumed: Old Testament/ New Testament = Hebrew Scriptures (the written Torah)/Rabbinic literature (the oral Torah). The parallel, however, is formal, not substantive. For the Gospels, the Hebrew Scriptures are asked to make sense of chapters in the life and teachings of Jesus and to provide a context that *validated* that life and those teachings. In contrast, the teachings of the rabbis derived not from the Hebrew Scriptures but from a long chain of oral tradition. The citing of a passage of the Hebrew Scriptures alongside a rabbinic teaching of law or theology served to *correlate* oral tradition with the written part of the same tradition. Rabbinic Judaism did not distinguish that oral tradition, handed on by the rabbis, from the revealed Scripture. Both oral and written traditions represented statements of God's will for Israel. If, as Brevard Childs states, "The evangelists read from the New [Testament] backward to the Old,"[1] we may say very simply, *the sages read from the written Torah forward to the oral one.*

---

[1] Brevard S. Childs, *Biblical Theology of the Old and New Testaments: Theological Reflection on the Christian Bible* (London: SCM, 1992), 720.

PART 3

THE SOURCES OF RABBINIC JUDAISM: LAW (HALAKAH)

10. HALAKAH

How do we know about rabbinic Judaism?

Our knowledge of rabbinic Judaism comes to us in writing. There are no archaeological sites that attest to that Judaism in particular, in the way in which the Dead Sea Scrolls and the community of Judaism that valued them are linked to the archaeology of the remains of the settlement and caves at Qumran. Synagogues that have been excavated may or may not conform to the Halakah. In some details, e.g., of provision for ritual baths, many private homes do. But for detailed knowledge of rabbinic Judaism, the sources are documents, preserved in manuscripts for long centuries until the advent of printing in the turn of the sixteenth century, when, along with the Bible, the rabbinic literature was very quickly published in movable type.

What was "the Halakah"?

The word in rabbinic writing for "law" is Halakah, from the Hebrew verbal root *halak,* "to go." Thus, Halakah was "the way": the norm for how things are to be done. The counterpart of law/Halakah is lore/Aggadah, which we address in Section 14.

Where in the writings of rabbinic Judaism do I find the law?

It is common in New Testament studies to refer to "the Law," meaning "the Torah," as "the Law and the Prophets." But the Torah, the Five Books of Moses, contains narrative, exhortation, and theology as much as law. Rabbinic Judaism differentiates law from lore, Halakah from Aggadah. The law of the Torah encompasses the statements governing normative conduct set forth in Scripture and in tradition, and the lore of the Torah takes in the narrative, prophecy, and theology presented by Scripture as mediated by tradition. The statements of normative theology (Aggadah) are no less authoritative, but they take a different form from those of normative conduct (Halakah).

By "law" people generally mean norms of concrete and practical conduct. In our setting law deals with secular questions of government and politics, civil relationships of the social order. Matters of religious belief and behavior are not appropriate topics for public law. But the distinction between religious and secular, between norms of ritual conduct and rules of civil behavior, does not register for Judaism. Scripture sets forth, side by side, laws of personal ethical behavior, e.g., not taking a false oath; laws of ritual conduct, e.g., observing the prohibitions of servile labor on the Sabbath; and refraining from conduct we should regard as the appropriate subject of legislation, e.g., not murdering, not stealing. The Ten Commandments illustrate the combination of laws of various categories that characterizes Scripture.

The Torah, in the books of Exodus, Leviticus, Numbers, and Deuteronomy, contains many laws, which we should regard as both secular and religious. These concern the Temple in Exodus, the priesthood and the offerings in Leviticus, the Temple offerings and certain other rites in Numbers, and the Israelite social order in Deuteronomy. Scripture sets forth numerous divine commandments for Israel to obey in constructing a kingdom of priests and a holy people, and these commandments involve moral, ethical, ritual matters, as much as they deal with the conduct of civil society that, in our culture, we assume law governs.

The rabbinic sages undertook to organize and systematize in a topical framework the laws set forth in Scripture, together with those handed on through oral tradition. They recast them in a logical construction, and they did this in the Mishnah, a singular document, ca. 200 (Section 11). The Mishnah was amplified by a compilation of supplements, the Tosefta, ca. 300 (Section 12), and the entire corpus of law was subjected to a process of analysis and criticism in the two Talmuds, the one—the Yerushalmi—of the land of Israel, ca. 400, and the other—the Bavli—of Babylonia, ca. 600 (Section 13). So we find the Law in the Torah, both oral and written, in Scripture, and in the unfolding code from the Mishnah through the Bavli.

What laws of Scripture are taken over and applied in the Halakah of rabbinic Judaism?

Every legal statement of Scripture, without a single exception, is taken over and given its place in the topically organized Halakah of rabbinic Judaism. Every law of Scripture is amplified and clarified through this work of reorganization and systematic exposition of general principles as adumbrated by concrete cases.

The work of systematization of the Halakah required the reorganization of Scripture's laws into topical expositions, rather than in the category-formations found suitable by Moses, some of them topical, some of them occasional and episodic. Category-formations define how the facts of the Halakah cohere. They show how they form more than arbitrary conglomerations of rules but rather cogent, propositional statements on various topics. Those of Scripture are defined by diverse traits, e.g., position in a narrative; those of the Mishnah are designated solely by topic.

An example of Scripture's systematic exposition of a topic is Lev 1–15, on the types of offerings in the Temple/tent of meeting in the wilderness, the consecration of the priesthood to present the offerings, and the laws of ritual purity that govern in the Temple/tent of meeting. An example of Scripture's episodic presentation of diverse rules in a single exposition is Lev 19, which takes as its organizing principle the realization of holiness or sanctification in diverse areas of everyday life, some practical, some ritual, some agricultural, some familial. The work of the Halakah as set forth by the Mishnah is to present the laws in accord with their subject matter.

Did rabbinic Judaism have laws on subjects not treated by the Hebrew Scriptures?

The Mishnah, and hence the category-formation of the law devised by rabbinic Judaism, does cover topics not introduced by Scripture but transmitted in oral tradition. The distinction between laws resting on Scripture and those based on tradition is explicit in the following:

> The absolution of vows hovers in the air, for it has nothing [in the Torah] upon which to depend.

> The laws of the Sabbath, festal offerings, and sacrilege—lo, they are like mountains hanging by a string,

for they have little Scripture for many laws.

Laws concerning civil litigations, the sacrificial cult, things to be kept cultically clean, sources of cultic uncleanness, and prohibited consanguineous marriages have much on which to depend.

And both these and those [equally] are the essentials of the Torah.

Mishnah Hagigah 1:8

The Torah thus relates to the Halakah in several distinct ways: some Halakic category-formations are autonomous of Scripture, some are wholly dependent upon Scripture, and some are connected to Scripture, either in a relationship of complete dependency or in a relationship of near-autonomy. Halakic category-formations, defined by the Mishnah, may relate to Scripture in one of the following four ways:

(1) dependent upon Scripture, merely developing points already set forth there; here we deal with Halakah that is symmetrical with Scripture's laws, going over the same ground and saying pretty much the same thing; or is it

(2) autonomous of Scripture, going its own way to explore issues of its own invention; here we address Halakah that is essentially autonomous of Scripture, which has not contributed the category or even a corpus of rules on the category;

(3) in-between but derivative; that is, Halakah deriving a topic and perhaps a corpus of facts from Scripture and fabricating a program of problems that Scripture has provoked;

(4) in-between yet fundamentally original; that is, deriving a topic and even some facts from Scripture but formulating a program of problems that Scripture has in no way suggested, invoking conceptions Scripture has not provided. The issue in the fourth classification, then, is, does Scripture define the provocative issues of a given topic, or do those generative problems take shape elsewhere than in the written part of the Mosaic revelation?

Some of the topics/category-formations of the Mishnah, hence of the Halakah, rest on tradition, not on Scripture, as indicated by (2) above and signaled by the description, ". . . hovers in the air, for it has nothing [in the Torah] upon which to depend" (as given in the Mishnah *Hagigah*, quoted above). All topics, both those with deep roots in Scripture and those without, form essentials of the law of the Torah.

11. THE MISHNAH

What are the sources of the Halakah?

Beyond Scripture, the principal source of the Halakah is the Mishnah, ca. 200 C.E., because that document defines the category-formations that organize and impart structure to the laws.

The Halakah as set forth in the Mishnah then is amplified by the Tosefta, a compilation of complementary and supplementary legal statements, ca. 300 C.E. There are also three compilations of exegeses of legal passages of Scripture, *Sifra* and the two *Sifrés*, ca. 300 C.E., and two Talmuds, one compiled in the Land of Israel under Roman rule, ca. 400 C.E., the other in Babylonia under Persian rule, ca. 600 C.E.

A further compilation of exegesis of both legal and theological passages of Scripture, deriving from the authorities cited in the Mishnah, Tosefta, *Sifra*, and the two *Sifrés*, is *Mekilta Attributed to R. Ishmael*. That serves important parts of the book of Exodus.

A table or chart showing the relationships both topical and chronological among these various documents follows:

Chronological and Topical Relationships among Major Sources of Judaism

Source	Date Completed	Topical Category
Scripture	prior to 70 C.E.	
Mishnah	ca. 200 C.E.	category formations
Tosefta	ca. 300 C.E.	supplementary legal texts
Sifra & *Sifrés*	ca. 300 C.E.	exegesis of legal texts
Mekilta Attributed to R. Ishmael	ca. 350 C.E.	supplementary to Exodus
Jerushalmi	ca. 400 C.E.	under Roman rule
Bavli	ca. 600 C.E.	under Iranian rule

What is the Mishnah?

The Mishnah is a six-part code of descriptive rules. The six divisions of the Mishnah are (1) agricultural rules; (2) laws governing appointed seasons, e.g., Sabbaths and festivals; (3) laws on the transfer of women and property along with women from one man (father) to another (husband); (4) the system of civil and criminal law (corresponding to what we today should regard as "the legal system"); (5) laws for the conduct of the cult and the Temple; and (6) laws on the preservation of cultic purity both in the Temple and under certain domestic circumstances, with special reference to the table and bed.

The Mishnah's principal intent in expounding a given topic is to organize data to show the principal classifications into which the facts are divided by their indicative traits, and to identify the hierarchy of those classifications. This approach, akin to that of natural history, is familiar from Section six:

> A high priest judges, and [others] judge him; gives testimony, and [others] give testimony about him;

> Mishnah *Sanhedrin* 2:1A–B

> The king does not judge, and [others] do not judge him; does not give testimony, and [others] do not give testimony about him;

> Mishnah *Sanhedrin* 2:2A–B

The facts that pertain to the high priest and the king are laid out in a pattern that permits not only classification but hierarchization. The upshot is, one of the points of acute interest in the presentation of any given topic is the principal components of that topic and how they relate.

What topics does the Mishnah cover?

The Halakic category-formations set forth norms for the religious and civil order of holy Israel, including matters that could not be realized at the time the Mishnah came to closure in ca. 200 C.E. For example, the Halakah encompasses Temple sacrifice when it deals with Appointed Times, Holy Things, and Purities, three of the six divisions of the Mishnah. So viewed whole, the Halakah should be regarded as a design for Israel restored to Land, Jerusalem, and the Temple at the end of days.

Agricultural Rules

The critical issue in the economic life, which means in farming, is in two parts, revealed in the first division. First, Israel, as tenant on God's holy Land, maintains the property in the ways God requires, keeping the rules which mark the Land and its crops as holy. Next, the hour at which the sanctification of the Land comes to form a critical mass, namely, in the ripened crops, is the moment ponderous with danger and heightened holiness. Israel's will so affects the crops as to mark a part of them as holy, the rest of them as available for common use. The human will is determinative in the process of sanctification.

The Division of Agriculture treats two topics: first, producing crops in accord with the Scriptural rules on the subject; second, paying the required offerings and tithes to the priests, Levites, and poor. The principal point of the Division is that the Land is holy, because God has a claim both on it and upon what it produces. God's claim must be honored by setting aside a portion of the produce for those for whom God has designated it. God's ownership must be acknowledged by observing the rules God has laid down for use of the Land. In sum, the Division is divided along these lines: (1) rules for producing crops in a state of holiness, and (2) rules for disposing of crops in accord with the rules of holiness.

Appointed Times

There are laws governing appointed seasons, e.g., Sabbaths and festivals. In the second division, what happens in the Land at certain times—at appointed times—marks off spaces of the Land as holy in yet another way. The center of the Land and the focus of its sanctification is the Temple. There the produce of the Land is received and given back to God, the one who created and sanctified the Land. At these unusual moments of sanctification, the inhabitants of the Land, socially existing in villages, enter a state of spatial sanctification. That is to say, the village boundaries mark off holy space, within which one must remain during the holy time. This is expressed in two ways. First, the Temple itself observes and expresses the special, recurring holy time.

Second, the villages of the Land are brought into alignment with the Temple, forming a complement and completion to the Temple's sacred being. The advent of the appointed times precipitates a spatial reordering of the Land, so that the boundaries of the sacred are matched and mirrored in village and in Temple. At the heightened holiness marked by these moments of Appointed Times, therefore, the occasion for an affective sanctification is worked out. Like the harvest, the advent of an appointed time, a pilgrim festival, also a sacred season, is made to express that regular, orderly, and predictable sort of sanctification for Israel which the system as a whole seeks.

The Division of Women

These define the role of women in the social economy of Israel's supernatural and natural reality. Women acquire definition wholly in relationship to men, who impart form to the Israelite social economy. The status of women is effected through both supernatural and natural, this-worldly action. What man and woman do on earth provokes a response in heaven, and the correspondences are perfect. So women are defined and secured both in heaven and here on earth, and that position is always and invariably relative to men. The principal interest for the Mishnah is the point at which a woman becomes, and ceases to be, holy to a particular man, that is, enters and leaves the marital union. These transfers of women are the dangerous and disorderly points in the relationship of woman to man, therefore, the Mishnah states, to society as well.

Damages: The System of Civil and Criminal Law

This corresponds to what we today should regard as "the legal system." The Division of Damages comprises two subsystems that fit together in a logical way. One part presents rules for the normal conduct of civil society. These cover commerce, trade, real estate, and other matters of everyday intercourse, as well as mishaps, such as damages by chattels and persons, fraud, overcharge, interest, and the like, in that same context of everyday social life. The other part describes the institutions governing the normal conduct of civil society, that is, courts of administration, and the penalties at the disposal of the government for the enforcement of the law. The two subjects form a single tight and systematic dissertation on the nature of Israelite society and its economic, social, and political relationships, as the Mishnah envisages them.

The main point of the first of the two parts of the Division is that the task of society is to maintain perfect stasis, to preserve the prevailing situation, and to secure the stability of all relationships. To this end, in the interchanges of buying and selling, giving and taking, borrowing and lending, it is important that there be an essential equality of interchange. No party in the end should have more than what he had at the outset, and none should be the victim of a sizable shift in fortune and circumstance. All parties' rights to, and in, this stable and unchanging economy of society are to be preserved. When the condition of a person is violated, so far as possible the law will secure the restoration of the antecedent status.

The other part of the Division describes the institutions of Israelite government and politics. This is in two main aspects: first, the description of the institutions and their jurisdiction, with reference to courts, conceived as both judicial and administrative agencies; and second, the extensive discussion of criminal penalties.

Holy Things: Laws for the Conduct of the Cult and the Temple

The Division of Holy Things presents a system of sacrifice and sanctuary: matters concerning the praxis of the altar and maintenance of the sanctuary. The praxis of the altar, specifically, involves sacrifice and things set aside for sacrifice and so deemed consecrated. The Mishnah's tractates divide themselves up into the following groups (in parentheses are tractates containing relevant materials): (1) Rules for the altar and the praxis of the cult; (2) Rules for the altar and the animals set aside for the cult; and (3) Rules for the altar and support of the Temple staff and buildings. In a word, this Division speaks of the sacrificial cult and the sanctuary in which the cult is conducted. The law pays special attention to the matter of the status of the property of the altar and of the sanctuary, both materials to be utilized in the actual sacrificial rites, and property the value of which supports the cult and sanctuary in general. Both are deemed to be sanctified, that is, "holy things." The Division of Holy Things centers upon the everyday and rules always applicable to the cult.

Purities

These are laws on the preservation of cultic purity, whether in the home or in the Temple. In the sixth division, once we speak of the one place of the Temple, we address, too, the cleanness which pertains to every place. A system of cleanness—taking into account what imparts uncleanness and how this is done, what is subject to uncleanness, and how that state is overcome—as a system is fully expressed, once more, in response to the participation of the human will. Without the wish and act of a human being, the system does not function. It is inert. Sources of uncleanness, which come naturally and not by volition, and modes of purification, which work naturally, and not by human intervention, remain inert until human will has imparted susceptibility to uncleanness, that is, introduced into the system, that food and drink, bed, pot, chair, and pan, which to begin with form the focus of the system. The movement from sanctification to uncleanness takes place when human will and work precipitate it.

How old are the Mishnah's traditions?

Rabbinic Judaism claimed that the teachings of the Mishnah are verbatim, derived from God's instruction to Moses, handed on from that ancient time to the time of the rabbinic sages cited in the Mishnah:

> What is the order of Mishnah teaching? Moses learned it from the mouth of the All-Powerful. Aaron came in, and Moses repeated his chapter to him and Aaron went forth and sat at the left hand of Moses. His sons came in and Moses repeated their chapter to them, and his sons went forth. Eleazar sat at the right of Moses, and Itamar at the left of Aaron.
>
> Then the elders entered, and Moses repeated for them their Mishnah chapter. The elders went out. Then the whole people came in, and Moses repeated for them their Mishnah chapter. So it came about that Aaron repeated the lesson four times, his sons three times, the elders two times, and all the people once.
>
> Then Moses went out, and Aaron repeated his chapter for them. Aaron went. His sons repeated their chapter. His sons went out. The elders repeated their chapter. So it turned out that everybody repeated the same chapter four times.
>
> Bavli *Eruvin* 54b 5:1.I.43B, D

While the claim of the rabbinic sages attests to their convictions on the origins of the Halakah of the Mishnah, verifying that claim is not easy. Everyone understands that the document attests to opinions held at the time of its closure, at ca. 200 C.E. What is at issue is, does the Mishnah tell us about times before its redaction? Does it tell us about its own prior layers of development?

The Mishnah and later documents often refer to times prior to their own redaction. No one has ruled out the possibility that the rabbinic writings contain facts deriving from long centuries prior to the closure of those documents. After all, Scripture is well-represented, and the law code encompasses survivals of ancient Near Eastern law from remote antiquity, i.e., enduring legal concepts. Not only so, but norms of correct conduct taken for granted in the Gospels intersect with rules of the Halakah set forth in the Mishnah and in related compilations. The Gospels then show that at least some of the Mishnah's rules go back to the period nearly two centuries prior to the closure of the Mishnah itself.

What then does the conventional date for the closure of the Mishnah, ca. 200 C.E., mark? It is the point at which the *system* constituted by the data viewed as a whole *in its present category-formations* was fully realized. Received facts are set forth to make a fresh, coherent statement. What the document's date of closure signifies is not the date of the discrete data but of the system constituted whole by that final statement. The context in which facts appearing in other contexts altogether entered into the system of the Mishnah, the role that they play there, the proportionate importance accorded to them—these are all matters that pertain to the Mishnah viewed whole and complete. And that document reached closure only in ca. 200 C.E., while utilizing ancient traditions to be sure.

Where do I find a translation of the document?

A complete translation that replicates the formal character of the Hebrew original is my *The Mishnah. A New Translation.* New Haven and London, 1987: Yale University Press.

12. BETWEEN THE MISHNAH AND THE TALMUDS

What is Pirqé Avot *and how does it relate to the Mishnah?*

Pirqé Avot, the "Sayings of the Fathers," a.k.a., tractate *Avot,* is made up of five chapters of wisdom-sayings, neither legal nor exegetical in character, but mainly a handbook of wise sayings for disciples of sages, especially those involved in administration of the law. These sayings, miscellaneous in character, are assigned to named authorities. Always published along with the Mishnah but autonomous of that document in every differentiating formal and programmatic attribute, the compilation cites authorities of the generation generally assumed to have flourished after the closure of the Mishnah and hence may be situated at ca. 250 C.E.—a mere guess.

Tractate *Avot* bears no formal, or substantive, relationship to the Mishnah. But the document serves as the Mishnah's first and most important documentary apologetic, stating in abstract and general terms the ideals for the virtuous life that are set forth by the Mishnah's sages and animate its laws. Its presentation of sayings of sages extending from Sinai to figures named in the Mishnah itself links the Mishnah to Sinai. The link consists of the chain of tradition handed on through the chain of sages itself. It follows that, because of the authorities cited in it, the Mishnah constitutes part of the Torah of Sinai, for by the evidence of the chain of tradition, the Mishnah too forms a statement of revelation, that is, "Torah revealed to Moses at Sinai." This is expressed in the opening sentence:

> Moses received {the} Torah at Sinai and handed it on to Joshua, Joshua to elders, and elders to prophets. And prophets handed it on to the men of the great assembly.

> Mishnah *Avot* 1:1A–B

The verbs *receive . . . hand on . . .* , in Hebrew yield the words *qabbalah,* tradition, and *masoret,* also tradition. The theological proposition that validates the Mishnah is that the Torah is a matter of tradition. The tradition goes from master to disciple, Moses to Joshua. And, further, those listed later on the same list include authorities of the Mishnah itself. That fact forms an implicit claim that (1) part of the Torah was, and is, orally formulated and orally transmitted, and (2) the Mishnah's authorities stand in the tradition of Sinai, so that (3) the Mishnah, too, forms part of the Torah of Sinai.

What is the Tosefta and why was it important? How old are its traditions?

A huge Halakic supplement to the Mishnah, four times larger than the document it amplifies, the Tosefta ("Supplements"), which reached closure by ca. 300 C.E., is like a vine on the Mishnah's trellis. It has no structure of its own. The Tosefta covers nearly the whole of the Mishnah's program but has little systematic program of its own. The document contains three kinds of writings.

(1) The first kind, about a third of the whole, consists of verbatim citations and glosses of sentences of the Mishnah. This part of the Tosefta dates from after the Mishnah reached closure, that is, after ca. 200.

(2) The second type, about half of the whole, is made up of free-standing statements that complement the sense of the Mishnah but do not cite a Mishnah-paragraph verbatim. These statements can be fully understood only in dialogue with the Mishnah's counterpart. This part of the Tosefta may or may not have originated in the period in which the Mishnah was taking shape, but probably dates from after 200.

(3) The third, about a sixth of the whole, comprises freestanding, autonomous statements, formulated in the manner of the Mishnah but fully comprehensible on their own. This part of the Tosefta can originate in the period in which Mishnah-sayings were being formalized.

The Tosefta sets out its statements on a given topic of the Mishnah in line with its three classifications of rules.

First, in a given topical exposition come statements that cite what the Mishnah's sentences say, and this ordinarily will occur in the order of the Mishnah's statements.

Second, in general, Mishnah-citation and gloss will be succeeded by Mishnah-amplification: sentences that do not cite the Mishnah's corresponding ones, but that cannot be understood without reference to the Mishnah's rule or sense. The first two kinds of statements are the ones that cannot be fully understood without knowledge of the Mishnah, which defines their context.

Third, in sequence, commonly, will be the small number of free-standing statements, which can be wholly understood on their own and without appeal to the sense or principle of the corresponding Mishnah-passage; and in some few cases, these compositions and even composites will have no parallel in the Mishnah at all.

What is Sifra?

Sifra sets forth a commentary to the book of Leviticus, written by the rabbinic sages probably between 250 and 350 C.E. A systematic commentary on the verses of Leviticus, *Sifra* explains the sense of Scripture and showing the relationship between the rules of the Mishnah on the topics covered by the book of Leviticus and the laws of that book. Its main point is that the rules of the Mishnah and their category-formations derive from the laws of Leviticus. For sizable passages, the sole point of coherence for the discrete sentences or paragraphs of *Sifra's* authorship derives from the base-verse of Scripture that is subject to commentary. A sizable proportion consists simply in the association of completed statements of the oral Torah with the exposition of the written Torah, the whole re-presenting as one whole Torah the dual Torah received by Moses at Sinai.

What is Sifré to Numbers?

Sifré to Numbers supplies a commentary to the book of Numbers, written ca. 250–350 C.E. by sages in the Land of Israel, presenting exegesis of a verse in the book of Numbers in terms of the theme or problems of that verse, hence, intrinsic exegesis; exegesis of a verse in Numbers in terms of a theme or polemic not particular to that verse, hence, extrinsic exegesis. (1) The syllogistic composition: Scripture supplies hard facts, which, properly classified, generate syllogisms. By collecting and classifying facts of Scripture, therefore, we may produce firm laws of history, society, and Israel's everyday life. (2) The fallibility of reason unguided by scriptural exegesis: Scripture alone supplies reliable basis for speculation. Laws cannot be generated by reason or logic unguided by Scripture. Scripture stands paramount; logic, reason, analytical processes of classification and differentiation, secondary. Reason not built on scriptural foundations yields uncertain results. The Mishnah itself demands scriptural bases.

A good example of how through narrative the three principal Midrash-exegesis of the Halakah conduct their work follows.

> "[So you shall remember and do (all my commandments and be holy to your God. I am the Lord your God who brought you out of the land of Egypt to be your God.) I am the Lord your God"...] (Num. 15:37–41):

> R. Nathan says, "You have not got {a} single religious duty that is listed in the Torah, the reward of the doing of which is not made explicit right alongside.

> "Go and learn the lesson from the religious duty of the fringes."

> There is the case {ma'aseh} of a man who was meticulous about carrying out the religious duty of the fringes. He heard that there was a certain whore in one of the coastal towns, who would collect a fee of four hundred gold coins. He sent her four hundred gold coins and made a date with her.

> When his time came, he came along and took a seat at the door of her house. Her maid came and told her, "That man with whom you made a date, lo, he is sitting at the door of the house."

> She said to her, "Let him come in."

> When he came in, she spread out for him seven silver mattresses and one gold one, and she was on the top, and between each one were silver stools, and on the top, gold ones. When he came to do the deed, the four fringes fell out [of his garment] and appeared to him like four witnesses. The man slapped himself in the face and immediately withdrew and took a seat on the ground.

> The whore too withdrew and took a seat on the ground.

> She said to him, "By the winged god of Rome! I shall not let you go until you tell me what blemish you have found in me."

> He said to her, "By the Temple service! I did not find any blemish at all in you, for in the whole world there is none so beautiful as you. But the Lord, our God, has imposed upon me a rather small duty, but concerning [even that minor matter] he wrote, 'I am the Lord your God who brought you out of the land of Egypt to be your God. I am the Lord your God,'— two times.

> " 'I am the Lord your God,' I am destined to pay a good reward.

" 'I am the Lord your God,' I am destined to exact punishment.' "

She said to him, "By the Temple service! I shall not let you go until you write me your name, the name of your town, and the name of your school in which you study Torah."

So he wrote for her his name, the name of his town, and the name of his master, and the name of the school in which he had studied Torah.

She went and split up her entire wealth, a third to the government, a third to the poor, and a third she took with her and came and stood at the school house of R. Hiyya.

She said to him, "My lord, accept me as a proselyte."

He said to her, "Is it possible that you have laid eyes on one of the disciples [and are converting in order to marry him]?"

She took the slip out that was in her hand.

He said to [the disciple who had paid the money but not gone through with the act], "Stand up and acquire possession of what you have purchased. Those spreads that she spread out for you in violation of a prohibition she will now spread out for you in full remission of the prohibition.

"As to this one, the recompense is paid out in this world, and as to the world to come, I do not know how much [more he will receive]!"

Sifré to Numbers CXV:v.5A, 6A–7Q

The narrative explains the value and importance of the show-fringes, the commandment concerning which the base verse, Num 14:37–41, sets forth as part of the proclamation of the Shema.

What is Sifré to Deuteronomy?

Out of cases and examples, sages seek generalizations and governing principles. Since in the book of Deuteronomy Moses explicitly sets forth a vision of Israel's future history, sages in *Sifré to Deuteronomy* examined that vision to uncover the rules that explain what happens to Israel. That issue drew attention from cases to rules, with the result that, in the book of Deuteronomy, they set forth a systematic account of Israel's future history, the key to Israel's recovery of command of its destiny. The methodical analysis does two things. First, the document's compilers take the details of cases and carefully re-frame them into rules pertaining to all cases. The authorship therefore asks those questions of susceptibility to generalization ("generalizability") that first-class philosophical minds raise. And it answers those questions by showing what details restrict the prevailing law to the conditions of the case, and what details exemplify the encompassing traits of the law overall. These are, after all, the two possibilities. The law is either limited to the case and to all cases that replicate this one, or the law derives from the principles exemplified, in detail, in the case at hand. Essentially, this authorship has reread the legal portions of the book of Deuteronomy and turned Scripture into what we now know is the orderly and encompassing code supplied by the Mishnah. To state matters simply, *Sifré to Deuteronomy* "Mishna-izes" Scripture.

Where do I find a translation of the documents?

I have translated all of these documents, as follows:

Pirqé Avot: Jacob Neusner, *Torah from Our Sages: Pirke Avot. A New American Translation and Explanation* (Chappaqua, N.Y.: Rossel, 1984). This work is now available in paperback from S. Orange, N.J.: Behrman House.

Tosefta: Jacob Neusner, *The Tosefta in English.* (2 vols.; Peabody, Mass.: Hendrickson, 2003).

Sifra: Jacob Neusner, *The Components of the Rabbinic Documents: From the Whole to the Parts: 1: Sifra.* (12 vols.; Atlanta, Ga.: Scholars Press for USF Academic Commentary Series, 1997; repr., Peabody, Mass.: Hendrickson, forthcoming).

Sifré to Numbers: Jacob Neusner, *The Components of the Rabbinic Documents: From the Whole to the Parts: Vol. 12: Sifré to Numbers.* (12 vols.; Atlanta, Ga.: Scholars Press for USF Academic Commentary Series, 1998; repr., Peabody, Mass.: Hendrickson, forthcoming).

Sifré to Deuteronomy: Jacob Neusner, *The Components of the Rabbinic Documents: From the Whole to the Parts: Vol. 7: Sifré to Deuteronomy* (12 vols.; Atlanta, Ga.: Scholars Press for USF Academic Commentary Serie 1997; repr., Peabody, Mass.: Hendrickson, forthcoming).

Mekhilta Attributed to R. Ishmael: Jacob Neusner, *The Components of the Rabbinic Documents: From the Whole to the Parts: Vol. 8: Mekhilta Attributed to R. Ishmael* (12 vols.; Atlanta, Ga.: Scholars Press for USF Academic Commentary Series 1997; repr., Peabody, Mass.: Hendrickson, forthcoming).

13. THE TALMUDS

What is a Talmud?

A Talmud, of which there are two, the one of the Land of Israel (a.k.a., the Yerushalmi, or Jerusalem Talmud), ca. 400 C.E., the other of Babylonia (a.k.a., the Bavli, or Babylonian Talmud), ca. 600 C.E., is a sustained, analytical reading and interpretation of a Mishnah-tractate. In a Talmud a systematic and critical program aims at explaining the meaning and concrete application of the Mishnah-rule, on the one side, and harmonizing one Mishnah-rule with others with which it intersects, on the other.

A Talmud accomplishes the work of Mishnah-commentary and explanation in particular by forming a moving ("dialectical") argument, progressing from point to point, in which all possibilities are systematically taken up and examined. What is talmudic about the two Talmuds is that mode of argumentative thought, which is a critical, systematic application of applied reason and practical logic, moving from a point starting with a proposition and (ordinarily) ending with a firm and articulated conclusion. The two Talmuds share many formal traits, although in character and most of their contents they differ radically.

How old are the Talmuds' traditions?

The Jerusalem and Babylonian Talmuds as we know them came to closure at 400 and 600 C.E., respectively. They refer back to past times and contain references to well-established facts. They take over some received materials from the Mishnah, Tosefta, and other prior documents, as well as writings produced between the closure of the prior documents, and the redaction of the Talmuds themselves. But the form in which we have them—the well-organized, systematic topical program, the coherent analytical method—was imposed only in the final generations of those that formulated and redacted the two documents.

How are the Talmuds organized?

The Talmuds are organized as commentaries to selected tractates of the Mishnah, thirty-nine for the Yerushalmi, thirty-seven for the Bavli. The Yerushalmi comments on the first four divisions of the Mishnah, the Bavli on the second through the fifth divisions.

Why are the Talmuds in both Hebrew and Aramaic?

When the Talmuds set forth authoritative statements of the Halakah, it is in Hebrew. When they conduct their analytical discussions of the law, it is in Aramaic. Hebrew is the language of the law, Aramaic, of the argument and analysis.

What is the Talmud of the Land of Israel/Yerushalmi?

The Yerushalmi is made up mostly of amplification and extension of passages of the Mishnah. Approximately 90% of the document comprises Mishnah-commentary, which consists of one of these four things: (1) text criticism; (2) exegesis of the meaning of the Mishnah, including glosses and amplifications; (3) addition of Scriptural proof texts of the Mishnah's central propositions; and (4) harmonization of one Mishnah passage with another such passage or with a statement of Tosefta. The Mishnah is read by the Yerushalmi as a composite of discrete and essentially autonomous rules, a set of atoms, not an integrated molecule; the most striking formal traits of the Mishnah are obliterated. The Mishnah as a whole and complete statement of a viewpoint no longer exists. Its propositions are reduced to details. Then, on occasion, the details may be restated in generalizations encompassing a wide variety of other details across the gaps between one tractate and another.

The Yerushalmi provides some indication of effort at establishing the correct text of various passages of the Mishnah. This nearly always is in the context of deciding the law. It is not a random search for a perfect text. It rather represents a deliberate and principled inquiry into the law as revealed by the phrasing of a passage. That is why, in the bulk of these passages, the legal consequences of one reading as opposed to another are carefully articulated, sometimes even tied to a range of other points subject to dispute. The Mishnah rarely finds it necessary to cite a Scriptural proof text for its propositions. The Yerushalmi, by contrast, whenever possible cites Scriptural proof texts for the propositions of the Mishnah.

What is the Talmud of Babylonia/Bavli?

The Bavli, a commentary to the second, third, fourth, and fifth divisions of the Mishnah, recasts received traditions into an intellectual framework of analysis and generalization. Generally it inquires into the sources in Scripture of rules in the Mishnah and the authorities behind unattributed laws of the Mishnah, and harmonizes passages of the Mishnah that appear to conflict. Also it contains large-scale commentaries to extended passages of Scripture; essays on theoretical problems; inquiries into modes and principles of scriptural exegesis that yield details of law, not necessarily in the context of Mishnah-exegesis.

While drawing on a variety of sources—Scripture, the Mishnah, the Tosefta, for example—the framers of the document in 500–600 C.E. reworked whatever they used into a cogent, orderly, and well-crafted piece of writing. The purpose of the Talmud of Babylonia is to clarify and amplify selected passages of the Mishnah. We may say very simply that the Mishnah is about life, and the Talmud is about the Mishnah. While the Mishnah records rules governing the conduct of the holy life of Israel, the holy people, the Talmud concerns itself with the details of the Mishnah. The one is descriptive and freestanding, the other analytical and contingent. Were there no Mishnah, there would be no Talmud.

The Bavli is a uniform document, beginning to end. Different from, much more than, a haphazard compilation of traditions, this Talmud shows itself upon examination to be a cogent and purposive writing, in which through a single determinate set of rhetoric devices, a single program of inquiry is brought to bear on many and diverse passages of two inherited documents, the Mishnah and Scripture. The voice is one and single because it is a voice that everywhere expresses the same limited set of sounds; the notes are arranged in one and the same way throughout. The Bavli's one voice, sounding through all tractates, is the voice of exegetes of the Mishnah. The document is organized around the Mishnah, and that order is not merely formal, but substantive. At *every* point, if the framers have chosen a passage of Mishnah-exegesis, that passage will stand at the head of all further discussion. *Every* turning point in every sustained composition and even in a large composite of compositions brings the editors back to the Mishnah, *always* read in its own order and *invariably* arranged in its own sequence.

Much more than four-fifths of all composites of the Bavli address the Mishnah and systematically expound that document. The other fifth (or still less) of a given tractate will comprise composites that take shape around (1) Scripture or (2) themes or topics of a generally theological or moral character. Distinguishing the latter from the former, of course, is merely formal; very often a scriptural topic will be set forth in a theological or moral framework, and very seldom does a composite on a topic omit all reference to the amplification of a verse or topic of Scripture. The proportion of a given tractate devoted to other-than-Mishnah-exegesis and amplification is generally not more than 10%. The Bavli speaks about the Mishnah in essentially a single voice, about fundamentally few things. Its mode of speech as much as of thought is uniform throughout. Diverse topics produce slight differentiation in modes of analysis. The same sorts of questions phrased in the same rhetoric—a moving, or dialectical, argument composed of questions and answers—turn out to pertain equally well to every subject and problem. The Talmud's discourse forms a closed system, in which people say the same thing about everything.

Five hermeneutical rules yielding theological facts govern throughout the Talmud of Babylonia:

Defining the Torah and the Context for Meaning

The Torah consists of freestanding statements/sentences, sometimes formed into paragraphs, more often not; and we are to read these sentences both on their own—for what they say—and also in the context created by the entirety of the Torah, oral and written. Therefore the task is to set side by side and show the compatibility of discrete sentences; documents mean nothing, the Torah being one. All sentences of the Torah, equally, jointly and severally, form the facts out of which meaning is to be constructed.

Specifying the Rules of Making Sense of the Torah

Several premises govern in our reading of the sentences of the Torah, and these dictate the rules of reading. These are: the Torah is perfect and flawless; the wording of the Torah yields meaning; the Torah contains, and can contain, nothing contradictory, incoherent, or otherwise contrary to common sense; the Torah can contain no statement that is redundant, banal, silly, or stupid.

Identifying Dialectics as the Correct Medium of Torah-Discourse

Since our principal affirmation is that the Torah is perfect, and the primary challenge to that affirmation derives from the named classifications of imperfection, the proper mode of analytical speech is argument. That is because if we seek flaws, we come in a combative spirit: proof and conflict, not truth and consequence. Only by challenging the Torah sentence by sentence, at every plausible point of imperfection, are we going to show in the infinity of detailed cases the governing fact of perfection. We discover right thinking by finding the flaws in wrong thinking, the logical out of the failings of illogic.

The Harmony of What Is Subject to Dispute, the Unity and Integrity of Truth

Finding what is rational and coherent: the final principle of hermeneutics is to uncover the rationality of dispute. Once commitment is to sustained conflict of intellect, it must follow that our goal can only be the demonstration of three propositions, everywhere meant to govern: first, disputes give evidence of rationality, meaning, each party has a valid, established principle in mind; second, disputes are subject to resolution; third, truth wins out. If we can demonstrate that reasonable sages can differ about equally valid propositions, for instance, which principle governs in a particular case, then schism affords evidence of not imperfection but profound coherence. The principles are affirmed, their application subjected to conflict. So too, if disputes worked out in extended, moving arguments, covering much ground, can be brought to resolution, as is frequently the case in either a declared decision or an agreement to disagree, then the perfection of the Torah once more comes to detailed articulation.

Knowing God through the Theology Expressed in Hermeneutics

In a protracted quest for the unity of the truth, what is always required through detailed demonstration is that beneath the laws is law; a few wholly coherent principles are inherent in the many and diverse rules and their cases. In that sustained quest, which defines the premise and the goal of all talmudic discourse, Israel meets God; in mind, in intellect, that meeting takes place.

Where do I find a translation of the documents?

The Jerusalem Talmud (Yerushalmi): Jacob Neusner, *The Talmud of the Land of Israel: An Academic Commentary to the Second, Third, and Fourth Divisions* (36 vols; Atlanta, Ga.: Scholars Press for USF Academic Commentary Series, 1998–1999; repr., Peabody, Mass.: Hendrickson, forthcoming).

The Babylonian Talmud (Bavli): Jacob Neusner, *The Talmud of Babylonia: An Academic Commentary* (28 vols.; Atlanta, Ga.: Scholars Press for USF Academic Commentary Series, 1994–1996, 1999; repr., Peabody, Mass.: Hendrickson, 2005).

PART 4

THE SOURCES OF RABBINIC JUDAISM: LORE (AGGADAH)

14. AGGADIC MIDRASH

What was "Aggadah"?

The word in rabbinic writing for "lore" is Aggadah, meaning "narrative." Aggadah sets forth theology, accomplished through the exegesis of Scripture and the systematic amplification of scriptural narratives. That work of extension of cases to rules yields generalizations subject to testing against the facts yielded by Scripture, nature, and history.

Is Aggadah the same as Haggadah?

The Hebrew word "to tell, to narrate," is *hagged,* producing the substantive, *haggadah.* The word *Aggadah* is the Aramaic form of the same word.

Reference to *The* Haggadah ordinarily pertains to the Passover Narrative, a retelling of elements of the story of the Exodus from Egypt in celebration of the Passover holiday at a home-banquet (Section 35).

Where do I find the Aggadah/Lore? Where do I find Scripture's Aggadah? Rabbinic Aggadah?

Scripture's Aggadah

The Pentateuch, from Genesis forward, tells the story of the formation of a holy family by Abraham and Sarah and the unfolding of that family's life in relationship to the Land that God promised to them. The family became a holy people through the experience of slavery in Egypt, salvation at the Red Sea, and revelation by God to Moses at Sinai. The books of Scripture that set forth that story, Exodus, Numbers,

Deuteronomy, are expounded in rabbinic Judaism. But, beyond the Pentateuch, the books of Joshua, Samuel, and Kings extend and continue the coherent story. Isaiah, Jeremiah, and Ezekiel, and the Twelve Minor Prophets, amplify matters as well.

Rabbinic Aggadah

The details of Scripture—particularly those books of Scripture that serve in synagogue liturgy, the Pentateuch and the Scrolls of Esther, Ruth, Lamentations, and Song of Songs—throughout are subjected to a close reading or exegesis. The purpose is clear and systematic for Aggadah as much as for Halakah: narratives, exhortations, and prophecies of Moses and the other prophets in the setting of Proverbs, Psalms, or Job, are translated into patterns and yield the theology that pervades them. The narratives and prophecies then are systematized, the rules that animate them being articulated and formed into a large and coherent theological construction for the Israelite social order.

What are the types of Aggadic Midrash?

There are three types of interpretation of Scripture characteristic of Midrash-compilations: episodic, philosophical, and theological. In the first, the focus of interest is on individual verses of Scripture, and interpreting those verses in the sequence in which they appear forms the organizing principle of sustained discourse. The earliest compilations, those in this section of the textbook, are organized mainly verse-by-verse, and in large measure they make their statements through comments on verses, over and over again saying the same thing in the same way about successive passages. These are the compilations that came to closure in the third century, ca. 200–300 C.E., as shown by the frequent citation of the Mishnah and the Tosefta verbatim in those compilations. They are *Sifra to Leviticus, Sifré to Numbers,* and *Sifré to Deuteronomy.*

In the second, the center of interest attends to the testing and validating of large-scale propositions, which, through the reading of individual verses, an authorship wishes to test and validate. In that rather philosophical trend in rabbinic Midrash-interpretation, the interpretation of individual verses takes a subordinated position, the appeal to facts of Scripture in the service of the syllogism at hand. This form of writing with Scripture so as to set forth a single, vast proposition, characterizes the second group of Midrash-compilations, those associated with the Talmud of the Land of Israel. These are *Genesis Rabbah, Leviticus Rabbah,* and *Pesiqta of Rab Kahana,* all of them supposed to have come to closure between ca. 450 and 500 C.E.

The third approach focuses upon the reading of phrases or verses so as to make a single, remarkably cogent theological-systematic statement. Here the form is the same as before, but the result is not. Instead of telling us a variety of things about many verses, the compilers of this third type of Midrash-compilation really wish to say one thing in many different ways. This approach to Midrash-compilation characterizes the documents associated with the Talmud of Babylonia. These are, in particular, *Lamentations Rabbah, Esther Rabbah I* (dealing with the book of Esther, chapters one and two), *Song of Songs Rabbah,* and *Ruth Rabbah.* A rough date for the conclusion of these compilations is ca. 600 C.E.

How about dating Midrash-compilations?

All dates, approximate though they are, really are guesswork. The one thing we may say for certain is that the first group is early, and, relative to that group, the second group, somewhat later, and the third group, the last in sequence. Nothing in any of the compilations plausibly permits us to date any document by reference to external events or (all the more so) evidence other than what the document itself gives us; so, plainly speaking, dates are guesswork. But, it is clear, as noted in the paragraph above, that there is a progression of interpretive activity. In the unfolding of the Midrash-compilations that form the other half of the Torah, both oral and written (that, in secular language, comprises the classics of Judaism—the half focused upon Scripture), we move (1) from the exegesis of phrases to make a fresh point, (2) through the reading of a variety of verses of Scripture so as to form a proposition to the compilation of readings of verses of Scripture, to (3) make a single, stunning, and encompassing proposition.

Is Aggadah normative in the way in which Halakah is normative in rabbinic Judaism?

Clearly, Halakah is normative, governing correct conduct. Certainly rabbinic Judaism recognized theological dogmas, which constituted its creed (cf. Section 8). But how about the Aggadah: what is its standing, and how is it authoritative? The answer is, at its foundations, the theology yielded by the Aggadah is normative, but these foundations could in matters of detail sustain diverse readings of Scripture and conflicting outcomes in matters of slight consequence.

What rendered Aggadah normative is its origin, which is in the rigorous, logical reading of Scripture: the close exegesis of God's word in his own wording. The rabbinic sages read Scripture—the facts it supplied or that oral tradition contributed—as philosophers read nature. They thought philosophically about Scripture. The logic that they uncovered imparted that rationality and coherence to the theological convictions they set forth, to the system they devised to account for the unity of being, the conformity of all reality to the few simple rules of reason that God embodied in his works of creation.

As philosophers sought to generalize out of the facts of nature, so sages brought system and order to the facts of Scripture, drawing conclusions, setting forth hypotheses, amassing data to them. Analytical principles comparable to those of natural history, specifically, guided them in their reading of the facts that Scripture provided. These involved, in particular, the classification and hierarchization of data in a taxonomical process of comparison and contrast: like followed like rules, unlike followed opposite rules. And the rules that classify also hierarchize, e.g., what is classified as sanctified or as unclean will then possess the traits that signify sanctification or uncleanness, and these traits will also order themselves, this time at levels of intensity.

How does the Aggadah make normative statements?

The basic method involves a search for abstraction out of concrete data. A variety of cases deriving from Scripture is subjected to generalization, and the whole is then set forth in the form of a generalization sustained by numerous probative cases. The generalization, moreover, is itself elaborated. Cases that validate the generalization are selected not at random but by appeal to common taxonomic traits, and then the generalization not only derives from the cases but from a very specific aspect thereof. These cases are all characterized by sudden and supernatural intervention in a crisis, such as the situation under discussion now requires. Or a set of kindred propositions is established through a sequence of cases; no effort is made to order the cases in a compelling sequence. It is adequate to state the generalization and then adduce probative cases out of Scripture. The whole represents the systematization of Scripture's evidence on a given topic, and it is the systematization of the data that yields a generalization.

15. *GENESIS RABBAH* AND *LEVITICUS RABBAH*

―――◦⦿◦―――

How was Genesis transformed in Genesis Rabbah?

Produced, like the Yerushalmi, after the triumph of Christianity and its adoption as the state religion of the Roman Empire, *Genesis Rabbah*, a systematic exegesis of the book of Genesis produced by the Judaic sages in ca. 450 C.E., makes the same point many times. It is that the deeds of the ancestors form signals and omens for the offspring, so Israel's history in patriarchal times prefigures Israel's history even in the present day. Then Jacob stands for contemporary Israel, and Esau, his opposite and his brother, stands for (now-Christian) Rome.

A systematic work, *Genesis Rabbah* conducts the search for the order yielded by the chaos of uninterpreted data that Scripture on its own provides. The governing mode of thought is that of natural philosophy. It involves the classification of data by shared traits, yielding descriptive rules, as well as the testing of propositions against the facts of data, with the whole work aimed at the discovery of underlying rules formed out of a multiplicity of details, that is to say, the proposing and testing, against the facts provided by Scripture, of the theses of Israel's salvation that demanded attention at that time in its history. But the issues were not so much philosophical as religious, in the sense that while philosophy addressed questions of nature and rules of enduring existence, religion asked about issues of history and God's intervention in time.

Genesis Rabbah in its final form emerges after that momentous century, the fourth century C.E., in which the Rome Empire passed from pagan to Christian rule under Constantine. At that time, in the aftermath of the Julian's abortive reversion to paganism, in ca. 360, which endangered the Christian character of the Roman empire, Christianity had adopted that politics of repression of paganism that rapidly engulfed Ju-

The upshot is that Scripture's facts are organized and sorted out in such a way as to present a generalization. Generalizations are to be formulated through that same process of collecting kindred facts and identifying the implication that all of them bear in common. But Scripture may also be asked to provide illustrative cases for principles that are formulated autonomously, as the result of analytical reasoning distinct from the sorting out of Scriptural precedents. Then Scripture is asked only to define in concrete terms what has been said abstractly. Successive propositions organize and rationalize a vast body of data, all of the facts pointing to the conclusions that are proposed as generalizations. The proof then lies once more in the regularity and order of the data that are collected and sorted out. What is normative in the Aggadic tradition is not the detail but the generalizations that it yields. These then guide the faithful in the myriad of everyday transactions, as individuals interpret the principles to apply to cases. The principles of the Aggadah are normative, the application sustains variation.

daism as well. The issue confronting Israel in the Land of Israel therefore proved immediate: the meaning of the new and ominous turn of history, the implications of Christ's worldly triumph for the other-worldly and supernatural people, Israel, whom God chooses and loves. The message of the exegete-compositors addressed the circumstance of historical crisis and generated remarkable renewal, a rebirth of intellect in the encounter with Scripture, now in quest of the rules not of sanctification— these had already been found—but of salvation. So the book of Genesis, which portrays how all things had begun, would testify to the message and the method of the end: the coming salvation of patient, hopeful, enduring Israel.

In the view of the framers of the compilation, the entire narrative of Genesis is so formed as to point toward the sacred history of Israel, the Jewish people: its slavery and redemption; its coming Temple in Jerusalem; its exile and salvation at the end of time. In the reading of the authors at hand, therefore, the powerful message of Genesis proclaims that the world's creation commenced a single, straight line of events, leading in the end to the salvation of Israel and through Israel of all humanity. That message—that history heads toward Israel's salvation—the sages derived from the book of Genesis and contributed to their own day. Therefore in their reading of Scripture a given story will bear a deeper truth about what it means to be Israel, on the one side, and what in the end of days will happen to Israel, on the other. True, their reading makes no explicit reference to what, if anything, had changed in the age of Constantine. But we do find repeated references to the four kingdoms, Babylonia, Media, Greece, Rome—and beyond the fourth will come Israel, fifth and last. So the rabbinic sages' message, in their theology of history, was that the present anguish prefigured the coming vindication of God's people.

The single most important proposition of *Genesis Rabbah* is that, in the story of the beginnings of creation, humanity, and Israel, we find the message of the meaning and end of the life of the Jewish people. The deeds of the founders supply signals for the children about what is going to come in the future. So the biography of Abraham, Isaac, and Jacob also constitutes a protracted account of the history of Israel later on. If the sages could announce a single syllogism and argue it systematically, that is the proposition upon which they would insist. (Christian) Rome claimed to be Israel, and, indeed, sages conceded, Rome shared the patrimony of Israel. That claim took the form of the Christians' appropriation of the Torah as "the Old Testament," so sages acknowledged a simple fact in acceding to the notion that, in some way, Rome too formed part of Israel. But it was the rejected part, the Ishmael, the Esau, not the Isaac, not the Jacob. The advent of Christian Rome precipitated the sustained, polemical, and rigorous and well-argued rereading of beginnings in light of the end. Rome then marked the conclusion of human history as Israel had known it. Beyond lay the coming of the true Messiah, the redemption of Israel, the salvation of the world, the end of time.

How was *Leviticus transformed in* Leviticus Rabbah?

Leviticus Rabbah, ca. 450 C.E., a compilation of thirty-seven propositional compositions on topics suggested by the book of Leviticus, argues that the rules of sanctification of the priesthood deliver a message of the salvation of all Israel. The compilation makes no pretense at a systematic exegesis of sequences of verses of Scripture, abandoning the verse by verse mode of organizing discourse. Each of the thirty-seven chapters proves cogent, and all of them spell out their respective statements in an intellectually economical, if rich, manner.

The message of *Leviticus Rabbah* is that the laws of history may be known, and that these laws, so far as Israel is concerned, focus upon the holy life of the community. If Israel then obeys the laws of society aimed at Israel's sanctification, then the foreordained history, resting on the merit of the ancestors, will unfold as Israel hopes. So there is no secret to the meaning of the events of the day, and Israel, for its part, can affect its destiny and effect salvation. The authorship of *Leviticus Rabbah* has thus joined the two great motifs, sanctification and salvation, by reading a biblical book, Leviticus, that is devoted to the former in the light of the requirements of the latter. In this way they made their fundamental point, which is that salvation at the end of history depends upon sanctification in the here and now.

To prove these points, the authors of the compositions make lists of facts that bear the same traits and show the working of rules of history. It follows that the mode of thought brought to bear upon the theme of history remains exactly the same as in the Mishnah: list-making, with data exhibiting similar taxonomic traits drawn together into lists based on common monothetic traits or definitions. These lists then through the power of repetition make a single enormous point or prove a social law of history. The catalogues of exemplary heroes and historical events serve a further purpose. They provide a model of how contemporary events are to be absorbed into the biblical paradigm. Since biblical events exemplify recurrent happenings, sin and redemption, forgiveness and atonement, they lose their onetime character. At the same time and in the same way, current events find a place within the ancient, but eternally present, paradigmatic scheme. So no new historical events, other than exemplary episodes in lives of heroes, demand narration because, through what is said about the past, what was happening in the times of the framers of *Leviticus Rabbah* would also come under consideration.

The focus of *Leviticus Rabbah's* laws of history is upon the society of Israel, its national fate and moral condition. Indeed, nearly all of the chapters of *Leviticus Rabbah* turn out to deal with the national, social condition of Israel, and this in three contexts: (1) Israel's setting in the history of the nations, (2) the sanctified character of the inner life of Israel itself, (3) the future, salvific history of Israel. So the biblical book that deals with the tabernacle in the wilderness, which sages understood to form the model for the holy Temple later on built in Jerusalem, now is shown to address the holy people. That is no paradox, rather a logical next step in the exploration of sanctification. Leviticus really discusses not the consecration of the cult but the sanctification of the nation—its conformity to God's will laid forth in the Torah, and God's rules. *Leviticus Rabbah* executes the paradox of shifting categories, applying to the nation—not a locative category—and its history the category that in the book subject to commentary pertained to the holy place—a locative category—and its eternal condition. The nation now is like the cult then, the ordinary Israelite now like the priest then. The holy way of life lived now, through acts to which merit accrues, corresponds to the holy rites then. The process of metamorphosis is full, rich, complete. When everything stands for something else, the something else repeatedly turns out to be the nation.

The authors of *Leviticus Rabbah* express their ideas, first, by selecting materials already written for other purposes and using them for their own, second, by composing materials, and third, by arranging both in *parashiyyot* (fifty-four lesson divisions of the Torah associated with the Babylonian tradition), an order through which propositions may reach expression. This involves both the modes of thought and the topical program, and also the unifying proposition of the document as a whole. (1) The principal mode of thought required one thing to be read in terms of another, one verse in light of a different verse (or topic, theme, symbol, idea), one situation in light of another. (2) The principal subject of thought is the moral condition of Israel, on the one side, and the salvation of Israel, on the other. (3) The single unifying proposition—the syllogism at the document's deepest structure—is that Israel's salvation depends upon its moral condition.

The recurrent message of the document may be stated in a brief way. God loves Israel, so gave them the Torah, which defines their life and governs their welfare. Israel is alone in its category (*sui generis*), so what is a virtue to Israel is a vice to the nations, life-giving to Israel, poison to the Gentiles. True, Israel sins, but God forgives that sin, having punished the nation on account of it. Such a process has yet to come to an end, but it will culminate in Israel's complete regeneration. Meanwhile, Israel's assurance of God's love lies in the many expressions of special concern, for even the humblest and most ordinary aspects of the national life: the food the nation eats, the sexual practices by which it procreates. These life-sustaining, life-transmitting activities draw God's special interest, as a mark of his general love for Israel. Israel then is supposed to achieve its life in conformity with the marks of God's love. The world to come will right all presently unbalanced relationships. What is good will go forward, what is bad will come to an end. The simple message is that the things people revere, the cult and its majestic course through the year, will go on; Jerusalem will come back, so too the Temple, in all their glory. Israel will be saved through the merit of the ancestors, atonement, study of Torah, practice of religious duties. The prevalence of the eschatological dimension in the formal structures, with its messianic and other expressions, here finds its counterpart in the repetition of the same few symbols in the expression of doctrine.

Salvation and sanctification join together in *Leviticus Rabbah*. The laws of the book of Leviticus, focused as they are on the sanctification of the nation through its cult, in *Leviticus Rabbah* indicate the rules of salvation as well. The message of *Leviticus Rabbah* attaches itself to the book of Leviticus, as if that book had come from prophecy and addressed the issue of the meaning of history and Israel's salvation. But the book of Leviticus came from the priesthood and spoke of sanctification. The paradoxical syllogism—the as-if reading, the opposite of how things seem—of the composers of *Leviticus Rabbah* therefore reaches simple formulation. In the very setting of sanctification we find the promise of salvation. In the topics of the cult and the priesthood we uncover the national and social issues of the moral life and redemptive hope of Israel. The repeated comparison and contrast of priesthood and prophecy, sanctification and salvation, turn out to produce a complement, which comes to most perfect union in the text at hand.

Where do I find a translation of the documents?

Genesis Rabbah: Jacob Neusner, *The Components of the Rabbinic Documents: From the Whole to the Parts: Vol. 9: Genesis Rabbah* (Atlanta,

Ga.: Scholars Press for USF Academic Commentary Series, 1998; repr., Peabody, Mass.: Hendrickson, forthcoming).

Leviticus Rabbah: Jacob Neusner, *The Components of the Rabbinic Documents: From the Whole to the Parts: Vol. 10: Leviticus Rabbah* (Atlanta, Ga.: Scholars Press for USF Academic Commentary Series, 1998; repr., Peabody, Mass.: Hendrickson, forthcoming).

16. *SONG OF SONGS RABBAH* AND *RUTH RABBAH*

How was the Song of Solomon transformed in Song of Songs Rabbah?

The Song of Songs (in the Christian Bible, "the Song of Solomon"—both titles referring to the opening line, "The Song of Songs, which is Solomon's") finds a place in the Torah because the collection of love songs in fact speaks about the relationship between God and Israel. The intent of the compilers of *Song of Songs Rabbah* is to justify that reading. What this means is that Midrash-exegesis turns to everyday experience—the love of husband and wife—for a metaphor of God's love for Israel and Israel's love for God. Then, when Solomon's song says, "O that you would kiss me with the kisses of your mouth! For your love is better than wine" (Song 1:2), sages of blessed memory think of how God kissed Israel. Reading the Song of Songs as a metaphor, the Judaic sages state in a systematic and orderly way their entire structure and system.

The sages who compiled *Song of Songs Rabbah* read the Song of Songs as a sequence of statements of urgent love between God and Israel, the holy people. How they convey the intensity of Israel's love of God forms the point of special interest in this document. For it is not in propositions that they choose to speak, but in the medium of symbols. The rabbinic sages set forth sequences of words that connote meanings, elicit emotions, stand for events, form the verbal equivalent of pictures or music or dance or poetry. Through the repertoire of these verbal symbols and their arrangement and rearrangement, the message the authors wish to convey emerges: not in so many words, but through words nonetheless. Sages chose for their compilation a very brief list of items among many possible candidates. They therefore determined to appeal to a highly restricted list of implicit meanings, calling upon some very few events or persons, repeatedly identifying these as the expressions of

God's profound affection for Israel, and Israel's deep love for God. The message of the document comes not from stories of what happened or did not happen but rather from the repetitious rehearsal of sets of symbols.

In reading the love songs of the Song of Songs as the story of the love affair of God and Israel, sages identify implicit meanings that are always few and invariably self-evident. No serious effort goes into demonstrating the fact that God speaks, or Israel speaks; the point of departure is the message and meaning the One or the other means to convey. To take one instance, time and again we shall be told that a certain expression of love in the poetry of the Song of Songs is God's speaking to Israel about (1) the Sea, (2) Sinai, and (3) the world to come; or at another level, (1) the first redemption, the one from Egypt, (2) the second redemption, the one from Babylonia, and (3) the third redemption, the one at the end of days. The repertoire of symbols covers Temple and schoolhouse, personal piety and public worship, and other matched pairs and sequences of coherent matters, all of them seen as embedded within the poetry. Here is an example of how Scripture's poetry is read as metaphor. The task of the reader is to discover a well-balanced interpretation, to discover that reality of the relation between God and Israel for which each image of the poem stands.

So Israel's holy life is metaphorized through the poetry of lover and beloved, Lover and Israel. Long lists of alternative meanings or interpretations end up saying just one thing, but in different ways. The implicit meanings prove very few indeed. When in *Song of Songs Rabbah* we have a sequence of items alleged to form a taxon, that is, a set of things that share a common indicative quality, what we have is a list. The list presents diverse matters that all together share, and therefore also set forth, a single fact or rule or phenomenon. That is why we can list them, in all their distinctive character and specificity, in a common catalogue of "other things" that pertain all together to one thing.

What message do the rabbinic sages find in the book of Ruth?

A commentary on the book of Ruth, the story of how the Moabite, Ruth, became an Israelite and the ancestress of the Messiah, David, *Ruth Rabbah* makes one paramount point through numerous details. It concerns the outsider who becomes the principal, Israel's Messiah's ancestress out of Moab, and this miracle is accomplished through mastery of the Torah. The main points of the document are these: (1) Israel's fate depends upon its proper conduct toward its leaders. (2) The leaders must not be arrogant. (3) Admitting the outsider depends upon the rules of the Torah. These differentiate among outsiders. Those who know the rules are able to apply them accurately and mercifully. (4) The proselyte is accepted because the Torah makes it possible to do so, and the condition of acceptance is complete and total submission to the Torah. Boaz taught Ruth the rules of the Torah, and she obeyed them carefully. (5) Those proselytes who are accepted are respected by God and are completely equal to all other Israelites. Those who marry them are masters of the Torah, and their descendants are masters of the Torah, typified by David. Boaz in his day and David in his day were the same in this regard. (6) What the proselyte therefore accomplishes is to take shelter under the wings of God's presence, and the proselyte who does so stands in the royal line of David, Solomon, and the Messiah. Over and over again, we see, the point is made that Ruth the Moabitess, perceived by the ignorant as an outsider, enjoyed complete equality with all other Israelites, because she had accepted the yoke of the Torah, married a great sage (Boaz), and through their descendants produced the Messiah-sage, David.

Scripture provided everything but the main thing: the paradox of the Messiah's deriving from the alien Land of Moab. But sages impose upon the whole their distinctive message, which is the priority of the Torah, the extraordinary power of the Torah to join the opposites—Messiah, utter outsider—into a single figure, and to accomplish this union of opposites through a woman. The femininity of Ruth is as critical to the whole as the Moabite origin: the two modes of the abnormal (from the rabbinic sages' perspective), outsider as against Israelite, woman as against man, therefore are invoked, and both for the same purpose, to show how, through the Torah, all things become one. That is the message of the document, and, seen whole, the principal message, to which all other messages prove peripheral.

The authorship decided to compose a document concerning the book of Ruth in order to make a single point. Everything else was subordinated to that definitive intention. Once the work got underway, the task was not one of exposition so much as repetition, not unpacking and exploring a complex conception, but restating the point, on the one side, and eliciting or evoking the proper attitude that was congruent with that point, on the other. The decision, viewed after the fact, was to make one statement in an enormous number of ways. It is that the Torah dictates Israel's fate. If you want to know what that fate will be, study the Torah, and if you want to control that fate, follow the model of the Messiah-sage. As usual, therefore, what we find is a recasting of the Deuteronomic-prophetic theology.

Where do I find a translation of the documents?

Song of Songs Rabbah: Jacob Neusner, *The Components of the Rabbinic Documents: From the Whole to the Parts: Vol. 5: Song of Songs Rabbah* (Atlanta, Ga.: Scholars Press for USF Academic Commentary Series, 1997; repr., Peabody, Mass.: Hendrickson, forthcoming).

Ruth Rabbah: Jacob Neusner, *The Components of the Rabbinic Documents: From the Whole to the Parts: Vol. 3: Ruth Rabbah* (Atlanta, Ga.: Scholars Press for USF Academic Commentary Series, 1997; repr., Peabody, Mass.: Hendrickson, forthcoming).

17. *LAMENTATIONS RABBAH*

How was Lamentations transformed in Lamentations Rabbah?

The theme of *Lamentations Rabbah* is Israel's relationship with God, and the message concerning that theme is that the stipulative covenant still and always governs that relationship. Therefore everything that happens to Israel makes sense and bears meaning; and Israel is not helpless before its fate but controls its own destiny. This is the whole message of the compilation, and it is the only message that is repeated throughout; everything else proves secondary and derivative of the fundamental proposition that the destruction of the Temple in Jerusalem in 70 C.E.—as much as in 586 B.C.E.—proves the enduring validity of the covenant, its rules, and its promise of redemption.

Lamentations Rabbah sets forth a covenantal theology, in which Israel and God have mutually and reciprocally agreed to bind themselves to a common Torah; the rules of the relationship are such that an infraction triggers its penalty willy-nilly, but obedience to the Torah likewise brings its reward, in the context envisaged by our compilers, the reward of redemption. The compilation sets forth a single message, which is reworked in only a few ways: Israel suffers because of sin, God will respond to Israel's atonement, on the one side, and loyalty to the covenant in the Torah, on the other. And when Israel has attained the merit that accrues through the Torah, God will redeem Israel. That is the simple, rock-hard and repeated message of this rather protracted reading of the book of Lamentations. Still, *Lamentations Rabbah* proves nearly as much a commentary in the narrowest sense—verse by verse amplification, paraphrase, exposition—as it is a compilation in the working definition of this inquiry of mine.

What holds the document together and gives it, if not coherence, then at least flow and movement, are the successive passages of (mere) exposition. All the more stunning, therefore, is the simple fact that, when all has been set forth and completed, there really is that simple message that God's unique relationship with Israel, which is unique among the nations, works itself out even now, in a time of despair and disappointment. The resentment of the present condition, recapitulating the calamity of the destruction of the Temple, finds its resolution and remission in the redemption that will follow Israel's regeneration through the Torah—that is the program, that is the proposition, and in this compilation, there is no other.

What are the specific doctrines of Lamentations Rabbah and how did rabbinic Judaism explain the destruction of the Temple of Jerusalem and God's response to that catastrophe?

Lamentations Rabbah focused on the themes of (1) Israel and God, with special reference to the covenant, the Torah, and the Land; (2) Israel and the nations, with interest in Israel's history, past, present, and future, and how that cyclical is to be known; (3) Israel on its own terms, with focus upon Israel's distinctive leadership; and (4) the book of Lamentations in particular. The rabbinic reading of the book of Lamentations repeats one point: the stipulative covenant still and always governs that relationship. Therefore everything that happens to Israel makes sense and bears meaning, and Israel is not helpless before its fate but controls its own destiny. Israel's relationship with God is treated with special reference to the covenant, the Torah, and the Land.

This is the one and whole message; everything else proves secondary and derivative of the fundamental proposition that the destruction proves the enduring validity of the covenant, its rules, and its promise of redemption. Israel's relationship with God is treated with special reference to the covenant, the Torah, and the Land. By reason of the sins of the Israelites, they have gone into exile with the destruction of the Temple. The founders of the family, Abraham, Isaac, and Jacob, also went into exile. Now the founders cannot be accused of lacking in religious duties, in attention to teachings of the Torah and prophecy, and in carrying out the requirements of righteousness (philanthropy) and good deeds, and the like.

The people are at fault for their own condition (*Lamentations Rabbah* I:i.1–7). Torah-study defines the condition of Israel, e.g., "If you have seen [the inhabitants of] towns uprooted from their places in the land of Israel, know that it is because they did not pay the salary of scribes and teachers" (II.i). So long as Judah and Benjamin were at home, God could take comfort at the loss of the ten tribes; once they went into exile, God began to mourn (II:ii). Israel survived Pharaoh and Sennacherib, but not God's punishment (III:i). After the disaster in Jeremiah's time, Israel emerged from Eden—but could come back (IV:i). God did not play favorites among the tribes; when any of them sinned, he punished them through exile (VI:i). Israel was punished because of the ravaging of words of Torah and prophecy, righteous men, religious duties, and good deeds (VII:i). The land of Israel, the Torah, and the Temple are ravaged, to the shame of Israel (Jer 9:19–21) (VIII:i). The Israelites practiced idolatry. Still more did the pagans. God was neglected by the people and was left solitary, so God responded to the people's actions (X:i). If you had achieved the merit (using the theological language at hand), then you would have enjoyed everything, but since you did not have the merit, you enjoyed nothing (XI:i). The Israelites did not trust God, so they suffered disaster (XIII.i). The Israelites scorned God and brought dishonor upon God among the nations (XV:i).

While God was generous with the Israelites in the wilderness, under severe conditions, he was harsh with them in civilization, under pleasant conditions, because they sinned and angered him (XVI:i). With merit one drinks good water in Jerusalem, without, bad water in the exile of Babylonia; with merit one sings songs and Psalms in Jerusalem, without, dirges and lamentations in Babylonia. At stake is peoples' merit, not God's grace (XIX:i). The contrast is drawn between redemption and disaster, the giving of the Torah and the destruction of the Temple (XX:i). When the Israelites went into exile among the nations of the world, not one of them could produce a word of Torah from his mouth; God punished Israel for its sins (XXI:i). Idolatry was the cause (XXII:i). The destruction of the Temple was possible only because God had already abandoned it (XXIV:ii). When the Temple was destroyed, God was answerable to the patriarchs for what he had done (XXIV:ii). The Presence of God departed from the Temple by stages (XXV:i).

Where do I find a translation of the document?

Lamentations Rabbah: Jacob Neusner, *The Components of the Rabbinic Documents: From the Whole to the Parts: Vol. 4: Lamentations Rabbah* (Atlanta, Ga.: Scholars Press for USF Academic Commentary Series, 1997; repr., Peabody, Mass.: Hendrickson, forthcoming).

PART 5

AGGADAH AND THE THEOLOGY OF RABBINIC JUDAISM

18. AGGADAH AND HISTORY

————◉————

What was the conception of history put forth by rabbinic Judaism in the Aggadah?

In its reworking of Scriptural narratives the Aggadah intersects with events that are deemed historical. But it portrays them as supernatural: the salvation at the Red Sea, the entry into the Land, the destruction of the Temple, and so on. These narratives then embody abstract theology in concrete terms. How did the rabbinic sages tell the tale of the Torah so as to make a statement of their theological system and structure?

The answer is, the Aggadah told the story of the Torah not as history but as cosmology; the story of the Torah is the story of the creation of the world. The record of history reveals the Creator's rules to govern the social order. The Torah, oral and written, spoke for Eternity: God's plan in creating the world. Rabbinic Judaism saw the Torah as the foundation of creation, and held that the Torah contained the secrets of life, both natural and social. This it showed in a powerful reading of Gen 1:1 in light of Prov 8:30–31;

> "In the beginning God created" (Gen. 1:1):
>
> R. Oshaia commenced [discourse by citing the following verse:] " 'Then I was beside him like a little child, and I was daily his delight [rejoicing before him always, rejoicing in his inhabited world, and delighting in the sons of men]' (Prov. 8:30–31).
>
> "The word [translated 'little child' also] means 'workman.' "
>
> [In the cited verse] the Torah speaks, "I was the work-plan of the Holy One, blessed be he."
>
> In the accepted practice of the world, when a mortal king builds a palace, he does not build it out of his own head, but he follows a work-plan.

And [the one who supplies] the work-plan does not build out of his own head, but he has designs and diagrams, so as to know how to situate the rooms and the doorways.

Thus the Holy One, blessed be he, consulted the Torah when he created the world.

So the Torah stated, "By means of 'the beginning' [that is to say, the Torah] did God create . . . " (Gen. 1:1).

And the word for "beginning" refers only to the Torah, as Scripture says, "The Lord made me as the beginning of his way" (Prov. 8:22).

Genesis Rabbah I:i.1A–B, 2A–H

The reading of Prov 8:30–31 takes as the speaker of the verse the Torah itself, and the Torah says, "I was beside him, like a master workman," or a work-plan. God then consulted the Torah when he created the world. Then Gen 1:1 is read in light of the interpretation of Prov 8:30–31. The Torah is referred to as "the beginning," thus "In the beginning" yields, "By means of the Torah."

The exegetes set forth a subtle and profound assertion of the Torah as the key to creation, the handbook of reality. In that context, to ask for a "conception of history" is to miss the very heart of the matter. In that context, rabbinic Judaism—"the Torah, oral and written"—defines itself beyond time. It does not set forth a conception of history at all, because it does not recognize history as a category for organizing the facts of reality.

What it sought instead was *patterns* that are realized by particular events. These patterns yield access to the rules that govern. These are to be discerned in the Torah. For us it is not easy to imagine a thought world in which patterns, rather than sequences of events treated as cause and effect, are asked to organize experience. Yet the Aggadah sets forth a thought world in which at stake are not beginnings and endings in an ordinal or (other) temporal sense. At issue, rather, are balances and proportions, the match of this to that, start to finish. True, that mode of thought is not commonplace outside of the rule-seeking sciences of nature and society.

How did that conception relate to the conception of history put forth by the Hebrew Scriptures from Genesis through Kings?

That fact will have surprised the authors of ancient Israelite Scripture, in particular those who set forth Genesis through Kings as a singular, continuous narrative. They saw events as purposive, revealing a pattern. By "history" as they portrayed the past, they meant an account of how events are so organized and narrated as to teach lessons. These chosen events reveal patterns, tell what people must do and why, what will happen tomorrow. The Pentateuchal and Prophetic writings of Scripture lay heavy stress on history in the sense just now given.

The legacy of prophecy, apocalypse, and history maintains that events bear meaning; God's message and judgment. Just as prophecy takes up the interpretation of historical events, so historians retell these events in the frame of prophetic theses. And out of the two—historiography as a mode of mythic reflection, prophecy as a means of mythic construction—emerges a picture of future history, that is, what is going to happen. That picture, framed in terms of visions and supernatural symbols, in the end focuses, as much as do prophecy and history writing, upon the here and now.

How did the Aggadah intersect with the Halakah when rabbinic Judaism defined an event?

The theology of rabbinic Judaism begins in the characterization of the rules for the social order embedded within, and embodied by, the Aggadah. But that theology to make a difference must end in the realization of those rules by the Halakah. So any account of the theology of history that forms the foundations of rabbinic Judaism must ask how the Halakah expresses that same theology that the Aggadah puts forth?

A Halakic document that intersects with Aggadic narrative, the Mishnah contains very few episodic tales and no large-scale conception of history. It organizes its system in non-historical terms. Instead of narratives, it gives descriptions of how things are done, that is, descriptive laws. Instead of reflection on the meaning and end of history, it constructs a world in which history plays little part. Instead of narratives full of didactic meaning, it provides lists of events so as to expose the traits that they share and thus the rules to which they conform.

The framers of the Mishnah explicitly refer to very few events, treating those they do mention within a focus quite separate from what happened—the unfolding of the events themselves. They rarely create or use narratives. More probative still, historical events do not supply organizing categories or taxonomic classifications. We find no tractate devoted to the destruction of the Temple, no complete chapter of the Mishnah detailing the events of Bar Kokhba, the failed Messiah of the second century C.E., nor even a sustained celebration of the events of the sages' own historical life. When things that have happened are mentioned, it is neither in order to narrate, nor to interpret and draw lessons from, the event. It is either to illustrate a point of law or to pose a problem of the law—always *en passant*, never in a pointed way.

How did the Halakah and the Aggadah converge in historical events?

How did the sages deal with the cataclysmic events that they acknowledged bore weighty meaning? Take for example the destruction of the Temple in 586 B.C.E. and again in 70 C.E. Although the sages surely mourned for the destruction and the loss of Israel's principal mode of worship, and certainly recorded the event of the ninth of Ab in 70 C.E., they did so in their characteristic way: they listed the event as an item in a catalogue of things that are like one another and so demand the same response. And having composed two such lists, they hierarchized them. But then the destruction no longer appears as a unique event. It is absorbed into a pattern of like disasters, all exhibiting similar taxonomic traits, events to which the people, now well-schooled in tragedy, knows full well the appropriate response. So catalogues of events, as much as lists of species of melons, served as brilliant apologetic by providing reassurance that nothing lies beyond the range and power of ordering system and stabilizing pattern.

> Five events took place for our fathers on the seventeenth of Tammuz, and five on the ninth of Ab.
>
> On the seventeenth of Tammuz (1) the tablets [of the Torah] were broken, (2) the daily whole offering was canceled, (3) the city wall was breached, (4) Apostemos burned the Torah, and (5) he set up an idol in the Temple.
>
> On the ninth of Ab (1) the decree was made against our forefathers that they should not enter the land, (2) the first Temple {586 B.C.E.} and (3) the second [Temple] {70 C.E.} were destroyed, (4) Betar was taken {in the war fought by Bar Kokhba}, and (5) the city of Jerusalem was plowed up [after the war {fought by Bar Kokhba against the Roman emperor} . . . Hadrian].
>
> When Ab comes, rejoicing diminishes.

4:7 In the week in which the ninth of Ab occurs it is prohibited to get a haircut and to wash one's clothes.

But on Thursday of that week these are permitted,

because of the honor due to the Sabbath. {One prepares for the Sabbath, which begins on Friday evening, on Thursday of any given week.}

On the eve of the ninth of Ab a person should not eat two prepared dishes, nor should one eat meat or drink wine.

Rabban Simeon b. Gamaliel says, "He should make some change from ordinary procedures."

R. Judah declares people liable {obligated} to turn over beds.

But sages did not concur with him.

Mishnah *Ta'anit* 4:6–7

M. Ta'anit 4:7 shows the context in which the list of *m. Ta'anit* 4:6 stands. The stunning calamities catalogued at *m. Ta'anit* 4:6 form groups, reveal common traits, so are subject to classification. Then the laws of *m. Ta'anit* 4:7 provide regular rules for responding to, coping with, these untimely catastrophes, all (fortuitously) in a single classification. So the raw materials of history are absorbed into the ahistorical, supernatural system of the Mishnah. The process of absorption and regularization of the unique and onetime moment is illustrated in the passage at hand.

The Mishnah absorbs into its encompassing system all events, small and large. With what happens the sages accomplish what they do with everything else: a vast labor of classification, an immense construction of the order and rules governing the classification of everything on earth and in Heaven. The disruptive character of history—onetime events of unique significance—scarcely impresses the rabbinic philosophers. They find no difficulty in showing that what appears unique and beyond classification has in fact happened before and so falls within the range of trustworthy rules and known procedures. Once history's components, onetime events, lose their distinctiveness, then history as a didactic intellectual construct, as a source of lessons and rules, also loses all pertinence.

So lessons and rules come from sorting things out and classifying them, that is, from the procedures and modes of thought of the philosopher seeking regularity. To this labor of classification, the historian's way of selecting data and arranging them into patterns of meaning to teach lessons, proves inconsequential. Onetime events are not what matters. The world is composed of nature and supernature. The repetitious laws that count are those to be discovered in Heaven and, in Heaven's creation and counterpart, on earth. Keep those laws and things will work out. Break them, and the result is predictable: calamity of whatever sort will supervene in accordance with the rules. But just because it is predictable, a catastrophic happening testifies to what has always been and must always be, in accordance with reliable rules and within categories already discovered and well explained. History is transformed and transcended by providing facts for theological construction.

19. TORAH

What, exactly, did rabbinic Judaism mean by "Torah"?

The word *Torah* stands for instruction—God's revelation to Moses at Sinai. It further refers to all authoritative teaching by sages, which enjoy the status of revelation by God to Moses at Sinai. The religion that the world calls "Judaism" calls itself "Torah," for the outsider names the religion, but the faithful define it by their lives together. Holy Israel has always looked to the Torah to find God and what God is, does, and wants of humanity. The doctrine of Torah moreover encompasses among much prized religious virtues and actions study of the Torah as the highest priority of Judaism. The word *Torah* bore seven distinct meanings:

(1) When the Torah refers to a particular thing, it is to a holy scroll containing divinely revealed words.

(2) The Torah may further refer to revelation, not as an object but as a corpus of doctrine.

(3) When one "does an act of Torah" the disciple "studies" or "learns," and the master "teaches," Torah. Hence while the word *Torah* never appears as a verb, it does refer to an act.

(4) The word also bears a quite separate sense, *torah* as category or classification or corpus of rules, e.g., "the torah of driving a car" is a usage entirely acceptable to some documents, including the books of Leviticus and Numbers. This generic usage of the word does occur.

(5) The word *Torah* very commonly refers to a status, distinct from and above another status, as "teachings of Torah" as against "teachings of scribes." For the two Talmuds that distinction is absolutely critical to the entire hermeneutic enterprise. But it is important even in the Mishnah.

(6) Obviously, no account of the meaning of the word *Torah* can ignore the distinction between the two Torahs, written and oral. It is important only in the secondary stages of the formation of the literature.

(7) Finally, the word *Torah* refers to a source of salvation, often fully worked out in stories about how the individual and the nation will be saved through Torah. In general, the sense of the word "salvation" is not complicated. It is simply salvation in the way in which Deuteronomy and the Deuteronomic historians understand it: kings who do what God wants win battles, those who do not, lose. So too here, people who study and do Torah are saved from sickness and death, and the way Israel can save itself from its condition of degradation also is through Torah.

That does not exhaust the possibilities. A striking and unexpected usage proves also highly suggestive:

> Said R. Aqiba, "I once went after R. Joshua to the privy and I learned the three things from him.
>
> "I learned that people defecate not on an east-west axis but on a north-south axis.
>
> "I learned that one urinates not standing but sitting.
>
> "And I learned that one wipes not with the right hand but with the left."
>
> Said Ben Azzai to him, "Do you behave so insolently toward your master?"
>
> He said to him, "It is a matter of Torah, which I need to learn."
>
> Ben Azzai says, "I once followed R. Aqiba into the privy, and I learned three things from him:
>
> "I learned that people defecate not on an east-west axis but on a north-south axis.
>
> "And I learned that people urinate not standing up but sitting down.
>
> "And I learned that people wipe themselves not with the right hand but with the left."
>
> Said R. Judah to him, "Do you behave all that insolently toward your master?"
>
> He said to him, "It is a matter of Torah, which I need to learn."
>
> R. Kahana went and hid under Rab's bed. He heard [Rab and his wife] "conversing" and laughing and doing what comes naturally. He said to him, "It appears that Abba's mouth has never before tasted 'the dish.'"
>
> He said, "Kahana, are you here! Get out! That's disgraceful!"

He said to him, "It is a matter of Torah, which I need to learn."

Bavli *Berakhot* 62a XIX.3B–4C

Here is a set of three curious stories that make the same jarring point: natural bodily processes, intimate chapters in the private life, both fall within the framework of Torah, which is to be taught by the sage and must be learned by the disciple. The details of the text need not detain us for long. The story shows us that "the Torah" referring to a specific set of authoritative Scriptures has lost its definite article. It now refers to authoritative teachings by a sage, teachings deriving from tradition to which the sage in particular has access and affecting every detail of ordinary life. The doctrine of "Torah" in Judaism then refers not to canonical writings alone but to God's will for holy Israel in every dimension of the everyday.

What is the standing of the oral part of the Torah?

The oral part of the Torah, conveyed in the teaching of the master to the disciple, enjoys higher standing than the written part of the Torah. The following is explicit in the matter:

> R. Haggai in the name of R. Samuel bar Nahman, "Some teachings were handed on orally, and some things were handed on in writing, and we do not know which of them is the more precious. But on the basis of that which is written, 'And the Lord said to Moses, Write these words; in accordance with these words I have made a covenant with you and with Israel' (Ex. 34:27), [we conclude] that the ones which are handed on orally are the more precious." R. Yohanan and R. Yudan b. R. Simeon—one said, "If you have kept what is preserved orally and also kept what is in writing, I shall make a covenant with you, and if not, I shall not make a covenant with you."

> The other said, "If you have kept what is preserved orally and you have kept what is preserved in writing, you shall receive a reward, and if not, you shall not receive a reward."

Yerushalmi *Hagigah* 1:8

Here we have absolutely explicit evidence that people believed part of the Torah had been preserved not in writing but orally. The point for the rabbinic sages found in Exod 34:27 is that two different sets of words are mentioned in the biblical passage. God says "Write these (first) words" and then God says "in accordance with these (other) words, I have made a covenant with you and with Israel." Thus there were two sets of words expressed by God, one to be written down; the other to be held orally. And the oral part, now preserved in the Mishnah and related writings, takes a high position indeed (because it is with these [other] words that the covenant was made).

What was rabbinic Judaism's attitude toward the Mosaic Law, given the fact that much of the Mosaic Judaism could not be practiced after 70 C.E.?

Clearly, important parts of the Torah, written and oral alike, could not be carried out from 70 C.E. onward. Approximately half of the category-formations of the Halakah, dealing with the Temple and its offerings and with most questions of purity, bore no relevance to everyday life once the Temple was destroyed. The laws could not be kept, but they could be studied and preserved as integral to the revealed will of God in the Torah. When the Messiah comes and restores Israel to the Land of Israel, the Temple to Jerusalem, and the offerings to the altar of the Temple in Jerusalem, then those laws will be reinstated. Until then, studying them represented an act of hope and Messianic affirmation.

20. GOD IN THE AGGADAH

What was the doctrine of God set forth by the Aggadah of rabbinic Judaism?

Rabbinic Judaism knows God through God's self-manifestation in the Torah—and otherwise, so that Judaism maintains, there should be no specific, reliable knowledge of God. The rabbinic doctrine of God is reliably set forth by the Shema and spelled out by the Aggadah. He is Creator of heaven and earth, who reveals the Torah and who redeems humanity at the end of days.

What we know about God we know because God's grace has permitted us to know—that alone. So the proposition is, the facts about God that are provided by the Torah themselves comprise an act of grace.

> {R. Aqiba says,} "Precious is the human being, who was created in the image [of God].
>
> "It was an act of still greater love that it was made known to him that he was created in the image [of God], as it is said, *For in the image of God he made man* (Gen. 9:6)."
>
> Mishnah *Avot* 3:14

This statement forms the paradigm of Judaic theology: not truth alone, but truth yielded by the Torah and enhanced because of the Torah's verification and validation. That is what it means to say; Israel knows God through the Torah. God is known because God makes himself known.

Was God in the Aggadah "the Old Testament God of vengeance"?

Does that knowledge, yielded by the Torah, mean that God is the angry and vengeful God of the Old Testament, as some suppose? In the one whole Torah, written as mediated by the oral, God appears as infinitely merciful and loving, passionate as a teenage lover, whom the Judaic community knows above all by the name, "the All-Merciful," who can be just because he is merciful, and who is merciful because he is just.

How is God portrayed as premise, presence, person, and personality?

The oral Torah portrays God in four ways: as premise, presence, person, and personality.

(1) God as premise occurs in passages in which a particular decision is reached because that people believe God created the world and has revealed the Torah to Israel. We know that God forms the premise of a passage because the particular proposition of that passage appeals to God as premise of all being, e.g., author and authority of the Torah. Things are decided one way, rather than some other, on that basis.

The premise that God has imposed requirements upon humanity in general, and Israel in particular, encompasses the entirely of the courpus of commandments present in the Torah, and the Mishnah sets forth the rules governing observance of these commandments. From that fact it must follow that God forms the principal premise of all Mishnaic dicourse, even though that premise rarely reaches explicit expression. That is, moreover, a statement, not of theory, but of everyday fact. Where the fact makes a difference can be easily specified. Let me give one instance. If one violates the law of the Torah, as set forth in the Mishnah, one transgresses the expressed will of God. One explicit statement of that view is as follows:

> Those [who participate in a loan on interest {practice usury}] violate a negative commandment: (1) the lender {the one who lends at usury}, (2) the borrower, (3) the guarantor {the one who guarantees the loan}, and (4) {the} witnesses. Sages say, "Also (5) the scribe."

> (1) They violate the negative commandment, *You will not give [him] your money upon usury* (Lev. 25:37). (2) And [they violate the negative command], *You will not take usury from him* (Lev. 25:36). (3) And [they violate the negative command], *You shall not be a creditor to him* (Ex. 22:25). (4) And [they violate the negative command], *Nor shall you lay upon him usury* (Ex. 22:25). (5) And they violate the negative command, *You shall not put a stumbling block before the blind, but you shall fear your God. I am the Lord* (Lev. 19:14).

Mishnah *Baba Mesi'a* 5:11

Here is an explicit statement, among many, that God through the Torah stands behind the laws of the Mishnah, and that those who violate the laws offend God while those who keep them please God. One fundamental trait of divinity is to lay forth and then guarantee rules of order and regularity in the world.

(2) God as presence stands for yet another consideration. It involves an authorship's referring to God as part of a situation in the here and now. When a law speaks of a wife's being accused of unfaithfulness to her husband, the law expects that God will intervene in a particular case, in the required ordeal, and so declare the decision for the case at hand. God is not only premise but very present in discourse and in making a decision.

(3) There is a setting in which God is held always to know and pay attention to specific cases, and that involves God as a "you," that is, as a person. For example, liturgy understands that God also hears prayer, hence is not only a presence but a person, a you, responding to what is said, requiring certain attitudes and rejecting others.

(4) God emerges as a vivid and highly distinctive personality, actor, conversation-partner, hero. In references to God as a personality, God is given corporeal traits. God looks like God in particular, just as each person exhibits distinctive physical traits. Not only so, but in matters of heart and mind and spirit, well-limned individual traits of personality and action alike endow God with that particularity that identifies every individual human being. When God is given attitudes but no active role in discourse, referred to but not invoked as part of a statement, God serves as person. When God participates as a hero and protagonist in a narrative, God gains traits of personality and emerges as God like humanity: God incarnate.

How does the Aggadah account for the diversity of portraits of God?

A definitive statement of the proposition that in diverse forms God appears to humanity is in the following:

> Said R. Levi, "The Holy One, blessed be he, appeared to them like an icon that has faces in all directions, so that if a thousand people look at it, it appears to look at them as well.
>
> "So too when the Holy One, blessed be he, when he was speaking, each Israelite would say, 'With me in particular the Word speaks.'

"What is written here is not, I am the Lord, your [plural] God, but rather, I am the Lord your [singular] God who brought you out of the land of Egypt (Ex. 20:2)."

That God may show diverse faces to various people is now established. The reason for God's variety is made explicit. People differ, and God, in the image of whom all mortals are made, must therefore sustain diverse images—all of them formed in the model of human beings:

Said R. Yosé bar Hanina, "And it was in accord with the capacity of each one of them to listen and understand what the Word spoke with him.

And do not be surprised at this matter, for when the manna came down to Israel, all would find its taste appropriate to their circumstance, infants in accord with their capacity, young people in accord with their capacity, old people in accord with their capacity.

"infants in accord with their capacity: just as an infant sucks from the teat of his mother, so was its flavor, as it is said, 'Its taste was like the taste of rich cream' (Num. 11:8).

"young people in accord with their capacity: as it is said, 'My bread also which I gave you, bread and oil and honey' (Ez. 16:19)

"old people in accord with their capacity: as it is said 'the taste of it was like wafers made with honey' (Ex. 16:31).

"Now if in the case of manna, each one would find its taste appropriate to his capacity, so in the matter of the Word, each one understood in accord with capacity.

"Said David, 'The voice of the Lord is [in accord with one's] in strength' (Ps. 29:4).

"What is written is not, in accord with his strength in particular, but rather, in accord with one's strength, meaning, in accord with the capacity of each one.

"Said to them the Holy One, blessed be He, 'It is not in accord with the fact that you hear a great many voices, but you should know that it is I who [speaks to all of you individually]: 'I am the Lord your God who brought you out of the land of Egypt' (Ex. 20:2)."

Pesiqta of Rab Kahana XII:xxv.3

The individuality and particularity of God rest upon the diversity of humanity. But, it must follow, the model of humanity—"in our image"—dictates how we are to envisage the face of God. And that is the starting point of our inquiry. The Torah defines what we know about God—but the Torah also tells us that we find God in the face of the other: in our image, after our likeness, means, everyone is in God's image, so if we want to know God, we had best look closely into the face of all humanity, one by one, one by one.

How is God wholly other?

The single most important narrative about the personality of God marks the point at which humanity cannot imitate God but must relate to God in an attitude of profound humility and obedience. In the Aggadah God is always God:

> Said R. Judah said Rab, "At the time that Moses went up on high, he found the Holy One in session, affixing crowns to the letters [of the words of the Torah].

> He said to him, 'Lord of the universe, who is stopping you [from regarding the document as perfect without these additional crowns on the letters]?'

> "He said to him, 'There is a man who is going to arrive at the end of many generations, and Aqiba b. Joseph is his name, who is going to interpret on the basis of each point of the crowns heaps and heaps of laws.'

> "He said to him, 'Lord of the universe, show him to me.'

> "He said to him, 'Turn around.'

> "He {Moses} went and took a seat at the end of eight rows, but he could not grasp what the people were saying. He felt faint. But when the discourse reached a certain matter, and the disciples said, 'My lord, how do you know this?' and he answered, 'It is a law given to Moses from Sinai,' he regained his composure.

> "He went and came before the Holy One. He said before him, 'Lord of the Universe, How come you have someone like that and yet you give the Torah through me?'

> "He said to him, 'Silence! That is how the thought came to me {That is how I have decided matters}.'"

> "He said to him, 'Be silent.'

"He said to him, 'Lord of the universe, you have {now} shown me his {mastery of the} Torah, now show me his reward.'

"He said to him, 'Turn around.'

"He turned around and saw his flesh being weighed out at the butcher-stalls in the market.

"He said to him, 'Lord of the universe, such is {his mastery of} Torah, {and} such is his reward?'

"He said to him, 'Silence!. That is how the thought came to me {That is how I have decided matters}.'"

Bavli *Menahot* 29b III.5

God makes all the decisions and guides the unfolding of the story. Moses who is called "our rabbi" and forms the prototype and ideal of the sage does not understand God's Torah. So God then tells him to shut up and accept his decree. God does what he likes, with whom he likes. In the end God is wholly other.

21. ISRAEL

What was the doctrine of Israel set forth by rabbinic Judaism?

To rabbinic Judaism "Israel" does not speak of a merely ethnic, this-worldly people. "Israel" refers to a supernatural community. It stands for the holy people whom God has called into being through Abraham and Sarah and their descendants, to whom the prophetic promises were made, and with whom the covenants were entered. "Israel" is a theological category, not a fact of sociology or ethnic culture or secular politics. Supernatural traits include being "chosen," "holy," subject to God's special love and concern.

Did rabbinic Judaism accept converts? What was their status?

A Gentile of any origin or status, slave or free, Greek or barbarian, African or European, male or female, may enter the "Israel" of rabbinic Judaism on equal terms with those born into the community, becoming children of Abraham and Sarah. If a Gentile keeps the Torah, he or she is saved. But by keeping the Torah, the Gentile has ceased to be Gentile and become Israelite, worthy even of the high priesthood:

". . . by the pursuit of which man shall live":

R. Jeremiah says, "How do I know that even a gentile who keeps the Torah, lo, he is like the high priest?

"Scripture says, 'by the pursuit of which man shall live.'"

And so Scripture says, "'And this is the Torah of the priests, Levites, and Israelites,' is not what is said here, but rather, 'This is the Torah of the man, O Lord God' (2 Sam. 7:19)."

And Scripture says, " 'open the gates and let priests, Levites, and Israelites will enter it' is not what is said, but rather, 'Open the gates and let the righteous nation, who keeps faith, enter it' (Is. 26:2)."

And so Scripture says, " 'This is the gate of the Lord. Priests, Levites, and Israelites . . . ' is not what is said, but rather, 'the righteous shall enter into it' (Ps. 118:20).

And so Scripture says, " 'What is said is not, 'Rejoice, priests, Levites, and Israelites,' but rather, 'Rejoice, O righteous, in the Lord' (Ps. 33:1)."

And so Scripture says, "It is not, 'Do good, O Lord, to the priests, Levites, and Israelites,' but rather, 'Do good, O Lord, to the good, to the upright in heart' (Ps. 125:4)."

"Thus, even a gentile who keeps the Torah, lo, he is like the high priest."

Sifra CXCIV:ii.15

God responds, also, to the acts of merit taken by Gentiles, as much as to those of Israel. The upshot is "Gentile" and "Israel" classify through the presence or absence of the same traits; they form taxonomic categories that can in the case of the Gentile change when that which is classified requires reclassification. That is to say, the classification of being a Gentile or 'of Israel' changes based on the actions and attitude of the individual in response to God.

Here an important qualification is required. Gentiles to be sure may become Israel, but while they are accepted when they present themselves properly, ordinarily they are not pressed to enter the kingdom of Heaven. The motivation must well up from within; Israelites do not encourage Gentiles to become Israel, because, in this world, clear penalties attach themselves to those who accept God's rule. It is not easy to be Israel. So Gentiles are not encouraged to become part of Israel, because of the rigors of such a commitment and the disadvantages incurred thereby; if he still persists, he is welcomed. This view of how, in this age, before the time of the resurrection and the judgment, Gentiles are to be dealt with is expressed in so many words as follows:

A person who comes to convert at this time—they say to him, "How come you have come to convert? Don't you know that at this time the Israelites are forsaken and harassed, despised, baited, and afflictions come upon them?" If he said, "I know full well, and I am not worthy [of sharing their suffering]," they accept him forthwith. And they inform him about some of the lesser religious duties and some of the weightier religious duties. He is informed about the sin of neglecting the religious duties involving gleanings, forgotten sheaf, corner of the field, and poorman's tithe. They further inform him about the penalty for not keeping the commandments.

Bavli *Yevamot* 47a–b 4:12.I.37B

The Gentile has to face the reality of Israel's condition in this world, but also the expectations that the Torah imposes, the matters formerly of no concern that now become occasions for sin, for example. What the Gentile does not know to make a difference, the Israelite learns presents the opportunity to violate God's will in the Torah.

The children of converts become Israelite without qualification. That is shown by an important fact. No distinction is made between the child of a convert and the child of a native-born Israelite. Since that fact bears concrete and material consequences, e.g., in the right to marry any other Israelite without distinction by reason of familial origin, it follows that the "Israel" of rabbinic Judaism must be understood in a wholly theological framework. This Judaism knows no distinction between children of the flesh and children of the promise and therefore cannot address a merely ethnic "Israel," because for rabbinic Judaism, "Israel" is always and only defined by the Torah received and represented by "our sages of blessed memory" as the word of God, never by the happenstance of secular history.

Was "Israel" an ethnic group or a nation?

No, "Israel" in rabbinic Judaism does not refer to an ethnic group or a nation in any secular sense. In rabbinic Judaism, "Israel" formed a social entity unlike any other in humanity. It was not a group formed by common ethnic or cultural traits, nor was it a nation among nations. Nor were the Jews a race.

Contemporary meanings imputed to the word "Israel" make the matter confusing. That theological social entity, "Israel," is not to be confused with the Jewish people, an ethnic group, let alone with the State of Israel, the modern nation-state. Thus "Israel" in Judaism compares to "the Torah," in that, just as the latter is not just another book, so the former is not just another social entity. Just as the story of the Torah speaks of transcendent matters, so the tale of Israel, in rabbinic Judaism, tells of God's relationship with humanity through the instrument God has chosen for self-manifestation: "You only have I known [singled out] of all the families of the earth; therefore I will punish you [I will call you to account] for all your iniquities." as the prophet Amos put it (Amos 3:2 RSV).

Was rabbinic Judaism racist?

No, rabbinic Judaism did not differentiate humanity by "race," whatever meaning be imputed to that category. It differentiated by relationship to God. There are only two divisions to humanity: (1) All those who accept God's rule and commandments in the Torah belong to the "Israel" of which rabbinic Judaism speaks, and (2) all those that do not then are deemed to reject God. "Israel," because it knows, loves, and obeys God as the Shema declares, is comprised by those that will rise from the grave, stand in judgment, and share in the restoration of Eden (cf. Section 3).

What difference did the distinction "Israel" vs. "non-Israel" make?

The Mishnah's use of "Israel" indicates the difference between "Israel" and "non-Israel." It defines "Israel" in antonymic relationships of two sorts: first, "Israel" as against "not-Israel," that is, Gentile, and second, "Israel" as against "priest," or "Levite." "Israel" thus serves as a taxonomic indicator, specifically part of a more encompassing system of hierarchization; "Israel" defined the frontiers, on the outer side of society, and the social boundaries within, on the other. In that context what was the sense of "Gentile"? The answer begins in the fact that the Mishnah does not distinguish among Gentiles, who represent an undifferentiated mass.

Whether or not a Gentile is a Roman or an Aramean or a Syrian or a Briton does not matter. Differentiation among Gentiles rarely, if ever, makes a difference. And "Israel" is not differentiated either. The upshot is that just as "Gentile" is an abstract category, so is "Israel." "Kohen" is a category, and so is "Israel." For the purposes for which Israel/priest are defined, no further differentiation is undertaken.

Who were the family of Abraham and Sarah ("Israel after the flesh")?

When the rabbinic sages wished to know what (an) "Israel" was, they reread the scriptural story of Scripture's "Israel"'s origins for the answer. To begin with, as Scripture told them the story, "Israel" was a man, Jacob, and his children are "the children of Jacob." That man's name was also "Israel," and, it followed, "the children of Israel" comprised the extended family of that man. By extension, "Israel" formed the family of Abraham and Sarah, Isaac and Rebecca, Jacob and Leah and Rachel. "Israel" therefore invoked the metaphor of genealogy to explain the bonds that linked persons unseen into a single social entity; the shared traits were imputed, not empirical (theological, not secular).

That social metaphor of "Israel"—a simple one, really, and easily grasped—bore consequences in two ways. First, children in general are admonished to follow the good example of their parents. The deeds of the patriarchs and matriarchs therefore taught lessons on how the children were to act. Of greater interest in an account of "Israel" as a social metaphor, "Israel" lived twice, once in the patriarchs and matriarchs, a second time in the life of the heirs as the descendants relived those earlier lives. The stories of the family were carefully reread to provide a picture of the meaning of the latter-day events of the descendants of that same family. Accordingly, the lives of the patriarchs signaled the history of Israel.

22. GENTILES

What was the Aggadic doctrine of the Gentiles?

The Aggadic doctrine of the Gentiles moves in these simple steps: (1) Israel differs from the Gentiles because Israel possesses the Torah and the Gentiles do not; (2) because they do not possess the Torah, the Gentiles also worship idols instead of God; and (3) therefore God rejects the Gentiles and identifies with Israel.

So Gentiles are idolators, and Israelites are those who worship the one, true God, who has made himself known in the Torah. Gentile idolators and Israelite worshippers of the one and only God part company at death. Israelites die and rise from the grave, Gentiles die and remain there. So, in substance, humanity viewed whole is divided between those who get a share in the world to come and who will stand when subject to divine judgment—Israel—and those who will not.

But the prophets promise that at the end of days, all humanity will recognize and worship the one, true God. Then there will be no Gentiles/idolaters.

Who were the children of Noah, and what did God want of them?

"The children of Noah" are the entirety of humanity after the Flood. They are subject through God's dealings with Noah to a number of commandments or religious obligations. God cares for Gentiles as for Israel, he wants Gentiles as much as Israel to enter the kingdom of Heaven, and he assigns to Gentiles opportunities to evince their acceptance of his rule. These key religious obligations apply to the children of Noah:

Concerning seven religious requirements were the children of Noah admonished:

setting up courts of justice, idolatry, blasphemy [cursing the Name of God], fornication, bloodshed, and thievery {and concerning cruelty to animals, e.g., not eating a limb cut from a living creature}.

Tosefta 'Avodah Zarah 8:4A–B

"On account of violating three religious duties are children of Noah put to death: on account of adultery, murder, and blasphemy"

Bavli *Sanhedrin* 57a 7:5 I.4A

The Gentiles thus sustain comparison and contrast with Israel, the point of ultimate division being death for the one, eternal life for the other.

Why did the Gentiles reject God?

The Gentiles rejected the Torah because the Torah deprived them of the very practices or traits that they deemed characteristic, essential to their being. That circularity marks the tale of how things were to begin with in fact describes how things always are; it is not historical but philosophical. The Gentiles' own character, the shape of their conscience, then, now, and always, accounts for their condition—which, by an act of will, as we have noted, they can change. What they did not want, that of which they were by their own word unworthy, is denied them. And what they do want condemns them. So when each nation comes under judgment for rejecting the Torah, the indictment of each is spoken out of its own mouth. Its own-self-indictment then forms the core of the matter. Given what we know about the definition of Israel as those destined to live and the Gentile as those not, we cannot find surprising that the entire account is set in that age to come to which the Gentiles are denied entry.

How has this catastrophic differentiation imposed itself between Israel and the Gentiles, such that the Gentiles, for all their glory in the here and now, won for themselves the grave, while Israel, for all its humiliation in the present age, inherits the world to come? When it was offered to them, the Gentiles rejected the Torah, and all else followed. And where do considerations of justice and fairness enter in? Torah dictates the fate of the Gentiles and denies them the Torah.

When they protest the injustice of the decision that takes effect just then, they are shown the workings of the moral order, as the following quite systematic account of the governing pattern explains:

> R. Hanina bar Pappa, and some say, R. Simlai, gave the following exposition [of the verse, "They that fashion a graven image are all of them vanity, and their delectable things shall not profit, and their own witnesses see not nor know" (Isa. 44:9)]: "In the age to come the Holy One, blessed be He, will bring a scroll of the Torah and hold it in his bosom and say, 'Let him who has kept himself busy with it come and take his reward.' Then all the gentiles will crowd together: 'All of the nations are gathered together' (Isa. 43:9). The Holy One, blessed be He, will say to them, 'Do not crowd together before me in a mob. But let each nation enter together with its scribes,

We note that the players are the principal participants in world history: the Romans first and foremost, then the Iranians, the other world rulers of the age:

> "The kingdom of Rome comes in first."

> "The Holy One, blessed be He, will say to them, 'How have you defined your chief occupation?'

> "They will say before him, 'Lord of the world, a vast number of marketplaces have we set up, a vast number of bathhouses we have made, a vast amount of silver and gold have we accumulated. And all of these things we have done only in behalf of Israel, so that they may define as their chief occupation the study of the Torah.'

> "The Holy One, blessed be He, will say to them, 'You complete idiots! Whatever you have done has been for your own convenience. You have set up a vast number of marketplaces to be sure, but that was so as to set up whorehouses in them. The bathhouses were for your own pleasure. Silver and gold belong to me anyhow: "Mine is the silver and mine is the gold, says the Lord of hosts" (Hag. 2:8). Are there any among you who have been telling of "this," and "this" is only the Torah: "And this is the Torah that Moses set before the children of Israel" (Dt. 4:44).' So they will make their exit, humiliated.

The claim of Rome—to support Israel in Torah-study—is rejected on grounds that the Romans did not exhibit the right attitude, always a dynamic force in the theology. Then the other world rule enters in with its claim:

> "When the kingdom of Rome has made its exit, the kingdom of Iran enters afterward."

"The Holy One, blessed be He, will say to them, 'How have you defined your chief occupation?'

"They will say before him, 'Lord of the world, We have thrown up a vast number of bridges, we have conquered a vast number of towns, we have made a vast number of wars, and all of them we did only for Israel, so that they may define as their chief occupation the study of the Torah.'

"The Holy One, blessed be He, will say to them, 'Whatever you have done has been for your own convenience. You have thrown up a vast number of bridges, to collect tolls, you have conquered a vast number of towns, to collect the corvée, and, as to making a vast number of wars, I am the one who makes wars: "The Lord is a man of war" (Ex. 19:17). Are there any among you who have been telling of "this," and "this" is only the Torah: "And this is the Torah that Moses set before the children of Israel" (Dt. 4:44).' So they will make their exit, humiliated.

"And so it will go with each and every nation."

                    Bavli 'Avodah Zarah 2a–b 1:1 I.2A, C, H–K, M–O, R

As native categories, Rome and Iran are singled out, "all the other nations" play no role, for reasons with which we are already familiar. Once more the theology reaches into its deepest thought on the power of intentionality, showing that what people want is what they get.

Now the Gentiles are not just Rome and Iran but others. Of special interest, the Torah is embodied in some of the Ten Commandments—not to murder, not to commit adultery, not to steal; then the Gentiles are rejected for not keeping the seven commandments assigned to the children of Noah. The upshot is that the reason that the Gentiles rejected the Torah is that the Torah prohibits deeds that the Gentiles do by their very nature.

Another teaching concerning the phrase, "He said, 'The Lord came from Sinai'":

When the Omnipresent appeared to give the Torah to Israel, it was not to Israel alone that he revealed himself but to every nation.

First of all he came to the children of Esau. He said to them, "Will you accept the Torah?"

They said to him, "What is written in it?"

He said to them, " 'You shall not murder' (Ex. 20:13)."

They said to him, "The very being of 'those men' [namely, us] and of their father is to murder, for it is said, 'But the hands are the hands of Esau' (Gen. 27:22). 'By your sword you shall live' (Gen. 27:40)."

At this point we cover new ground: other classes of Gentiles that reject the Torah. Now the Torah's own narrative takes over, replacing the known facts of world politics, such as the earlier account sets forth, and instead supplying evidence out of Scripture as to the character of the Gentile group under discussion:

So he went to the children of Ammon and Moab and said to them, "Will you accept the Torah?"

They said to him, "What is written in it?"

He said to them, "'You shall not commit adultery' (Ex. 20:13)."

They said to him, "The very essence of fornication belongs to them [us], for it is said, 'Thus were both the daughters of Lot with child by their fathers' (Gen. 19:36)."

So he went to the children of Ishmael and said to them, "Will you accept the Torah?"

They said to him, "What is written in it?"

He said to them, "'You shall not steal' (Ex. 20:13)."

They said to him, "The very essence of their [our] father is thievery, as it is said, 'And he shall be a wild ass of a man' (Gen. 16:12)."

And so it went. He went to every nation, asking them, "Will you accept the Torah?"

For so it is said, "All the kings of the earth shall give you thanks, O Lord, for they have heard the words of your mouth" (Ps. 138:4).

Might one suppose that they listened and accepted the Torah?

Scripture says, "And I will execute vengeance in anger and fury upon the nations, because they did not listen" (Mic. 5:14).

At this point we turn back to the obligations that God has imposed upon the Gentiles. These obligations have no bearing upon the acceptance of the Torah; they form part of the ground of being, the condition of existence, of the Gentiles. Yet even here, the Gentiles do not accept God's authority in matters of natural law:

And it is not enough for them that they did not listen, but even the seven religious duties that the children of Noah indeed accepted upon themselves they could not uphold before breaking them.

When the Holy One, blessed be He, saw that that is how things were, he gave them to Israel.

Sifré to Deuteronomy CCCXLIII:iv.1S–T

The various Gentile nations rejected the Torah for specific and reasonable considerations, concretely, because the Torah prohibited deeds essential to their being. This point is made in so many words, then amplified through a parable. Israel, by contrast, is prepared to give up life itself for the Torah.

23. SUFFERING AND RESURRECTION

What explains the prosperity of the wicked and the suffering of the righteous?

What the Torah reveals about God is his justice and mercy. Then how to explain human suffering, for example, when bad things happen to good people, and good things to bad? The same premises that guided sages' thinking about Israel and the Torah, the Gentiles and idolatry, required deep thought indeed on the ultimate anomaly of a logic animated by the principle of God's rational justice: the actualities of everyday life. How then reveal God's justice in the chaotic detritus of private lives? It is through articulation of the doctrine of reward and punishment, the insistence on the justice of God in whatever happens, and the doctrine of the resurrection of the dead. The rabbinic sages never for one minute doubted that the world order of justice encompassed those private lives. This they stated in countless ways, the simplest being the representation of Hillel's statement encased in a fragmentary narrative:

> [One day he was walking along the river and] he saw a skull floating on the water and said to it, "Because you drowned others, they drowned you, and in the end those who drowned you will be drowned."

> Mishnah *Avot* 2:6

Somewhere, somehow, the wicked get their comeuppance. The just God sees to it, in the coming Judgment if not in this world. But what about the righteous? Is their just reward equally certain?

Why does humanity bear responsibility for its condition, and what is the role of free will?

If the nations are responsible for their condition, so is Israel, so are Israelites. So too is the rule of justice, and justification, for private lives.

Everything begins with the insistence that people are responsible for what they do, therefore for what happens to them, as much as Israel dictates its destiny by its own deeds. Justice reigns, whatever happens. The reason that man (therefore, groups formed by men) is responsible for his own actions is that he enjoys free will. Man is constantly subject to divine judgment. He has free choice, hence may sin. God judges the world in a generous way, but judgment does take place:

> {R. Aqiba says,} "Everything is foreseen, and free choice is given. In goodness the world is judged. And all is in accord with the abundance of deed[s]."

> Mishnah *Avot* 3:15

God may foresee what is to happen, but man still exercises free will. His attitude and intentionality make all the difference. Because man is not coerced to sin, nor can man be forced to love God or even obey the Torah, an element of uncertainty affects every life. That is the point at which man's will competes with God's. It follows that, where man gives to God what God wants but cannot coerce, or what God wants but cannot command—love, generosity, for instance—there, God responds with an act of uncoerced grace. But in all, one thing is reliable, and that is the working of just recompense for individual action. Expectations of a just reward or punishment, contrasting with actualities, therefore precipitate all thought on the rationality of private life: what happens is supposed to make sense within the governing theology of a just order.

The principle that man is responsible for what he does is established in the very creation of the "First Man." Just as individuation is explained by appeal to the figure of Adam, so now, man's responsibility for his own deeds is adumbrated and exemplified by Adam. Adam acknowledged that he bore full responsibility for his own fate, and built into the human condition, therefore, is that same recognition:

> It is written, "Thus said the Lord, What wrong did your fathers find in me that they went far from me and went after worthlessness and became worthless?" (Jer. 2:5)

> " 'The first Man found no wrong with me, but you have found wrong with me.'

> "To what may the first Man be compared?

> "To a sick man, to whom the physician came. The physician said to him, 'Eat this, don't eat that.'

"When the man violated the instructions of the physician, he brought about his own death.

"[As he lay dying,] his relatives came to him and said to him, 'Is it possible that the physician is imposing on you the divine attribute of justice?'

"He said to them, 'God forbid. I am the one who brought about my own death. This is what he instructed me, saying to me, 'Eat this, don't eat that,' but when I violated his instructions, I brought about my own death.

"So too all the generations came to the first Man, saying to him, 'Is it possible that the Holy One, blessed be He, is imposing the attribute of justice on you?'

"He said to them, 'God forbid. I am the one who has brought about my own death. Thus did he command me, saying to me, 'Of all the trees of the garden you may eat, but of the tree of the knowledge of good and evil you may not eat' (Gen. 2:17). When I violated his instructions, I brought about my own death, for it is written, 'On the day on which you eat it, you will surely die' (Gen. 2:17)."

Pesiqta of Rab Kahana XIV:v.1A, D–K

God is not at fault for Adam's fall; Adam brought about his own death. The exercise of free will brought him down; he did it to himself, and so do all of us. So justice governs, and people may appeal to that sense for the fitting penalty for the sin to explain what happens in ordinary, everyday affairs.

Why do the righteous suffer?

The righteous suffer as recipients of God's favor; it is God who is testing them.

"The Lord tries the righteous, but the wicked and him who loves violence his soul hates" (Ps. 11:5):

Said R. Jonathan, "A potter does not test a weak utensil, for if he hits it just once, he will break it. What does the potter test? He tests the strong ones, for even if he strikes them repeatedly, they will not break. So the Holy One, blessed be he, does not try the wicked but the righteous: 'The Lord tries the righteous' (Ps. 11:5)."

Genesis Rabbah LV:ii.1A–C

The suffering of the righteous pays tribute to their strength and is a mark of their virtue. That is shown by appeal to both analogies (potter) and Scripture. Suffering then shows God's favor for the one who suffers, indicating that such a one is worthy of God's attention and special interest.

How is suffering part of God's plan?

That suffering is a valued gift explains the critical importance of the theological principle that one should accept whatever God metes out to him, even suffering. In a context defined by the conviction that suffering forms a gift from a benevolent, just God, we cannot find surprising that loving God should involve accepting punishment as much as benefit. This is stated in so many words: One is obligated to bless over evil as one blesses over the good, as it is said,

> And you shall love the Lord your God with all your heart, with all your soul, and with all your might (Dt. 6:5). With all your heart—with both of your inclinations, with the good inclination and with the evil inclination. And with all your soul—even if He takes your soul. And with all your might— with all of your money.

Mishnah *Berakhot* 9:5B–E

Accordingly, the correct attitude toward suffering entails grateful acknowledgement that what God metes out is just and merciful. The same matter is amplified in the following exegesis of the same verses of Scripture:

> R. Aqiba says, "Since it is said, 'with all your soul,' it is an argument *a fortiori*, that we should encompass, 'with all your might.'
>
> "Why then does Scripture say, 'with all your might'?
>
> "It is to encompass every single measure that God metes out to you, whether the measure of good or the measure of punishment."

Sifré to Deuteronomy XXXII:v.1

So the sages persuaded themselves that somehow the world conformed to rationality defined by justice. True, the claim that anguish and illness, premature death and everyday suffering fit under the rules of reasonable world order; that insistence that when the wicked prosper, justice still may be done—these propositions, necessary to the system, may well have transcended the here and now and conformed to a higher reality.

How does the resurrection of the dead resolve monotheism's theology of suffering?

Resurrection of the dead is the only solution to the problem of evil available to ethical monotheism, with its doctrine of a truly just and merciful God. Some folk suffer more than others, and not uncommonly the wicked prosper and the righteous do not. Justice will be done only when the world is perfected. With that conviction's forming the foundation of their very definition of world order, divided between those who will overcome the grave, Israel with the Torah, and those who will not, the Gentiles with idolatry, the rabbinic sages found in hand a simple solution. The righteous suffer in this world and get their just reward in the world to come, but the wicked enjoy this world and suffer in the world to come. Since the theology of the rabbinic Judaism to begin with distinguished the Torah and life from idolatry and death, what happens in this world and in this life does not tell the whole story. And when—but only when—that entire story is told, the received formulation of the problem of evil no longer pertains, and the final anomalies are smoothed out.

24. INTENTIONALITY

How is man like God?

Free will reaches concrete expression in the deeds a man does by reason of the plans or intentions that he shapes on his own. The high value accorded by God to man's voluntary act of accepting God's dominion, the enthusiastic response made by God to man's supererogatory deeds of uncoerced love and uncompelled generosity, the heavy emphasis upon the virtues of self-abnegation and self-restraint—these emblematic traits of the coherent theology attest to the uncertainty of man's response that, from the beginning, God has built into creation. For the one power that lies beyond the rules of reason, that defies predicting, is man's power to make up his own mind.

Man bears a single trait that most accords with the likeness of God. It is his possession of free will and the power of the free exercise thereof. In his act of will God makes just rules, and in his, man willfully breaks them. Man matches God in possessing freedom of will. And therein sages found the source of world disorder. Man's will was the sole power in the world that matched the power of God. And it is that variable in creation that accounts for the present imperfection of creation. To understand why, we recall that by his act of will God created the orderly world of justice, one that exhibits abundant, indicative marks of perfection. Then whence chaos embodied by disorder and dissonance? And, when the rules that embody rationality—that guarantee measure for measure above all—cease to describe the everyday experience of mankind and the here and now of Israel, where shall we find the reason why? In the logic of a world order based on exact justice, in the Torah God accords to man a statement of his own will, a commandment, and one who issues a command both wants the command to be obeyed but also accords to the other the power to disobey. That is the very premise of commandments.

What is intentionality?

By "intentionality" in the context of normative rules of law sages mean the attitude that motivates a given action, the intention of the person who performs the action that defines what he hopes to accomplish—effect, affect, or prevent. That intentionality, or expression of an attitude, governs the action's classification, e.g., as to effect or lack of effect, as to acceptability or lack of acceptability, e.g., in recitation of prayer. While a single word, *kavvanah*, corresponds directly to intentionality, the broader category of intentionality is shown by context to pertain even where that particular word *kavvanah* does not appear. Other words also serve to convey the same meaning, e.g., the Hebrew word, *leb*, "heart."

Concrete actions take on consequence only by reference to the intention with which they are carried out. For example, what matters in the offerings is intentionality; the size of the offering makes no difference, only the intent of the person who presents it:

> It is said of the burnt offering of a beast, *An offering by fire, a smell of sweet savor* (Lev. 1:9) and of the bird offering, *An offering by fire, a smell of sweet savor* (Lev. 1:17) and [even] of the meal offering, *An offering by fire, a smell of sweet savor* (Lev. 2:9)—

> to teach that all the same are the one who offers much and the one who offers little, on condition that a man will direct his intention to Heaven.

Mishnah Menahot 13:11

The entire cult represents an act of human volition and is evaluated solely on that basis, so that if a sacrifice were carried out without proper intentionality, it does not accomplish its purpose, e.g., atonement. Take the matter of the sin offering, for example. A sin is atoned for by a sin offering—but that is only when the act is inadvertent. A deliberate action is not covered, so Mishnah-tractate *Shabbat* 11:6J–K: "This is the general principle: All those who may be liable to sin offerings in fact are not liable unless at the beginning and the end, their sin is done inadvertently." That is, the sin offering expiates sin only if the act was done without the intention of rebelling against the commandments of the Torah. If it was a deliberate sin, there are means of atonement (cf. Section 27).

What is the relationship between intentionality and action?

Intentionality governs, we already anticipate, because it has the power to classify actions, one sort of action being valid, another, invalid. This we have already seen in a variety of practical, legal contexts. It is intentionality of the actor, then, that defines the effect of an action; the same action, performed in the same way, may then produce diverse results, based on the will that one brings to bear upon the action. In religious duties, the effect of intentionality proves especially critical. That is to say, the intention to carry out one's obligation must accompany the act that effects that obligation; otherwise, the act bears no effect, so Mishnah-tractate *Berakhot* 2:1A–C:

> One who was reading [the verses of the *Shema*] in the Torah and the time for the recitation [of the *Shema*] arrived: If he directed his heart [towards fulfilling the obligation to recite the *Shema*], he fulfilled his obligation [to recite]. And if [he did] not [direct his heart], he did not fulfill his obligation.

Intentionality may also prevent a negative result. That we know from the distinction between involuntary manslaughter and murder, which Scripture makes explicit. Along these same lines, in the view of sages, the intentional violation of the law always invalidates the consequent action. What is done in violation of the law but not by intention, by contrast, may well be accepted, since it was not an act of rebellion against the Torah, e.g., Mishnah-tractate *Terumot* 2:3.1A–C:

> One who immerses [unclean] utensils on the Sabbath {when it is not permitted to do so}—[if he does] so unintentionally {not realizing that it is the Sabbath}, he may use them; [but if he does so] intentionally {intending to violate the Sabbath}, he may not use them.

Why is intentionality critical to the theological system of the Aggadah?

For the sages, therefore, it was man's rebellion, beyond God's control but within God's dominion, that explains change. And change, imperfection, the ephemerality of affairs—these signal the actualities of disorder in a world meant for perfection, stasis, balance throughout. God proposes, man disposes. Chaos begins not in God but in man, in that trait of man that endows man with the same power that the Creator has, to exercise free will to carry out one's intentions: to conceive and to do. Since God has made an orderly world, only his counterpart on earth, man, can account for the disruption of world order. For the sole player in the cosmic drama with the power to upset God's plans is man. He alone is like God, "in our image, after our likeness." In their penetrating reflection on the power of intentionality, sages explain chaos, and that prepares the way for their investigation of sin and its remedy. For the one power that lies beyond the rules of reason, that defies predicting, is man's power to make up his own mind.

25. SIN

—————◈—————

Why is the doctrine of sin critical to the Aggadic theology of rabbinic Judaism?

Sin explains the condition of Israel. And sin comes in consequence of sinful attitudes of rebellion against God. Death comes about by reason of sin, as is stated in so many words, in a great many passages, of which the following is representative:

> "So too all the generations came to the first Man, saying to him, 'Is it possible that the Holy One, blessed be He, is imposing the attribute of justice on you?'
>
> "He said to them, 'God forbid. I am the one who has brought about my own death. Thus did he command me, saying to me, 'Of all the trees of the garden you may eat, but of the tree of the knowledge of good and evil you may not eat' (Gen. 2:17). When I violated his instructions, I brought about my own death, for it is written, 'On the day on which you eat it, you will surely die' (Gen. 2:17)."

> *Pesiqta of Rab Kahana* XIV:v.1J–K

Death does not define the purpose of the life of Adam and Eve but violates the teleology that governed God's making of them.

The governing theory of Israel, that had Israel kept the Torah from the beginning, the Holy People would never have had any history at all but would have lived in a perfect world at rest and balance and order, is now invoked. There would have been nothing to write down, no history, no Scripture beyond the Pentateuch and Joshua, had Israel kept the Torah. I can imagine no more explicit statement of how the world order is disrupted by sin, and, specifically, sinful attitudes, than the following:

Said R. Ada b. R. Hanina, "If the Israelites had not sinned, to them would have been given only the Five Books of the Torah and the book of Joshua alone, which involves the division of the Land of Israel."

Bavli Nedarim 22a–b 3:1 I.18

Adam ought to have stayed in Eden. With the Torah in hand, Israel, the new Adam, ought to have remained in the Land, beyond the reach of time and change, exempt from the events of interesting times. Sin ruined everything, for Adam, for Israel, bringing about the history recorded in Scripture—not a very complicated theodicy.

How does sin express an attitude of rebellion against God?

Defined in the model of the first sin, the one committed by man in Eden, sin is an act of rebellion against God. Rebellion takes two forms. As a gesture of omission, sin embodies the failure to carry out one's obligation to God set forth in the Torah. As one of commission, it constitutes an act of defiance. In both cases sin comes about by reason of man's intentionality to reject the will of God, set forth in the Torah. However accomplished, whether through omission or commission, an act becomes sinful because of the attitude that accompanies it. That is why man is responsible for sin, answerable to God in particular, who may be said to take the matter personally, just as it is meant. The consequence of sin is death for the individual, exile and estrangement for holy Israel, and disruption for the world. That is why sin accounts for much of the flaw of creation.

It follows, as we now realize, that the consequences of the correspondence of God and man account for all else. If the one power in all of creation that can and does stand against the will of God is man's will or intentionality, then man bears responsibility for the flawed condition of creation, and God's justice comes to its fullest expression in the very imperfection of existence, a circularity that once more marks a well-crafted, severely logical system. But free will also forms the source of remission; God's mercy (cf. Section 26), intervenes when man's will warrants. Specifically, God restores the perfection of creation through his provision of means of atonement through repentance. But that presents no anomaly but conforms to the encompassing theory of matters. For repentance represents yet an act of human will that is countered with a commensurate act of God's will. The entire story of the world, start to finish, therefore records the cosmic confrontation of

God's will and man's freedom to form and carry out an intention contrary to God's will. The universe is not animate but animated by the encounter of God and, in his image, after his likeness, man—the story, the only story, that the oral Torah recapitulates from, and in completion of, the written Torah.

What is at stake in sin is succinctly stated: it accounts for the deplorable condition of the world, defined by the situation of Israel. But sin is not a permanent feature of world order. It is a detail of an orderly progression, as God to begin with had planned, from chaos, which gave way to creation, to the Torah, which after the Flood through Israel restored order to the world, and onward to the age of perfection and stasis.

What are particularly critical sins?

What has already been said about sin as an act of rebellion bears the implication that an act may or may not be sinful, depending upon the attitude of the actor, a view that our inquiry into intentionality has adumbrated. In fact only a few actions are treated as *eo ipse* sinful. Chief among them are, specifically, murder, fornication, and idolatry. Under all circumstances a man must refrain from committing such actions, even at the cost of his own life. These represent absolute sins:

"For the earth is filled with violence" (Gen. 6:13):

Said R. Levi, "The word for violence refers to idolatry, fornication, and murder.

"Idolatry: 'For the earth is filled with violence' (Gen. 6:13).

"Fornication: 'The violence done to me and to my flesh be upon Babylonia' (Jer. 51:35). [And the word for 'flesh' refers to incest, as at Lev. 18:6].

"Murder: 'For the violence against the children of Judah, because they have shed innocent blood' (Joel 4:19).

"Further, the word for 'violence' stands for its ordinary meaning as well."

Genesis Rabbah XXXI:vi.1

Since these were the deeds of the men of the generation of the Flood that so outraged God as to bring about mass destruction, they form a class of sin by themselves. The children of Noah, not only the children of Israel, must avoid these sins at all costs.

But there is a sin that Israel may commit that exceeds even the cardinal sins. Even those three are forgivable, but rejection of the Torah is not:

> R. Huna, R. Jeremiah in the name of R. Samuel bar R. Isaac: "We find that the Holy One, blessed be he, forgave Israel for idolatry, fornication, and murder. [But] for their rejection of the Torah he never forgave them."

What is the scriptural basis for that view?

> It is not written, "Because they practiced idolatry, fornication, and murder," but rather, "And the Lord said, 'Because they have forsaken my Torah.'"

> Said R. Hiyya bar Ba, " 'If they were to forsake me, I should forgive them, for they may yet keep my Torah. For if they should forsake me but keep my Torah, the leaven that is in [the Torah] will bring them closer to me.'"

> R. Huna said, "Study Torah [even if it is] not for its own sake, for, out of [doing so] not for its own sake, you will come [to study it] for its own sake."

> Yerushalmi *Hagigah* 1:7 I:3A–E

Still, that the classification of an action, even of the most severe character, depends upon the intentionality or attitude of the actor governs even here.

An Israelite's rejection of not God but the Torah is forthwith set into the context of will or intentionality. God does not object to insincerity when it comes to study of the Torah, because the Torah itself contains the power to reshape the will of man (as framed succinctly by sages elsewhere, "The commandments were given only to purify the heart of man," "God craves the heart," and similar formulations). God can forgive Israel for forsaking him, because if they hold on to the Torah, they will find their way back. The Torah will reshape Israel's heart. And then, amplifying that point but moving still further from the main proposition, comes Huna's sentiment that studying the Torah does not require proper intentionality, because the Torah in due course will effect the proper intentionality. Two critical points emerge. First, intentionality plays a central role in the discussion of principal sins. Second, sin ordinarily does not form an absolute but only a relative category, which is to say, an action that is sinful under one set of circumstances, when the intent is wicked, is not sinful but even subject to forgiveness under another set of circumstances.

What is the relationship between intentionality, arrogance, and humility?

Given sages' focus upon intentionality, it is not surprising that the matched traits of arrogance and humility should take priority in their systematic thinking about the imperfections of the world order. God favors the humble and accepts humility as equivalent to offerings in the Temple, responding to prayers of the humble:

> Said R. Joshua b. Levi, "Come and take note of how great are the humble in the sight of the Holy One, blessed be he.
>
> "For when the sanctuary stood, a person would bring a burnt-offering, gaining thereby the reward for bringing a burnt-offering, or a meal-offering, and gaining the reward for a meal offering.
>
> "But a person who is genuinely humble does Scripture treat as if he had made offerings of all the sacrifices,
>
> "as it is said, 'The sacrifices [plural] of God are a broken spirit' (Ps. 51:19).
>
> "And not only so, but his prayer is not rejected, as it is said, 'A broken and contrite heart, O God, you will not despise' (Ps. 51:19)."
>
> Bavli Sotah 5b 1:1–2.V.25A–E

All things are relative to one relationship: humility vs. arrogance. Specific sins, such as adultery, are placed into that larger context of a failure of right attitude. Adultery is an expression of arrogance, and so too is jealousy. So specific sin is an expression of a general attitude of arrogance, and virtue, of humility. The marital bond expresses that same faithfulness that is required of Israel in relationship to God. Sin contrasts with faithfulness, since the opposite of faithfulness is arrogance, the opposite of sin, humility.

26. REPENTANCE

What is repentance (teshubah) and why is it God's final solution to the human problem?

Repentance is integral to the Aggadic theology of rabbinic Judaism; it holds the entire system together. It is what effects the regeneration of man: an act of will to overcome a willful act.

How so? Man both complemented and corresponded to God, and it was man's freedom, meaning, his effective will and power of intentionality, that matched God's will. When these conflict, man's arrogance leads him to rebel against God, sin resulting. And from sin comes the imperfection of world order, change, inequity, imbalance. Punished and remorseful, man gives up his arrogant attitude and conforms his will to God's. God responds with mercy, freely accepting the reformation that is freely offered. Then world order restored, that perfection effected at the outset is regained for Israel, which means, for God's part of mankind. Eden, now the Land of Israel, is recovered, Adam, now embodied in Israel, is restored to his blissful place. For the Israelite death dies, man rises from the grave to life eternal. For Israel the Gentiles' rule comes to an end, and Israel regains the Land. Repentance then marks the recovery of the world as God wanted it to be, which is to say, the world in which Israel regains its promised place.

The logic of repentance is simple and familiar. It is a logic that appeals to the balance and proportion of all things. If sin is what introduces rebellion and change, and the will of man is what constitutes the variable in disrupting creation, then the Aggadic theology of rabbinic Judaism makes provision for restoration through the free exercise of man's will. That requires (1) an attitude of remorse, (2) a resolve not to repeat the act of rebellion, and (3) a good-faith effort at reparation, in all, transformation from rebellion against, to obedience to, God's will. World order, disrupted by an act of will, regains perfection through an act of will that complements and corresponds to the initial, rebellious one. That is realized in an act of willful repentance.

Repentance effects the required transformation of man and inaugurates reconciliation with God. Through a matched act of will, now in conformity with God's design for creation, repentance therefore restores the balance upset by man's act of will. So the act of repentance, and with it atonement, takes its place within the theology of perfection, disruption, and restoration, that all together organizes—shows the order of— the world of creation.

Repentance, action, and attitude: how do they relate?

Teshubah then involves not humiliation but reaffirmation of the self in God's image, after God's likeness. It follows that repentance forms a theological category encompassing moral issues of action and attitude, wrong action, arrogant attitude, in particular. Repentance forms a step in the path to God that starts with the estrangement represented by sin: doing what I want, instead of what God wants, thus rebellion and arrogance. Sin precipitates punishment, whether personal for individuals or historical for nations, which brings about repentance for sin, which, in turn, leads to atonement for sin and, it follows, reconciliation with God. That sequence of stages in the moral regeneration of sinful humanity, individual or collective, defines the context in which repentance finds its natural home.

True, the penitent corrects damage one has actually carried out to his fellow man. But apart from reparations, the act of repentance involves only the attitude, specifically substituting feelings of regret and remorse for the arrogant intention that lead to the commission of the sin. If the person declares regret and undertakes not to repeat the action, the process of repentance gets underway. When the occasion to repeat the sinful act arises and the penitent refrains from doing it again, the process comes to a conclusion. So it is through the will and attitude of the sinner that the act of repentance is realized; the entire process is carried on beyond the framework of religious actions, rites, or rituals. The power of repentance overcomes sins of the most heinous and otherwise unforgivable character.

The following is explicit that no sin overwhelms the transformative power of repentance. It lists sinners, those who oppressed Israel and tried to destroy her, like Haman, Sisera, Sennacherib:

Naaman was a resident proselyte.

Nebuzaradan was a righteous proselyte.

Grandsons of Haman studied Torah in Bene Beraq.

Grandsons of Sisera taught children in Jerusalem.

Grandsons of Sennacherib taught Torah in public.

And who were they? Shemaiah and Abtalion.

Bavli *Gittin* 57b 5:6 I.26B–G

Shemaiah and Abtalion are represented as masters of the Torah. The act of repentance transforms the heirs of the destroyers of Israel and the Temple into the framers of the redemptive oral Torah. A more extreme statement of the power of any attitude or action defies imagining—even the fact of our own day that a distant cousin of Adolph Hitler has converted to Judaism and serves in the reserves of the Israel Defense Army.

What stake does God have in man's repentance?

That to such a remarkable extent God responds to man's will, which time and again has defined the dynamics of complementarity characteristic of the oral Torah's theology, accounts for the possibility of repentance. As much as mercy completes the principle of justice, so repentance forms the complement to sin; without mercy, represented here by the possibility of repentance, justice as God defines justice cannot endure. For were man to regret sin and see things in God's way without a corresponding response from God, God would execute justice but not mercy, and, from sages' perspective, the world would fall out of balance. To them, therefore, it is urgent that God have his own distinctive message to the sinner, separate from the voices of Wisdom, Prophecy, and even the Pentateuch (the Torah narrowly defined), of the written Torah:

Said R. Phineas: "'Good and upright [is the Lord; therefore he instructs sinners in the way]' (Ps. 25:8).

"Why is he good? Because he is upright.

"And why is he upright? Because he is good.

"'Therefore he instructs sinners in the way'—that is, he teaches them the way to repentance."

Now we interrogate the great compendia of God's will, wisdom, prophecy, then turn to God himself, and ask how to treat the sinner:

They asked wisdom, "As to a sinner, what is his punishment?"

She said to them, "Evil pursues the evil" (Prov. 13:21).

They asked prophecy, "As to a sinner, what is his punishment?"

She said to them, "The soul that sins shall die" (Ez. 18:20).

They asked the Holy One, blessed be he, "As to a sinner, what is his punishment?"

He said to them, "Let the sinner repent, and his sin will be forgiven for him."

This is in line with the following verse of Scripture: "Therefore he instructs sinners in the way" (Ps. 25:8).

"He shows the sinners the way to repentance."

Yerushalmi Makkot 2:6 I:4

The response of Wisdom presents no surprise; it is the familiar principle of measure for measure. Prophecy concurs. But God has something more to say. Accordingly, the proposition concerns the distinctive mercy of God, above even the Torah. What does prophecy say about the punishment of the sinner? But the question serves to demonstrate the uniquely merciful character of God, the way in which God is God.

What is the relationship between sin and punishment on the one hand, and repentance and mercy on the other?

The power of repentance is disproportionate, out of all balance with sin. By contrast, the penalty for sin never exceeds the gravity of the sin. We may say that, while, when it comes to sin, God effects exact justice, when it comes to repentance, God accords mercy out of all proportion to the arrogance of the act of rebellion. The act of will that is represented by repentance vastly outweighs in effect the act of will that brings about sin. That is because one may commit many sins, but a single act of repentance encompasses them all and restores the balance that those sins all together have upset. So repentance makes sense, in its remarkable power, only in the context of God's mercy. It follows that any account of repentance and atonement must commence with a clear statement of God's mercy, the logical precondition for the act of repentance.

Now as to the matter of divine mercy, God's mercy vastly exceeds his justice, so when God metes out reward, he does so very lavishly. We note Tosefta *Sotah* 4:1:

> I know only with regard to the measure of retribution that *by that same measure by which a man metes out, they mete out to him* (M. Sot. 1:7A). How do I know that the same is so with the measure of goodness. . . .

God's power to forgive sin, however formidable, and to reward virtue, however slight, is expressed in his acts of mercy. And the mercy of God comes to expression in his deeds:

> "The Lord is good to all, and his tender mercies are over all his works" (Ps. 145:9):
>
> Said R. Joshua b. Levi, " 'The Lord is good to all, and his tender mercies are over all, for they are his works.' "
>
> Said R. Samuel bar Nahman, " 'The Lord is good to all, and his tender mercies are over all, for lo, by his very nature, he extends mercy.' "
>
> R. Joshua in the name of R. Levi: " 'The Lord is good to all, and out of his store of tender mercy he gives [mercy] to his creatures.' "
>
> R. Abba said, "Tomorrow a year of scarcity will come, and people will show mercy to one another, on account of which the Holy One, blessed be he, is filled with mercy for them." [This point will now be illustrated.]
>
> *Genesis Rabbah* XXXIII:iii.1

The attitude of mercy that characterizes God must shape man's will, and that comes about when man needs mercy from Heaven and learns out of necessity to show mercy to other men. When God sees men treating one another mercifully, then God responds with an act of mercy of his own.

27. ATONEMENT

What is atonement and why is atonement integral to repentance?

Through the act of repentance, a person who has sinned leaves the status of sinner, but he must also atone for the sin to gain forgiveness. Then the statement of remorse and voluntary change of will is confirmed by an action, specifically, atonement in one of three media.

What are the media of atonement? How do the sacrifice of the sin offering in the Temple, death, and the Day of Atonement figure?

Three distinct media of atonement for sin are sacrifice, death, and the advent of the Day of Atonement.

First comes atonement for inadvertent sin, acts that violate God's will but are not done intentionally. A sin offering in the Temple in Jerusalem, presented for unintentional sins, atones. What atones for what is inadvertent has no bearing upon what is deliberate. The willful sin can be atoned for only if repentance has taken place, that is to say, genuine regret, a turning away from the sin, after the fact therefore transforming the sin from one that is deliberate to one that is, if not unintentional beforehand, then at least unintentional afterward. Then death, on the one side, or the Day of Atonement, on the other, work their enchantment.

Death, second, marks the final atonement for sin, which bears its implication for the condition of man at the resurrection. Because one has atoned through sin (accompanied at the hour of death by a statement of repentance, "May my death be atonement for all my sins," in the liturgy), when he is raised from the dead, his atonement for all his sins is complete. The judgment after resurrection becomes for most a formality. That is why "all Israel has a portion in the world to come," with the exception of a few whose sins are not atoned for by death, and that is by their own word.

Third is the Day of Atonement, Yom Kippur. That solemn "Sabbath of Sabbaths" accomplishes atonement: "for on this day shall atonement be made for you, to cleanse you; from all your sins you shall be clean before the LORD." (Lev 16:30 RSV). The Day of Atonement provides atonement, as the written Torah makes explicit, for the sins of the year for which one has repented, and that accounts for the elaborate rites of confession that fill the day.

Here is how the media of atonement of death, for a lifetime, and the Day of Atonement, for the year just past, are sorted out:

A sin offering and an unconditional guilt offering atone.

Death and the Day of Atonement atone when joined with repentance.

Repentance atones for minor transgressions of positive and negative commandments.

And as to serious transgressions, [repentance] suspends the punishment until the Day of Atonement comes along and atones.

He who says, "I shall sin and repent, sin and repent"—

they give him no chance to do repentance.

{If he said,} "I will sin and the Day of Atonement will atone,"—the Day of Atonement does not atone.

For transgressions done between man and the Omnipresent, the Day of Atonement atones.

For transgressions between man and man, the Day of Atonement atones, only if the man will regain the good will of his friend.

Mishnah *Yoma* 8:8A–9E

The first statement sorts out the workings of repentance, death, the Day of Atonement, and atonement. We see that repentance on its own serves for the violation of commandments, for that involves God; when another man is involved in a man's sin, then the this-worldly counterpart to repentance, which is reparation and reconciliation, is required.

Reconciliation with God and with the other person: how are these joined?

The process of reconciliation with God encompasses a number of steps and components, not only repentance; and repentance, for its part, does not reach concrete definition in the formulation of the process. This is how the Bavli deals with precisely the problem of intransigence on the part of the victim, citing the Mishnah-rule just above:

> For transgressions done between man and the Omnipresent, the Day of Atonement atones.
>
> For transgressions between man and man, the Day of Atonement atones, only if the man will regain the good will of his friend.
>
> Mishnah *Yoma* 8:9D–E

The matter of reconciling the other is now spelled out:

> Said R. Isaac, "Whoever offends his fellow, even if through what he says, has to reconcile with him, as it is said, 'My son, if you have become surety for your neighbor, if you have struck your hands for a stranger, you are snared by the words of your mouth . . . do this now, my son, and deliver yourself, seeing you have come into the power of your neighbor, go, humble yourself, and urge your neighbor' (Prov. 6:1–3). If it is a money-claim against you, open the palm of your hand to him [and pay him off], and if not, send a lot of intermediaries to him."
>
> Said R. Hisda, "He has to reconcile with him through three sets of three people each: 'He comes before men and says, I have sinned and perverted that which was right and it did not profit me' (Job 33:27)."
>
> Said R. Yosé bar Hanina, "Whoever seeks reconciliation with his neighbor has to do so only three times: 'Forgive I pray you now . . . and now we pray you' (Gen. 50:17).
>
> "And if he has died, he brings ten people and sets them up at his grave and says, 'I have sinned against the Lord the God of Israel and against this one, whom I have hurt.'"
>
> Bavli *Yoma* 87a–b 8:8–9 VI.2

The matter has its own limits. Beyond the specified point, the penitent has carried out his obligation as best he can, and nothing more is to be done.

Can one attain preemptive atonement for sin?

What about deliberate and willful violation of the law, encompassing repentance, before the fact? If to begin with one has insinuated repentance into the sinful act itself, declaring up front that afterward one will repent, the power of repentance is lost, the act of will denying the *ex post facto* possibility altogether. That is the point of Mishnah-tractate *Yoma* 8:9A–C, which is now amplified. For, we now observe, the issue of attitude takes over, and it is in the end the fundamental attitude that governs. If to begin with the willful act is joined to an act of will affecting the *ex post facto* circumstance, all is lost; one's attitude to begin with nullifies all further possibilities.

He who says, "I shall sin and repent" will never suffice to carry out repentance.

"I will sin and the Day of Atonement will accomplish atonement"—the Day of Atonement will not accomplish atonement.

"I shall sin and the day of death will wipe away the sin"—the day of death will not wipe away the sin.

R. Eliezer b. R. Yosé says, "He who sins and repents and then proceeds in an unblemished life does not move from his place before he is forgiven.

"He who says, 'I shall sin and repent' is forgiven three times but no more."

Fathers According to Rabbi Nathan XL:v.1

That is why there is no such thing as preemptive atonement, that is, planning in advance to atone for a sin. The attitude of arrogance embodied in the notion, "I shall sin and the Day of Atonement will atone for the sin" vitiates the process of atonement.

God forgives sinners who atone and repent and asks of humanity that same act of grace—but no greater. For forgiveness without a prior act of repentance violates the rule of justice but also humiliates the law of mercy, cheapening and trivializing the superhuman act of forgiveness by treating as compulsive what is an act of human, and divine, grace. Sin is to be punished, but repentance is to be responded to with forgiveness, as the written Torah states explicitly: "You shall not take vengeance or bear a grudge against the sons of your people, but you shall love your neighbor as yourself" (Lev 19:18a–b RSV). The role of the sinful other is to repent, the task of the sinned-against is to respond to and accept repentance, at which point, loving one's neighbor as oneself becomes the just person's duty, so repentance forms the critical center of the moral transaction in a contentious and willful world.

28. THE MESSIAH

When will the Messiah come?

When Israel's will conforms to the will of God, then God will respond to the act of repentance by restoring Adam to Eden, Israel to the lost Land, and consequently to bring about resurrection and eternal life. The Messiah's task is to respond to Israel's regeneration by raising the dead. When will he come? When Israel wants—when else?

This is expressed in a colloquy that announces the Messiah will come when all Israel keeps a single Sabbath. And that will take place when Israel wants it to take place. It requires only an act of will on the part of Israel to accept one of the Ten Commandments. Then in a broader restatement of matters, the entire redemptive process is made to depend upon Israel's repentance:

> The Israelites said to Isaiah, "O our Rabbi, Isaiah, What will come for us out of this night?"
>
> He said to them, "Wait for me, until I can present the question."
>
> Once he had asked the question, he came back to them.
>
> They said to him, "Watchman, what of the night? What did the Guardian of the ages say [a play on 'of the night' and 'say']?"
>
> He said to them, "The watchman says: 'Morning comes; and also the night. [If you will inquire, inquire; come back again]'" (Is. 21:12).
>
> They said to him, "Also the night?"
>
> He said to them, "It is not what you are thinking. But there will be morning for the righteous, and night for the wicked, morning for Israel, and night for idolaters."

Now comes the main point in the exchange: when will this happen? It will happen when Israel wants. And what is standing in the way is Israel's arrogance, to be atoned for by Israel's remorseful repentance:

> They said to him, "When?"
>
> He said to them, "Whenever you want, He too wants [it to be]—if you want it, he wants it."
>
> They said to him, "What is standing in the way?"
>
> He said to them, "Repentance: 'come back again'" (Is. 21:12).

This is stated in the clearest possible way: one day will do it.

> R. Aha in the name of R. Tanhum b. R. Hiyya, "If Israel repents for one day, forthwith the son of David will come.
>
> "What is the scriptural basis? 'O that today you would hearken to his voice!'" (Ps. 95:7).

Now comes the introduction of the Sabbath as a test case:

> Said R Levi, "If Israel would keep a single Sabbath in the proper way [as God and Adam and Eve kept the Sabbath in Eden], forthwith the son of David will come.
>
> "What is the scriptural basis for this view? 'Moses said, Eat it today, for today is a Sabbath to the Lord; [today you will not find it in the field]' (Ex. 16:25).
>
> "And it says, '[For thus said the Lord God, the Holy One of Israel], 'In returning and rest you shall be saved; [in quietness and in trust shall be your strength.' And you would not]'" (Is. 30:15). By means of returning and [Sabbath] rest you will be redeemed.

Yerushalmi Ta'anit 1:1 II:5G–V

The main point, then, is the linkage of repentance to the coming restoration of Israel to the Land, the dead to life, by the Messiah. But the advent of the Messiah depends wholly upon Israel's will. If Israel will subordinate its will to God's, all else will follow.

How will Israel know who the Messiah is—and is not?

What we already have learned about repentance has made inevitable the very odd juxtaposition that signals who the Messiah is and is not: the contrapuntal relationship of arrogance and repentance, sinfulness and reconciliation. Here is how the false Messiah shows why he cannot save Israel, and in so many words, it is because of his blasphemous arrogance. The story concerns Bar Kokhba ("son of the star"), known also as Ben Koziba or Bar Koziba, general of the Jewish army that fought against Rome to restore the Temple in Jerusalem and Israel's self-rule, 132–135 C.E. In this narrative Aqiba, a leading sage, called him the Messiah:

> Rabbi would interpret the verse, "There shall come forth a star out of Jacob" (Num. 24:17) in this way: "Do not read the letters of the word for 'star' as 'star' but as 'deceit.'"

> When R. Aqiba saw Bar Koziba, he said, "This is the royal messiah."

> R. Yohanan b. Torta said to him, "Aqiba, grass will grow from your cheeks and he will still not have come."

We are now told why Aqiba is wrong:

> Eighty thousand trumpeters besieged Betar. There Bar Koziba was encamped, with two hundred thousand men with an amputated finger.

> Sages sent word to him, saying, "How long are you going to produce blemished men in Israel?"

> He said to them, "And what shall I do to examine them [to see whether or not they are brave]?"

> They said to him, "Whoever cannot uproot a cedar of Lebanon do not enroll in your army."

> He had two hundred thousand men of each sort [half with an amputated finger, half proved by uprooting a cedar].

Now comes the explicit statement of the false Messiah's arrogance toward Heaven:

> When they went out to battle, he would say, "Lord of all ages, don't help us and don't hinder us!"

> That is in line with this verse: "Have you not, O God, cast us off? And do not go forth, O God, with our hosts" (Ps. 60:12).

It would be difficult to find a passage more directly opposed to sages' fundamental theological convictions than Bar Kokhba's explicit rejection of God's help in favor of his own strength.

Now a separate story underscores the unsuitable character of this particular Messiah, namely, the mark of arrogance represented by temper. Losing one's temper is a mark of arrogance toward Heaven, and here Bar Kokhba does just that:

> For three and a half years Hadrian besieged Betar.
>
> R. Eleazar the Modiite was sitting in sack cloth and ashes, praying, and saying, "Lord of all the ages, do not sit in judgment today, do not sit in judgment today."
>
> Since [Hadrian] could not conquer the place, he considered going home.
>
> There was with him a Samaritan, who said to him, "My lord, as long as that old cock wallows in ashes, you will not conquer the city.
>
> "But be patient, and I shall do something so you can conquer it today."

The first act is one of gossip:

> He went into the gate of the city and found R. Eleazar standing in prayer.
>
> He pretended to whisper something into his ear, but the other paid no attention to him.

From slander the conspiracy turns to false witness, taking God's name in vain:

> People went and told Bar Koziba, "Your friend wants to betray the city."
>
> He sent and summoned the Samaritan and said to him, "What did you say to him?"
>
> He said to him, "If I say, Caesar will kill me, and if not, you will kill me. Best that I kill myself and not betray state secrets."

The false Messiah proved a false judge as well, rejecting even the testimony in his hands and the plea of the honest sage:

> Nonetheless, Bar Koziba reached the conclusion that he wanted to betray the city.
>
> When R. Eleazar had finished his prayer, he sent and summoned him, saying to him, "What did this one say to you?"
>
> He said to him, "I never saw that man."
>
> He kicked him and killed him.

At that moment an echo proclaimed: "Woe to the worthless shepherd who leaves the flock, the sword shall be upon his arm and upon his right eye" (Zech. 11:17).

Said the Holy One, blessed be He, "You have broken the right army of Israel and blinded their right eye. Therefore your arm will wither and your eye grow dark."

Forthwith Betar was conquered and Ben Koziba was killed.

That God has responded to the arrogance of the Messiah is now underscored. On his own, Hadrian could have accomplished nothing. It was God who killed the Messiah, not Hadrian:

They went, carrying his head to Hadrian. He said, "Who killed this one?"

They said, "One of the Goths killed him," but he did not believe them.

He said to them, "Go and bring me his body."

They went to bring his body and found a snake around the neck.

He said, "If the God of this one had not killed him, who could have vanquished him?"

That illustrates the following verse of Scripture: "If their Rock had not given them over. . . . " (Dt. 32:30).

Lamentations Rabbah LVIII:ii.4A, 5A–B, 7–8, 10A–b, F–W

The same attitude is set forth in a further story of the arrogance of the army of the Messiah, which repeated the Messiah's plea to heaven, "Let him not help us nor hinder us," and which was defeated not by Hadrian's army but by God:

There were two brothers in Kefar Haruba, and no Roman could pass by there, for they killed him.

They decided, "The whole point of the thing is that we must take the crown and put it on our head and make ourselves kings."

They heard that the Romans were coming to fight them.

They went out to do battle, and an old man met them and said, "May the Creator be your help against them."

They said, "Let him not help us nor hinder us!"

Because of their sins, they went forth and were killed.

They went, carrying his head to Hadrian. He said, "Who killed this one?"

They said, "One of the Goths killed him," but he did not believe them.

He said to them, "Go and bring me his body."

They went to bring his body and found a snake around the neck.

He said, "If the God of this one had not killed him, who could have vanquished him?"

That illustrates the following verse of Scripture: "If their Rock had not given them over. . . . " (Dt. 32:30).

Lamentations Rabbah LVIII:ii.19A–L

Arrogance toward God, rather than repentance and remorse, thus characterize the false Messiah. If, then, Israel wants to bring about the restoration, whether the individual to life or Israel to the Land, it will accomplish repentance: an act of humility to which God will respond by sending the Messiah, the humble sage.

The failed Messiah of the second century, Bar Kokhba, above all, exemplifies arrogance against God. He lost the war because of that arrogance. His emotions, attitudes, sentiments, and feelings form the model of how the virtuous Israelite is not to conceive of matters. The heart of the matter then is Israel's subservience to God's will, as expressed in the Torah and embodied in the teachings and lives of the great rabbinic sages. When Israel fully accepts God's rule, then the Messiah will come. Until Israel subjects itself to God's rule, the Jews will be subjugated to pagan domination. Since the condition of Israel governs, Israel itself holds the key to its own redemption: an act of humility and self-abnegation is what is required.

29. RESURRECTION OF THE DEAD

What is the doctrine of the resurrection from the dead?

At the end of days, through the Messiah, God will raise the dead. Death does not mark the end of the individual human life, nor exile the last stop in the journey of Holy Israel. Israelites will live in the age of the world to come, all Israel in the Land of Israel; and Israel will comprehend all who know the one true God. The restoration of world order that completes the demonstration of God's justice encompasses both private life and the domain of all Israel. For both the restorationist theology provides eternal life; to be Israel means to live. So far as the individual is concerned, beyond the grave, at a determinate moment, man (1) rises from the grave in resurrection, (2) is judged, and (3) enjoys the world to come. For the entirety of Israel, congruently: all Israel participates in the resurrection, which takes place in the Land of Israel, and enters the world to come.

Where do we find that doctrine in a creedal setting?

Besides the full exposition of the matter in the Mishnah, Tosefta, Yerushalmi, and Bavli to *Sanhedrin* chapter eleven, the doctrine of the resurrection of the dead is prominent in the liturgical creed. It is located at the second benediction of *The Standing Prayer* (Amidah), recited three times daily, every day of the year; a doctrine in rabbinic Judaism does not get more official than that:

Your might, Lord, is eternal,

Your saving power brings the dead to life again.

You sustain the living with loving kindness;

With great mercy you bring the dead to life again.

You support the fallen, heal the sick, free the captives;

You keep faith with those who sleep in the dust.

Who can compare with your might, Lord and King,

You are master over life and death and deliverance.

Faithful are you in bringing the dead to life again.

Praised are you, Lord, master over life and death.[1]

Here is a fully articulated belief in the resurrection of the dead, with the implicit conviction that that marks the end of days.

Why is resurrection a logical necessity of monotheism?

The absolute given, a logical necessity of a theology revealing God's justice, maintains that individual life goes forward from this world, past the grave, to the world to come, and people are both judged and promised eternal life. That is a necessary doctrine for a system that insists upon the rationality and order of the universe under God's rule. Without judgment and eternal life for the righteous, this world's imbalance cannot be righted, nor can God's justice be revealed. Monotheism without an eschatology of judgment and the world to come leaves unresolved the tensions inherent in the starting point: God is one, God is merciful and just in light of the observed injustices of life. That is why the starting point of the theology dictates its conclusion: the deeds one does in this world bear consequences for his situation in the world to come, and the merit attained through this-worldly deeds, e.g., of generosity, persists; individuals retain their status as individuals through all time to come.

Who is raised from the grave, and who is not?

In a predictable application of the governing principle of divine justice, measure for measure, those who do not believe in the resurrection

---

[1] Jules Harlow, ed., *Weekday Prayer Book* (New York: The Rabbinical Assembly, 1966), 53–54.

of the dead will be punished by being denied what they do not accept. Some few others bear the same fate. To be Israel means to rise from the grave, and that applies to all Israelites. The entire holy people will enter the world to come, that is, Israel will enjoy the resurrection of the dead and eternal life. "Israel" then is anticipated to be the people of eternity. Excluded from the category of resurrection and the world to come, then, are only those who by their own sins have denied themselves that benefit. These are those who deny that the teaching of the world to come derives from the Torah, or who deny that the Torah comes from God, or who are hedonists. Rabbinic exegesis of Scripture also yields the names of three kings who will not be resurrected, as well as four commoners and certain specified generations: those of the Flood, the Dispersion, the inhabitants of Sodom, the generation of the wilderness, the party of Korah, and the Ten Tribes.

> All Israelites have a share in the world to come,
>
> as it is said, *Your people also shall be all righteous, they shall inherit the land forever; the branch of my planting, the work of my hands, that I may be glorified* (Is. 60:21).

That single statement serves better than any other to define Israel in the oral Torah. Now we forthwith take up exceptions:

> And these are the ones who have no portion in the world to come:
>
> He who says, the resurrection of the dead is a teaching which does not derive from the Torah, and the Torah does not come from Heaven; and an Epicurean.

> Mishnah *Sanhedrin* 10:1A–D

From classes of persons, we turn to specified individuals who are denied a place within Israel and entry in the world to come; all but one are Israelites, and the exception, Balaam, has a special relation to Israel, as the gentile prophet who came to curse but ended with a blessing:

> Three kings and four ordinary folk have no portion in the world to come.
>
> Three kings: Jeroboam, Ahab, and Manasseh.

> Mishnah *Sanhedrin* 10:2A–B

Then come entire generations of Gentiles before Abraham, who might have been considered for eternal life outside of the framework of God's self-manifestation, first to Abraham, then in the Torah. These are the Generation of the Flood, the Generation of the Dispersion, and the Men of Sodom.

What about judgment ("the last judgment") in the Aggadic theology?

The details of judgment that follow resurrection prove less ample and are not so clearly focused. The basic account stresses that God will judge with great mercy. But the oral Torah presents no fully-articulated story of judgment. Within the documents of the oral Torah, we have little narrative to tell us how the judgment will be carried on. Even the detail that through repentance and death man has already atoned, which is stated so explicitly in the context of repentance and atonement, plays no role that I can discern in discussions of the last judgment. What we do know concerns two matters. When does the judgment take place? By what criteria does God decide who inherits the world to come? As to the former: the judgment is comparable to the annual judgment for man's fate in the following year. It will happen either at the beginning of the New Year on the first of Tishré, when, annually, man is judged, or on the fifteenth of Nisan, when Israel celebrates its freedom from Egyptian bondage and begins its pilgrimage to Sinai. The detail is subject to dispute, leaving the main point to stand as normative doctrine. As to the latter, the criteria are those announced at Mishnah-tractate *Sanhedrin* 10:1: All Israel except for . . . Excluded then are those that deny the Torah, meaning, idolaters.

What constitutes heaven and hell?

Heaven is the restoration of Adam and Eve to Eden, of Israel to the Land of Israel. Hell is to die forever, the utter annihilation of one's individual person.

The final judgment lasts for a period of time, not forever, and at that point the resurrected who have endured in judgment pass to the world to come or eternal life. Those judged for death remain in the grave. When the judgment comes, it will last for twelve (or six) months; this we know because Scripture is explicit. We have only to identify the correct verse of Scripture:

Also he [Aqiba] would list five things which [last for] twelve months:

(1) the judgment of the generation of the Flood is twelve months;

(2) the judgment of Job is twelve months;

(3) the judgment of the Egyptians is twelve months;

(4) the judgment of Gog and Magog in the time to come is twelve months;

and (5) the judgment of the wicked in Gehenna is twelve months,

as it is said, It will be from one month until the same month [a year later] (Is. 66:23).

Mishnah Eduyyot 2:10A–G

The point is established by identifying five classes of persons that come under judgment and assigning them all to the term of judgment specified by the prophet. What about the others, who, when judged, are rejected? Those who do not pass judgment then are condemned and do not pass on to eternal life, and these are Israelites or Gentiles who have a special relation to Israel. Other Gentiles—idolaters—do not even figure in judgment at all. They do not rise from the grave.

30. THE WORLD TO COME

What are the components of the Aggadic doctrine of the world to come?

The governing theology sets forth its main components in a simple narrative, and very often, a single sentence captures the story. Here is such a version of the complete tale of the world to come in one short sentence: *When Israel returns to God, God will restore their fortunes.* The sentence remains brief enough with the added adjectival clause, *in the model of Adam and Eve in Eden.* Everything else amplifies details. That simple sentence is explicitly built on the verb-root for "return," encompassing "restore," *shub,* yielding *teshubah,* "repentance" as well as the causative form of the verb, *hashib,* thus "return" or "restore." It thereby defines the condition, (intransitive) return or repentance, for the advent of the age to come, which encompasses the action, (transitively) to return matters to their original condition.

How exactly does the Aggadah envision the world to come?

The world to come marks the final condition of world order: its restoration to God's original plan. It signifies the realization of correct and perfect relationships between God and man, God and Israel in particular. Those who reject God having been disposed of, the age to come finds its definition in the time of total reconciliation between God and man. It is the age when man loves God and accepts his dominion and completes the work of repentance and atonement for acts of rebellion. While, clearly, that reconciliation of God and man takes place in individual life, in which case we may use the language of salvation, it also governs the public life of Israel, in which case we may speak of redemption.

What do sages have in mind when they speak of the world to come—
concrete actualities, or intangible feelings and attitudes, impalpable matters of the spirit? May we suppose that we deal with a mere narration, in
mythic form, of what in fact represents an inner, other-worldly, intangible
and spiritual encounter? That is to say, if all that is at stake is abstract patterns of relationships that happen to come to expression in tales of the
eschaton, one might suppose that the conception, "the world to come,"
simply serves as another way of saying, "man reconciled with God." Then,
through paradigmatic thinking, sages should be represented as finding in
the myth a vivid and palpable way of speaking of the inner life of
intentionality and attitude. That is a possible reading of the character of
the discourse at hand. But I think that that would drastically misrepresent
the worldly reality, the concrete actuality, of the rabbinic sages' account of
matters, their intent to speak to the here and now—"today, if you will it!"

When they speak of the world to come, the sages mean a world
that is public and shared, not private and inner-facing. It is not a world
of relativities and relationships as these intangibles are concretely sym-
bolized, but a world of real encounter. Sages know a palpable God who
punishes arrogance and rewards humility, in both instances in worldly
ways. Prayers are answered with rain or healing, virtue responded to
with grace bearing material benefit, acts of generosity with miracles.
Heaven intervenes in matters of health and sickness, in the abundance
or scarcity of crops, in good fortune and ill. Sages insist upon an exact
correspondence between practicalities and transcendent relationships.
The spiritualization of matters earthly would seriously misinterpret
what is at stake here. When sages see the world to come as the climax
and conclusion of the processes of creation that commenced with Eden,
they envisage the world that comes within their everyday gaze, the
people they see out there, in the street, not only imagine in here, in the
heart. Take the resurrection for instance. When the dead are raised from
the grave, they will stink and need new clothes:

> Raba contrasted [these two verses]: "It is written, 'I kill and I make alive'
> (Deut. 32:39) and it is written, 'I wound and I heal' (Deut. 32:39). [The for-
> mer implies that one is resurrected just as he was at death, thus with blem-
> ishes, and the other implies that at the resurrection all wounds are healed].

> "Said the Holy One, blessed be he, 'What I kill I bring to life,' and then,
> 'What I have wounded I heal.'"

> Bavli *Sanhedrin* 91b 11:1–2 I.25

From that simple affirmation we may extrapolate much else. At the
advent of the world or age to come, exactly what happens, in the process

of restoration of world order to the condition of Eden, and of Israel to the Land of Israel? Samuel's minimalist view, "There is no difference between the world to come and the days of the Messiah, except the end of the subjugation of the exilic communities of Israel" (Bavli-tractate *Sanhedrin* 91b), alerts us to the breadth of opinion on how the days of the Messiah will differ from the world to come. But it is clear that a clear sequence governs. First comes salvation in the aspect of resurrection and judgment pertains to individuals, and then, immediately following judgment, the world or age to come marks the time of redemption for the holy people, Israel. And the bulk of the evidence supports the view that the age to come differs from this age, as well as from the time of the Messiah, in more ways than the political one that Samuel selects as primary.

What is going to happen in the age to come? Israel will eat and drink, sing and dance, and enjoy God, who will be lord of the dance. What about the restored Temple? The war of Gog and Magog having concluded, the dead having been returned to the Land and raised, the next stage in the restoration of world order requires the reconstruction of the Temple, where, as we recall, God and man, Heaven and earth, meet.

> "Then Jacob called his sons and said, 'Gather yourselves together, that I may tell you what shall befall you in days to come:'"
>
> R. Simon said, "He showed them the fall of Gog, in line with this usage: 'It shall be in the end of days ... when I shall be sanctified through you, O Gog' (Ez. 38:[16]). 'Behold, it shall come upon Edom' (Is. 34:5)."
>
> R. Judah said, "He showed them the building of the house of the sanctuary: 'And it shall come to pass in the end of days that the mountain of the Lord's house shall be established' (Is. 2:2)."
>
> Rabbis say, "He came to reveal the time of the end to them, but it was hidden from him."

> *Genesis Rabbah* XCVIII:ii.7A–D

So in the now-familiar sequence of restoration, (1) final war, (2) advent of the Messiah and the resurrection and judgment, and (3) the age to come, next in sequence must be (4) the restoration of Israel to the Land, and (5) rebuilding the Temple, destroyed by reason of Israel's sin. Since the bulk of offerings in the Temple set forth by Moses in the written Torah had focused upon atonement for sin and guilt, what purpose would the Temple, and its surrogate, the synagogue, now serve? There is only a single one. In the age to come, responding to redemption, all offerings but the thanksgiving offering, appropriately, will cease, all prayers but thanksgiving prayers will cease.

31. AGGADAH AND HALAKAH

How did theology and law, Aggadah and Halakah, combine in rabbinic Judaism to advance the restoration of Israel?

Rabbinic Judaism aims at restoring humanity to Eden. This takes place in the embodiment of Israel restored to the Land of Israel through the Messiah's intervention into human history. Through the realization of the Torah's laws, viewed as a discipline in the education of Israel as Adam regenerate, the rabbinic sages would accomplish God's purpose.

That is why Halakah, normative law, defined "the way" for Israel to go. Accordingly, the theology yielded by the Aggadah and the law formulated in the Halakah together constituted a complete and encompassing system of Israel's social order. The Aggadah provided the narrative, the Halakah, the realization of the narrative, in a single coherent statement. When you grasp that, you understand rabbinic Judaism.

How do Adam and Israel compare? The task of the Torah: what makes Israel the regenerate Adam?

The single most important exercise in the search for patterns emerges in parallel details of two stories, Adam's and Israel's. And everything follows from that discovery of the rabbinic sages. They identified the master-narrative of the human condition in the parallel stories of Adam and the loss of Eden, Israel and the loss of the Land. Israel lost the Land twice, first in 586 B.C.E. to the Babylonians, then in 70 C.E. to the Romans. It regained the Land once, and would be restored to the Land a second, and final time, with the coming of the Messiah, judgment, and the resurrection of the dead to eternal life in the Land made Eden. This paradigm begins in narrative-exegesis of Scripture but reaches its full expression in principal parts of the Halakah.

Defining the worldview and theory of Israel of rabbinic Judaism, the text before us derives from *Genesis Rabbah*. Here Scripture is turned into a vast corpus of facts, and the task of the rabbinic sage is to discern out of those facts the patterns and regularities that signal the workings of laws, just as in natural history the philosopher turns the facts of nature into natural laws.

Now to the text, comparing Israel to "a man," that is, Adam:

> R. Abbahu in the name of R. Yosé bar Haninah: "It is written, 'But they [Israel] are like a man [Adam], they have transgressed the covenant' (Hos. 6:7).

> " 'They are like a man,' specifically, like the first man." [We shall now compare the story of the first man in Eden with the story of Israel in its land.]

Now in line with Hosea's declaration that Israel is like Adam, the sage identifies God's action in regard to Adam with a counterpart action in regard to Israel, in each case matching verse for verse, beginning with Eden and Adam. Adam is brought to Eden as Israel is brought to the Land, with comparable outcomes:

> " 'In the case of the first man, I brought him into the garden of Eden, I commanded him, he violated my commandment, I judged him to be sent away and driven out, but I mourned for him, saying "How . . ." '[which begins the book of Lamentations, hence stands for a lament, but which, as we just saw, also is written with the consonants that also yield, 'Where are you'].

> " 'I brought him into the garden of Eden,' as it is written, 'And the Lord God took the man and put him into the garden of Eden' (Gen. 2:15).

> " 'I commanded him,' as it is written, 'And the Lord God commanded . . .' (Gen. 2:16).

> " 'And he violated my commandment,' as it is written, 'Did you eat from the tree concerning which I commanded you' (Gen. 3:11).

> " 'I judged him to be sent away,' as it is written, 'And the Lord God sent him from the garden of Eden' (Gen. 3:23).

> " 'And I judged him to be driven out.' 'And he drove out the man' (Gen. 3:24).

> " 'But I mourned for him, saying, "How . . ." ' 'And he said to him, "Where are you" ' (Gen. 3:9), and the word for 'where are you' is written, 'How. . . .' "

Now comes the systematic comparison of Adam and Eden with Israel and the Land of Israel:

" 'So too in the case of his descendants, [God continues to speak,] I brought them [Israel] into the Land of Israel, I commanded them, they violated my commandment, I judged them to be sent out and driven away but I mourned for them, saying, "How. . . ." '"

" 'I brought them into the Land of Israel.' 'And I brought you into the land of Carmel' (Jer. 2:7).

" 'I commanded them.' 'And you, command the children of Israel' (Ex. 27:20). 'Command the children of Israel' (Lev. 24:2).

" 'They violated my commandment.' 'And all Israel have violated your Torah' (Dan. 9:11).

" 'I judged them to be sent out.' 'Send them away, out of my sight and let them go forth' (Jer 15:1).

" '. . . and driven away.' 'From my house I shall drive them' (Hos. 9:15).

" 'But I mourned for them, saying, "How. . . ." ' 'How has the city sat solitary, that was full of people' (Lam. 1:1)."

Genesis Rabbah XIX:ix. 2

We end with Lamentations, the writing of mourning produced after the destruction of the Temple in Jerusalem in 586 by the Babylonians. Here we end where we began, Israel in exile from the Land, like Adam in exile from Eden. But the Torah is clear that there is a difference, which we shall address in its proper place: Israel can repent.

How is Israel exemplary of Adam?

These persons, Israel and Adam, form not individual and particular, onetime characters, but exemplary categories. Israel is Adam's counterpart, Israel is the other model for Man, the one being without the Torah, the other possessing, and possessed by, the Torah. Adam's failure defined Israel's task, marked the occasion for the formation of Israel. Israel came into existence in the aftermath of the failure of Creation with the fall of Man and his ultimate near-extinction; in the restoration that followed the Flood, God identified Abraham to found in the Land, the new Eden, a supernatural social entity to realize his will in creating the world. Israel above all embodies God's abode in humanity, his resting place on earth. The entire Halakic system of rabbinic Judaism forms an elaboration of that conception. And it is the Torah that makes all the difference, given as it is "to purify the heart of humanity."

PART 6

HALAKAH AND THE THEOLOGY OF RABBINIC JUDAISM: HOW DOES THE LAW EMBODY THE TORAH'S NARRATIVE THEOLOGY?

32. NARRATIVE PATTERN AND THE HALAKAH

―――◈―――

How does the Halakah embody the Torah's narrative theology?

The rabbinic sages searched the stories and laws of Scripture for patterns yielding laws subject to generalization. That was their approach to the past, to history (cf. Section 18). It also characterized their reading of Scripture's own legal passages, the hundreds of concrete laws that fill Exodus, Leviticus, Numbers, and Deuteronomy. The outcome of this quest for order and regularization was the Halakah: Scripture's cases made into exemplary rules for Israel's social order. But as we shall now see, the quest for law was guided by the master-narrative that the rabbinic sages discerned in Scripture. That point of intersection of norm and narrative is where the Halakah and the Aggadah unite, the one defining, the other explaining, right action.

Focused as it is on Scripture's narrative, the Halakah sets forth a systematic and coherent response to Genesis's account of the tragic situation of Man from Eden onward. The Halakah lays out an account of how the entire social order may be constructed to realize Eden, this time with Man fully and willingly accepting life under God's rule. Through examining the Halakah in its native categories or tractates, these propositions are shown to animate the entire Halakic corpus, which is thus proved to embody a theological system.

I group the Halakic tractates of the Mishnah (thus also of the Tosefta-Yerushalmi-Bavli) by their role in the exposition of the Aggadic-theological narrative, in each case spelling out how a component of the question is dealt with. The subject matter of the tractates is signaled by the title in each case.

Where and when is Eden?

What is the narrative of *Shevi'it* (the cessation of agricultural labor in the Seventh Year), *Orlah* (the prohibition of produce of a fruit tree for the first three years after planting), *Kil'ayim* (the prohibition of mixed seeds), *Shabbat-Eruvin* (the Sabbath, the sharing of ownership of property on the Sabbath)?

By "Eden" Scripture means that moment and condition, whole and at rest that God sanctified; "Eden" stands for creation in perfect repose. In the Halakah, Eden stands for not a particular place but nature in a defined condition, at a particular moment: creation in Sabbath repose, sanctified. Then a place in repose at the climax of creation, at sunset at the start of the seventh day, whole and at rest, embodies, realizes Eden. The Halakah means to systematize the condition of Eden, to define Eden in its normative traits, and also to localize Eden within Israel, the people. How so? Eden is the place to the perfection of which God responded in the act of sanctification at the advent of the seventh day. While the Land, in the Torah's explicit account of matters, claims the right to repose on the seventh day and in the seventh year of the septennial cycle, it is the location of Israel wherever that may be at the advent of sunset on the eve of the seventh day of the week of creation that recapitulates Eden.

Who owns Eden?

What is the narrative of *Ma'aserot* (tithing), *Terumot* (priestly rations), *Hallah* (dough offering), *Ma'aser Sheni* (second tithe), *Bikkurim* (firstfruits), *Pe'ah* (leaving the corner of the field for the poor), and *Demai* (doubtfully tithed produce)?

The story expands to within the motif of Eden, the matter of ownership and possession as media for the expression of the relationship between Man and God. God accorded to Adam and Eve possession of nearly everything in Eden, retaining ownership—the right to govern according to his will—for himself. The key to the entire system of interaction between God and Israel through the Land and its gifts emerges in the Halakah of *Ma'aserot*, tithing, and its companions. These bodies of the Halakah explicate the difference between possession and ownership. God owns the world, which he made. But God has accorded to man the right of possession and usufruct of the earth and its produce. This he did twice, once to Man—Adam and Eve—in Eden, the second time to Israel in the Land of Israel. And to learn the lesson that Man did not master, that possession is not ownership but custody and stewardship, Israel has to acknowledge the claims of the Creator to the glory of all creation, which is the Land. This Israel does by giving back God's share of the produce of the Land at the time, and in the manner, that God defines.

What about the Israelite Adam and Eve?

What is the narrative of *Qiddushin* (betrothals), *Ketubbot* (marriage contracts), *Nedarim* (vows), *Nazir* (the special vow of the Nazirite), *Sotah* (the wife accused of infidelity), *Gittin* (divorces), and *Yevamot* (levirate marriages)?

The Halakah of the family, covering the act of sanctification of a woman by a man (*Qiddushin*), the marriage agreement (*Ketubbah*), vows and special vows (*Nedarim, Nazir*), the disposition of a charge of unfaithfulness against a woman (*Sotah* = Num 5), and the severance of the marital bond of sanctification through a writ of divorce or death, only occasionally invokes the metaphor of Adam and Eve in Eden. How here does Eden figure? The connection is made articulate by the (possibly later) liturgical framework in which the Halakah plays itself out. There, in the liturgy of the marriage canopy, the act of creation of Man is recapitulated, the bride and groom explicitly are compared to Adam and Eve.

What about sin and atonement in the Halakah?

What role in the narrative is played by *Sheqalim* (the Temple tax), *Tamid* & *Yoma* (the daily whole offering, the offering of the Day of Atonement), *Zevahim* & *Menahot* (animal offerings, meal offerings), *'Arakhin* (pledges of personal valuation to the Temple), *Bekhorot* (firstborn), *Me'ilah* (sacrilege), and *Temurah* (exchanges of an unconsecrated animal for an already consecrated one)?

The Halakah takes account of the tragedy of Eden and provides for a new moral entity, a reformed transaction accorded that entity, one not available to Adam and Eve. For God at Eden made no provision for atonement for sin, but, in the unfolding of Man's story, God grasped the full measure of Man's character and drew the necessary conclusion and acted on it. Endowed with autonomous will, Man has the power to rebel against God's will. Therefore the Halakah finds urgent the question, How is Man, subject to God's rule, to atone for the sin that, by his rebellious

nature, Man is likely to commit? The Torah to answer that question for-
mulates the rules that govern Man both (1) when under God's dominion and (2) when in rebellion against God's will. These represent the two
aspects of the one story that commences with Eden, leads to the formation of Israel through Abraham, Isaac, and Jacob, God's antidotes to
Adam, and climaxes at Sinai. But Israel also is Man, so that story accom-
modates both Adam's fall and Israel's worship of the golden calf, and, as
the denouement, Adam and Eve's exile from Eden and Israel's ultimate
exile from the Land.

What about intentionality and the civil order?

How do the generative themes of the Aggadah come to expression
in the Halakah of *Keritot* (extirpation), *Sanhedrin-Makkot* (court-inflicted
penalties, floggings), *Bava Qamma-Bava Metzi'a-Bava Batra* (the civil law),
Horayot (the law covering sin on the part of rulers), and *Shevu'ot* (court
oaths)?

The Halakah dictates the character of (its) Israel's civil order—its
political institutions and system of criminal justice. It undertakes a labor
of differentiation of power, indicating what agency or person has the
power to precipitate the working of politics as legitimate violence. When
we understand the differentiating force that imparts to politics its activity and dynamism, we grasp the theology that animates the structures of
the politics and propels the system. The details of the Halakah, in particular the sanctions assigned to various infractions, effect the taxonomy of
power, which forms an implicit exegesis of the story of Eden, translated
into reflection on the power of intentionality.

Are the enemies of Eden tangible or invisible?

What is the place in the theological narrative carried out in the
Halakah covering the tangible enemies in *'Avodah Zarah* (idolatry), and
the invisible enemy: death in the Halakah of *Ohalot* (corpse uncleanness), *Nega'im* (the uncleanness of the skin ailment analogous to corpse
uncleanness), *Zavim* and *Niddah* (the uncleanness of the improperly
functioning sexual organs, menstrual uncleanness)?

The enemies of Eden take shape around the grand struggle between life and death, in the here and now meaning Israel and the Gentiles, sanctification and cleanness as against death and uncleanness.

Specifically, the world beyond the limits of Israel forms an undifferentiated realm of idolatry and corpse uncleanness. Then how is Israel to negotiate life with the world of Gentiles and their idolatry, corpses and their contamination? Among the sources of uncleanness, tangible and invisible, we begin with the Gentiles and proceed to corpse and comparable kinds of uncleanness. But the two—Gentiles, corpses—form a single domain. The former bears exactly the same uncleanness as the latter. Gentiles, defined as idolators, and Israelites, defined as worshippers of the one and only God, part company at death. For the moment Israelites die—only to rise from the grave. Gentiles die for eternity. The roads intersect at the grave, each component of humanity taking its own path beyond. Israelites—meaning, those possessed of right conviction—will rise from the grave, stand in judgment, but then enter upon eternal life, to which no one else will enjoy access.

What is the arena for the contest between death and life?

How are uncleanness and sanctification counterposed in *Makhshirin* (liquids that impart susceptibility to uncleanness when deliberately spread about), *Teharot* (uncleanness of food and doubtful situations), *Uqtzin* (uncleanness of parts of produce), and *Kelim* (uncleanness of utensils and how it is removed)?

The sources of change and disruption that threaten the cleanness, hence the sanctification, of the Temple are the same sources that threaten the norm of cleanness of the household. If the same uncleanness affects the Temple and the table, then the only difference is one of degree, not of kind, as the Halakah states explicitly. And the rest follows. The web of relationships between sanctification and uncleanness spins itself out into every corner of the Israelite household, where the system makes a difference. And it is the will of the householder that determines the difference that the distinction between clean and unclean is going to make. Everything is relative to the householder's will; he has it in his power to draw the household table into alignment with the altar in the Temple, that is to say, to place the table and the food set thereon into relationship, onto a continuum, with the altar and the Holy Things of the cult. This he can accomplish through an act of will that motivates an attitude of constant watchfulness in the household for those very sources of contamination that Scripture identifies as danger to the Lord's altar in the Jerusalem Temple.

How is death overcome?

What are the antidotes to uncleanness set forth in *Parah* (preparing purification water to remove corpse uncleanness), *Mikwa'ot* (immersion pools for the removal of ordinary uncleanness), *Tevul Yom* (the diminished degree of uncleanness of one who has immersed and awaits sunset to complete the process of purification at the advent of the new day), and *Yadayim* (the uncleanness attaching to the hands)?

From death and its affect upon food and drink, that is, the uncleanness caused by, and analogous to, death, we turn to the media for the restoration of life. Still water unaffected by human agency restores the natural condition disrupted by uncleanness other than that of the corpse and its analogues. Purification water systematically subjected to human intervention—by constant attention and deliberate action from start to finish—alone removes corpse uncleanness. We have then to account for the exclusion of man from the one process using still water, the radical insistence upon his inclusion, in full deliberation, within the other using purification water. Uncleanness that comes about by reason of any cause but death and its analogues is removed by the Heaven's own dispensation, not by man's intervention: rainfall and sunset suffice. Ordinary purification is done by nature, resulting from natural processes. But as to persons and objects that have contracted uncleanness from death, nature on its own cannot produce the kind of water that bears the power to remove that uncleanness and restore the condition of nature. Only man can. And man can do this only by the highest level of concentration, the most deliberate and focussed action. Man's act of will overcomes the uncleanness of death, just as man's act of deliberate rebellion brought about death to begin with. Man restores what man has disrupted. Had the Halakah wished in its terms and categories to accomplish a reprise of the story of man's fall, it could not have made a more eloquent statement than it does in the contrast between the Halakah of *Mikwa'ot* and that of *Parah*.

Where and what is the Kingdom of God?

How does the Halakah embody *Accepting the Yoke of the Kingdom of Heaven and the Commandments* in *Berakhot* (reciting the Shema, the Prayer, and other blessings), *Hullin* (foods for domestic, non-cultic use), *Megillah* (declaiming the Scroll of Esther; laws concerning declaiming the Torah and prophets), *Rosh HaShanah* (the New Year, sounding the shofar), *Pesahim* (the Paschal offering, the Passover seder), *Sukkah* (the hut for the Festival of Huts), *Moʿed Qatan* (working on the intermediate days of the festivals of Passover and Huts; laws of burial), *Betzah* (the relationship between the Sabbath and the festival days), and *Taʿanit* (public fasts in time of trouble or drought)?

As much as Man by his nature rebels against God, Man tutored by the commandments willingly accepts God's will and therefore his rule. What are the Halakah's media for the reformation, regeneration, and renewal of Man? The Halakah here legislates for not Eden but the Kingdom of God. For Sinai's answer to Eden's question transcends the matter of sin and atonement and encompasses the conduct of the ordinary, everyday life lived under God's rule. The normative deals with the normal, so the final solution to God's dilemma with Man—how to accord Man free will but to nurture in Man freely-given love for God—lies in the Torah. That way of life in accord with God's rule means to form the *Paideia*, the character-building education to transform Man by making Israelite Man's freely-given obedience to God as natural as was the First Man's contumacious rebellion against God. That is why the Halakic provision for life in God's kingdom moves from the ordinary day and its duties to the table and its everyday nourishment, then to the meeting with God that is seasonal and temporal, and finally to the climax of the system, confrontation with routine crisis.

33. THE SABBATH

What was the theological significance of the Sabbath in the Halakah?

The Ten Commandments in Exodus portray the Sabbath as a memorial to creation:

> Remember the Sabbath day to keep it holy. Six days you shall labor and do all your work, but the seventh day is a Sabbath to the Lord your God . . . for in six days the Lord made heaven and earth, the sea and all that is in them, and rested on the seventh day; therefore the Lord blessed the Sabbath day and hallowed it.

> Exod 20:8–11

The Israelite household at rest on the Sabbath day recapitulates the celebration of God at the moment of the conclusion and perfection of creation. Then the Israelite household, like creation at sunset marking the end of the sixth day of creation, is sanctified: separated from the profane world and distinguished as God's domain. With all things in place and in order, at the sunset that marks the advent of the seventh day, the rest that marks the perfection of creation descends. Then the Israelite stays in his place and enters the state of repose.

The advent of the Sabbath imposes upon the household a set of rules of sanctification. The Torah has set the stage. The Sabbath marks the celebration of creation's perfection (Gen 2:1–3). Food for the day is to be prepared in advance (Exod 16:22–26, 29–30). Fire is not to be kindled on that day, thus no cooking (Exod 35:2–3). Servile labor is not to be carried on in that day by the householder and his dependents, encompassing his chattel (Exod 20:5–11, 23:12, 31:12–17, 34:21). The where matters as much as the when and the how: people are supposed to stay in their place: "Let each person remain in place, let no one leave his place on the seventh day" (Exod 16:29), understanding by place the private domain of the household. But ownership of private domains may be commingled, so that many households form a single property for the purposes of moving about and carrying objects on the Sabbath.

What type of actions is forbidden on the Sabbath?

Israel on the Sabbath in the Land like God on the Sabbath of Eden rests from the labor of creation. And that brings us to the question, what labor is forbidden? That question is answered in two settings.

First, the analogy of conduct in the Temple is introduced. Work that on the Sabbath day is permissible in connection with God's house, the Temple, is forbidden in connection with the Israelite household. It is the one that finds the definition of forbidden labor in those activities required for the construction and maintenance of the tabernacle, which is to say, God's residence on earth.

> People are liable only for classifications of labor the like of which was done in the tabernacle. They sowed, so you are not to sow. They harvested, so you are not to harvest. They lifted up the boards from the ground to the wagon, so you are not to lift them in from public to private domain. They lowered boards from the wagon to the ground, so you must not carry anything from private to public domain. They transported boards from wagon to wagon, so you must not carry from one private domain to another.

> Bavli *Shabbat* 49b 4:2 I.4B

Sages found in the analogy of how, in theory, the tabernacle was maintained, the classifications of labor that pertain. In the tabernacle these activities are permitted, even on the Sabbath. In God's house, the priests and Levites must do for God classifications of work that on the Sabbath the Israelites cannot do outside of the Temple.

Second, out of a myriad of detailed laws, certain governing principles emerge, which are: on the Sabbath it is prohibited deliberately to carry out in a normal way a completed act of constructive labor, one that produces enduring results, one that carries out one's entire intention (the whole of what one planned, one has accomplished, in exactly the proper manner). It is not an act of labor that itself is prohibited (as the Ten Commandments in Exodus and Deuteronomy would have it), but an act of labor of a very particular definition.

What is striking is, no prohibition impedes performing on the Sabbath an act of labor in an *other-than-normal* way. In theory, one may go out into the fields and plough, if he does so in some odd manner. He may build an entire house, so long as it collapses promptly. He may write a single letter, but not two, which form a word. The issue of activity on the Sabbath therefore is removed from the obvious context of work, conventionally defined. Now the activity that is forbidden is of a very particular sort, modeled in its indicative traits after a quite specific paradigm.

Constructive labor is prohibited. A person is not forbidden to carry out an act of destruction, or an act of labor that produces no lasting consequences. He may start an act of labor if he does not complete it. He may accomplish an act of labor in some extraordinary manner. None of these acts of labor are forbidden, even though, done properly and with consequence, they represent massive violations of the Halakah. Nor is part of an act of labor that is not brought to conclusion prohibited. Nor is it forbidden to perform part of an act of labor in partnership with another person who carries out the other requisite part. Nor does one incur culpability for performing an act of labor in several distinct parts, e.g., over a protracted, differentiated period of time. A person may not willingly carry out the entirety of an act of constructive labor, start to finish. The issue is not why not, since we know the answer: God has said not to do so. The question is, whence the particular definition at hand?

Clearly, a definition of the act of labor that is prohibited on the Sabbath has taken over and recast the commonsense meaning of the commandment not to labor on the Sabbath. For considerations enter that recast matters from an absolute to a relative definition. One may tie a knot—but not one that stands. One may carry a package, but not in the usual manner. One may build a wall, only if it falls down. And one may do pretty much anything without penalty—if he did not intend matters as they actually happened. The metaphor of God in Eden, as sages have reflected on the story of Creation, yields the governing principles that define forbidden labor. What God did in the six days of creation provides the model.

What are the principles that define an act of labor forbidden on the Sabbath?

Let us review the main principles item by item. They involve the three preconditions.

(1) The act must fully carry out the intention of the actor, as creation carried out God's intention.

(2) The act of labor must be carried out by a single actor, as God acted alone in creating the world.

(3) An act of labor is the like of one that is required in the building and maintenance of God's residence in this world, the tabernacle.

The act of labor prohibited on the Sabbath involves two considerations. The act must be done in the ordinary way, just as Scripture's account leaves no doubt, God accomplished creation in the manner in which he accomplished his goals from creation onward, by an act of speech. And, weightier still, the forbidden act of labor is one that produces enduring consequences. God did not create only to destroy, but he created the enduring world. And it goes without saying, creation yielded the obvious consequences that the act was completely done in all ways, as God himself declared. The act was one of consequence, involving what was not negligible but what man and God alike deemed to make a difference. Sages would claim, therefore, that the activity that must cease on the Sabbath finds its definition in the model of those actions that God carried out in making the world.

What are the governing narratives of the Sabbath?

To act like God on the Sabbath the Israelite rests; he does not do what God did in creation. The key words, therefore, are in the shift from the here and now of time in which one works like God, to the *then* and *there* when one desists from working, just as God did at the moment the world was finished, perfected, and sanctified. Israel gives up the situation of man in ordinary time and space, destructive, selfish, dissatisfied and doing. Then, on the Sabbath, and there, in the household, with each one in place, Israel enters the situation of God in that initial, that perfected and sanctified then and there of creation: the activity that consists in sustaining life, sharing dominion, and perfecting repose through acts of restraint and sufficiency. Then where and what is Eden? Eden is Israel, the holy people. And when does Eden take place? Eden takes place on the Sabbath—just as in the beginning and in the end-time.

34. PURITY AND IMPURITY

What was the meaning of purity and what was the source of impurity?

Purity bears both moral and ritual meanings in the Halakah of rabbinic Judaism. Scripture lists a variety of sources of impurity or uncleanness (not a hygienic category but a ritual one), most (but not all) of them modeled after the principal source of uncleanness, which is death in the form of the corpse and what is comparable to a corpse, e.g., the skin ailment described at Lev 13–14. One who has contracted uncleanness is forbidden to enter the Temple or participate in the cult. The Temple celebrated life and had to be kept clean of death and its effects. The priests had to eat their priestly rations from the altar of the Lord in a state of purity.

In addition, Israelites, chief among them the Pharisees or "abstainers," who compared their table at home to the table of the Lord in the Temple in Jerusalem, wanted to keep the purity laws even outside of the Temple, at home (cf. Section 43). They too would keep the laws of cultic purity, as if they were priests in the Temple. The ritual meaning of purity and uncleanness competed with the moral one: to be clean of sin. That is expressed in the following:

> R. Pinhas b. Yair says, "Heedfulness leads to cleanliness, cleanliness leads to cleanness {purity}, cleanness leads to abstinence, abstinence leads to holiness, holiness leads to modesty, modesty leads to the fear of sin, the fear of sin leads to piety, piety leads to the Holy Spirit, the Holy Spirit leads to the resurrection of the dead, and the resurrection of the dead comes through Elijah, blessed be his memory."

Mishnah Sotah 9:15MM

In this ladder of virtue, the starting point is to be alert to sources of hygienic uncleanliness as well as of cultic uncleanness. When one is alert to the possibilities of cultic contamination, he may aspire to a state of purity, and this leads to holiness. Holiness forms a step in the way toward moral virtues, modesty, fear of sin, piety. So purity was a condition one attained by avoiding sources of contamination, death and what was comparable to death, and by undergoing a process of purification in a body of still water when one had contracted contamination.

How did purity represent a position in the contest between life and death?

Most of the Halakic exposition of purity and uncleanness pertains to the domestic setting, the household, as much as to the Temple. The household like the Temple forms the arena for the contest between life and death. The principal activities of the household—creating, sustaining life—also involve acts of sanctification (in creating life) and the maintenance of the model of sanctity (in sustaining life): the whole mirroring the space, time (as at the Sabbath), and activity of the Temple. That is why Israel confronts the sources of contamination; its task is constantly to remain alert and watchful, lest those contaminations that signify death affect Israel.

Israel consequently must watch not only what it eats and drinks and wears and where it stands and sits and lies. Israel also must pay attention to what the food it eats may have touched, who may have stood or sat upon the clothing that the Israelite wears and the beds on which he takes a rest. To preserve the condition it ought always to enjoy, which is, the state of sanctification, Israel has then to maintain a constant surveillance of the present and past of the world in which it lives and the people among whom it makes its life. Marrying without carefully investigating the genealogy of the Israelite family into which one marries can produce *mamzerim* [meaning "of illegal lineage," Heb. pl. of *mamzer*] and sitting on a bench without finding out who has sat there before can produce uncleanness that can contaminate much else, and eating a piece of bread without knowing where it has been and who has touched it can diminish one's standing in the hierarchy of sanctification.

Did intentionality play a role in that contest?

The web of relationships between sanctification and uncleanness spins itself out into every corner of the Israelite household, where the system makes a difference. And it is the will of the householder that determines the difference that the distinction between clean and unclean is going to make. Everything is relative to the householder's will; he has it in his power to draw the household table into alignment with the altar in the Temple, that is to say, to place the table and the food set thereon into relationship, onto a continuum, with the altar and the Holy Things of the cult. This he can accomplish through an act of will that motivates an attitude of constant watchfulness for those very sources of contamination that Scripture identifies as a danger to the Lord's altar in the Jerusalem Temple. Such an attitude of watchfulness then comes to realization in actions that confirm the attitude and embody the intentionality: take note, avoid, watch out for this, that, and the other thing. That is because the faithful of the Halakah think of themselves as Temple priests but situate themselves in the ordinary world.

In the actual Temple, avoiding sources of uncleanness, e.g., corpses, menstruating women, people suffering a flux, posed no enormous problems; most of the virulent sources of uncleanness were walled out to begin with. But in the household and in the marketplace who knows what can happen—and commonly does? And bumping into someone quite inadvertently, who can trace the history of each person, his or her encounter with a corpse, her period, for instance, or with someone who has had such an encounter or sat on a chair on whom a menstruating woman or a man with flux has sat? The possibilities for cultic contamination, controlled in the cult, prove limitless outside. But then, the Halakah aims at imposing order and a certain rationality, a well-construed assessment of probabilities, upon that chaos of the unclean and the profane. So much for the construction of a world of sanctification and desacralization in response to the householder's will and intention. Now we turn to what lies beyond his power, to matters upon which his attitude and plan have no bearing: the sources of uncleanness that do function *ex opere operato* and that, when they do, take what is sacred and render it unclean, inaccessible to its ordinary purpose and task: sustaining the life of holy Israel.

On the side of life eternal, Israel abides within God's kingdom, both unseen and seen, tangible, visible, and temporal. To aspire to live in God's kingdom bears a variety of meanings, but the simplest and most explicit calls upon Israel to be holy like God: "You shall be holy; for I the Lord your God am holy." (Lev 19:2 RSV). Just as the holiness of the Temple, where God abides and Israel meets him, is to be defended from the sources of uncleanness that represent death, so the Israelite household, its table, utensils and food, as much the bed, are to be protected against those same enemies. In the model of Eden, Man bears responsibility for his part in the confrontation. Where exactly does the will of Man enter into the contest between life and death? That question occupies us in our inquiry into how Israel takes its position within the Kingdom of God, choosing life. And, by now predictably, the answer will be, by an act of will Israel enters the contest.

How is the household treated as comparable to the Temple?

When Scripture defines sources of uncleanness, it is to protect from death and for life the camp of Israel, which sages understand to refer to the Temple and its altar. In the Temple what is at stake is nourishing God through the offerings, and nourishing the priesthood through their share of the offerings to God. Any analogy built upon the Temple will therefore focus upon how nourishment is carried on, and within that governing analogy, the Temple's rules of how food is preserved for the altar and the priests and how it is rendered unsuitable for them will take center stage. But the altar is not the only locus of life against death. Just as God's altar is to be kept free of uncleanness, so too is the Israelite table. And the act of procreation is explicitly identified as one to be protected from uncleanness. In that way the Halakah places the household upon a continuum of sanctification with the Temple. In light of the character of the forces of uncleanness, choosing nourishment alongside procreation as the principal occasion for acting out the sanctification of the household in the model of the Temple presents no surprise.

How does the Halakah place the household of holy Israel in the holy Land upon the same continuum as the Temple? This it does by providing rules for cultic cleanness and uncleanness in the Temple and among the priests—in connection with preparation of secular food for the household at home. Food, together with the pots and pans and other utensils used in connection with preparing and eating it, and, by extension, the other domestic furniture of the household, is explicitly placed upon that continuum when the food is prepared in accord with the rules of cleanness that pertain to the altar and the Temple in Jerusalem. Food and its appurtenances, broadly construed, then may be removed from the status of cleanness, within the hierarchical framework of sanctification, and plunged into the status of uncleanness, by exactly those same sources of uncleanness that render a priest or an offering unclean and unfit for the sanctity of the Temple altar and courtyard. So along with the desacralization of the bed, more broadly, of the household at the point of sanctification of the union of husband and wife, food for the domestic table may lose its position on the continuum of cleanness and holiness that observance of the rules of cultic cleanness may accord to it.

What was rabbinic Judaism's conception of ritual sanctification vis-a-vis moral sanctification?

What about moral uncleanness and moral sanctification? Rabbinic Judaism defined in moral terms the Torah's imperatives concerning holiness. That is shown in the exposition of the commandment, "You shall be holy, for I the Lord your God am holy" (Lev 19:2):

> "You shall be holy, for I the Lord your God am holy" (Lev. 19:2):
>
> That is to say, "if you sanctify yourselves, I shall credit it to you as though you had sanctified me, and if you do not sanctify yourselves, I shall hold that it is as if you have not sanctified me."
>
> Abba Saul says, "The king has a retinue, and what is the task thereof? It is to imitate the king."
>
> Sifra CXCV:i.3A–B, E

To be holy is to imitate God, to be like God. Lev 19 immediately introduces, as articulations of sanctification, a systematic articulation of the Ten Commandments, for instance, honor of parents, not making images of God, care for the poor, not stealing, not deceiving, not swearing falsely, fearing God by not insulting the deaf or placing a stumbling block before the blind (Lev 19:14). The systematic exposition of the concretization of holiness ends with the golden rule, "You shall not take vengeance or bear a grudge against your fellow. You shall love your neighbor as yourself, I am the Lord" (Lev 19:18). The commandment to love is deemed fundamental by rabbinic Judaism in its reading of Scripture, and it is embedded in the exposition of sanctification.

35. FESTIVALS

---◆◆◆---

What was the meaning of the festivals?

The Judaic year follows the lunar calendar, so the appearance of the new moon marks the beginning of a month, and that is celebrated. But the Judaic year also correlates with the solar seasons. The lunar year is 354 days, the solar, 365. The lunar year from time to time is adjusted to the solar seasons by the inclusion of an additional lunar month. The key turnings of the solar year define the festal calendar: the first full moon after the vernal equinox, March 21, and the first full moon after the autumnal equinox, September 21.

These mark the time of heightened celebration. To understand how the rhythm of the year unfolds, however, we begin with the new moon of the month of Tishré, corresponding to September-October. That marks the New Year, Rosh Hashanah. Ten days later comes the Day of Atonement, commemorating the rite described in Lev 16, and marking God's judgment and forgiveness of humanity. Five days afterward is the full moon, which is the beginning of the Festival of Huts or Tabernacles, in Hebrew, Sukkot; that festival lasts for eight days and ends with a day of solemn assembly, Shemini Aseret, and of rejoicing of the Torah, Simhat Torah. So nearly the whole month of Tishré is spent in celebration: eating, drinking, praying, studying, enjoying and celebrating God's sovereignty, creation, revelation, redemption, as the themes of the festivals and solemn celebrations of the season work themselves out.

The next major sequence of celebration, as we realize, follows the first new moon after the vernal equinox, which begins the month of Nisan and culminates, at its full moon, with Passover, in Hebrew, *pessah,* which commemorates the Exodus of Israel from Egypt and celebrates Israel's freedom, bestowed by God. Fifty days thereafter comes the Festival of Weeks/Pentecost, in Hebrew, Shavuot, which commemorates the giving of the Torah at Mount Sinai. Other occasions for celebration exist, but, apart from the Sabbath, the New Year, Day of Atonement, and the pilgrim Festivals of Tabernacles, Passover, and Pentecost are the main holy days.

What was the meaning of Passover?

Called the feast of unleavened bread and the season of our freedom, the Passover festival preserves very ancient rites in a new framework. It is, for example, absolutely prohibited to make use of leaven, fermented dough, and the like. The agricultural calendar of ancient Canaan was marked by the grain harvest, beginning in the spring with the cutting of barley and ending with the reaping of the wheat approximately seven weeks later. The farmers would get rid of all their sourdough, which they used as yeast, and old bread as well as any leaven from last year's crop. The origins of the practice are not clear, but that the Passover taboo against leaven was connected with the agricultural calendar is beyond doubt. Just as the agricultural festivals were historicized, likewise much of the detailed observance connected with them was supplied with historical "reasons" or explanations. In the case of the taboo against leaven the reason was that the Israelites had to leave Egypt in haste and therefore had to take with them unleavened bread, for they had not time to permit the bread to rise properly and be baked. Therefore Israelites eat the *matzah,* unleavened bread.

A Narrative, or Haggadah, at a home banquet, marks the commencement of the Festival of Passover. It is highlighted by the following:

> We were the slaves of Pharaoh in Egypt; and the Lord our God brought us forth from there with a mightily hand and an outstretched arm. And if the Holy One, blessed be He, had not brought our fathers forth from Egypt, then surely we, and our children, and our children's children, would be enslaved to Pharaoh in Egypt. And so, even if all of us were full of wisdom and understanding, well along in years and deeply versed in the tradition, we should still be bidden to repeat once more the story of the exodus from Egypt; and he who delights to dwell on the liberation is one to be praised.

The story of Israel then is spelled out, and in the course of the narrative, Israel comes to definition:

> Long ago our ancestors were idol-worshippers but now the Holy One has drawn us to his service. So we read in the Torah: And Joshua said to all the people, "Thus says the Lord, God of Israel: From time immemorial your fathers lived beyond the river Euphrates, even to Terah, father of Abraham and of Nahor, and they worshipped idols. And I took your father

Abraham from beyond the river and guided his footsteps throughout the land of Canaan. I multiplied his offspring and gave him Isaac. To Isaac I gave Jacob and Esau. And I set apart Mount Seir as the inheritance of Esau, while Jacob and his sons went down to Egypt."

All of it is deeply relevant to those present, for it says who the assembled family really are, and for whom they really stand. Here, then, "Israel" explicitly defines itself: a family become a people, saved by God from bondage. Thus the family states at the conclusion of the Passover Haggadah, recapitulating the entire narrative of Judaism's Israel:

> Again and again, in double and redoubled measure, are we beholden to God the All-Present: that He freed us from the Egyptians and wrought His judgment on them; that He sentenced all their idols and slaughtered all their first-born; that He gave their treasure to us and split the Red Sea for us; that He led us through it dry-shod and drowned the tyrants in it; that He helped us through the desert and fed us with the manna; that He gave the Sabbath to us and brought us to Mount Sinai; that He gave the Torah to us and brought us to our homeland, there to build the Temple for us, for atonement of our sins.

Here we find the definition of that "us" that constitutes Israel, a definition formed of a sequence of events that have designated that group.

What was the meaning of Pentecost/Weeks?

Continuous with Passover, the second of the three festivals of the calendar of Judaism, Weeks/Shavuot, celebrates God's freely giving, and Israel's willingly receiving, the Torah at Sinai. First the slaves are liberated, at Passover, then they gain the freedom incised on the tablets of the Torah, on Pentecost. Israel then accepts God's dominion in the covenant of Sinai. Weeks/Shavuot is also called Pentecost ("fifty") because it falls fifty days beyond Passover, that is, Weeks falls on the fifty-first day from the full moon of Nisan, the occasion of Passover, for "On the third new moon [the third month] after the people of Israel had gone forth out of the land of Egypt, on that [same] day they came into the wilderness of Sinai" (Exod 19:1 RSV). In the natural calendar of the Land of Israel, Weeks marks the end of the barley harvest and the beginning of the wheat harvest. In the sacred calendar of Judaism, the festival of Weeks embodies the second component of Judaism's story of Israel: the Israel defined by the event at Sinai: all those present and accounted for by declaring, in one voice, "All the words which the LORD has spoken we will do" (Exod 24:3 RSV).

Weeks is celebrated primarily in public worship in the synagogue, in the declamation of the Ten Commandments and the study of the Torah. The stage is set by the custom of the faithful to spend the entire night of the festival, from the sundown that marks the beginning, to sunrise, in community Torah-study under synagogue auspices. That is followed by morning services. So the congregation has reenacted Israel's action at Sinai, receiving and meditating on the revealed Torah.

But at the morning worship the congregation then is given a jarring message, as unanticipated, in its way, as the surprising message of Passover about the family representing a covey of freed slaves. Specifically, Israel assembled in the synagogue hears, in addition to the obligatory declamation of the Pentateuch and the prophets, the book of Ruth. That book tells the story of how a woman deriving from Moab, which abused Israel when Israel wandered in the wilderness, and the male heirs of which are excluded from Israel by reason of churlishness, chose to make herself part of Israel by accepting the yoke of the Torah and the dominion of God. So Israel is Israel by reason of the Torah, not only by genealogy and ethnic identification.

What was the meaning of Tabernacles/Huts?

Called simply "The Festival," the Festival of Huts, in Hebrew, Sukkot (frequently translated, in fancy language, as "Tabernacles"), forms the climax of the autumnal holy day season, the counterpart to the sequence of Passover and Weeks after the vernal equinox. Just as the vernal season begins at Passover and concludes fifty days later at Weeks, so a span of time is covered in the fall as well. It concerns itself not with freedom and the giving of the Torah but sin, forgiveness, and rejoicing.

The Festival of Huts places Israel beyond the Sea and Sinai, wandering about in the wilderness, where by reason of rebellion against God, Israel wandered for forty years. Israel then is reminded that it is a people that has sinned, but that God can and does forgive. The sojourn in the wilderness embodies the story. There they remained until the entire generation of the wilderness had died out, and Israel was ready to enter the promised land. Passover places Israel's freedom into the context of the affirmation of life beyond sin, Sukkot returns Israel to the fragility of abiding in the wilderness, as Moses explicitly states:

> And the Lord said to Moses, "Say to the people of Israel, On the fifteenth day of this seventh month and for seven days is the feast of booths [huts] to the Lord. . . . You shall dwell in booths for seven days; all that are native

in Israel shall dwell in booths, that your generations may know that I made the people of Israel dwell in booths when I brought them out of the land of Egypt: I am the LORD your God."

Leviticus 23:33–34, 42–43 RSV

The principal observance of the Festival is the construction of a frail hut, for temporary use. In it Israel lives once more in the condition of that sinful generation, eating meals and (where the climate permits) sleeping out-of-doors. What defines the hut is the roofing, which must cast more shade than light, but not be fully covered over. Roofing of branches, leaves, fruit, and flowers allows light to show through, and at night, the stars. At this time of harvest bounty it is good to be reminded of man's travail and dependence upon heavenly succor. The hut or Sukkah is an abode that cannot serve in the rainy season that is coming, announced by the new moon that occasions the festival. Israel is to take shelter, in reverting to the wilderness, in any random, ramshackle hut, covered with what nature has provided but in form and in purpose what man otherwise does not value. The Sukkah in its transience matches Israel's condition in the wilderness, wandering between Egypt and the Land, death and eternal life. What the Festival of Huts registers is the fragility and culpability of liberated, covenanted Israel.

36. A UNIFYING RULE

What are the 613 commandments?

The written Torah not only commands Israel to "... be holy, for I the LORD your God am holy" (Lev 19:2 RSV), it defines holiness in the performance of religious duties, commandments (*mitzvot*), which sanctify those that do them, and which are many. At the same time the Torah offers general rules of sanctification of the community of Israel, for example, "... you shall love your neighbor as yourself" (Lev 19:18 RSV).

Accordingly, the master narrative of Judaism describes in vast detail the rules for living in God's kingdom under the yoke of the Torah. The commandments, enumerated at 613, 365 matching the days of the solar year, and 248 corresponding to the number of bones of the body, govern everyday life and transactions, both social and personal. Through myriads of details, it is, then, easy to lose sight of the purpose of the whole. Hence, as Moses did in Lev 19:2 and 19:18, so too the rabbinic sages made every effort at teaching the purpose of the laws of the Torah, finding the main point realized in the details. In a series of stories and sayings, they declared what they deemed to form the heart and soul, the center of the system as a whole.

Is there a single purpose that explains the entire Halakic system?

Among many efforts at summarizing life under the law of the Torah, the most comprehensive is attributed to R. Simlai, in the following composition:

> R. Simelai expounded, "Six hundred and thirteen commandments were given to Moses, three hundred and sixty-five negative ones, corresponding to the number of the days of the solar year, and two hundred forty-eight positive commandments, corresponding to the parts of man's body."

"David came and reduced them to eleven: 'A Psalm of David: Lord, who shall sojourn in thy tabernacle, and who shall dwell in thy holy mountain? (i) He who walks uprightly and (ii) works righteousness and (iii) speaks truth in his heart and (iv) has no slander on his tongue and (v) does no evil to his fellow and (vi) does not take up a reproach against his neighbor, (vii) in whose eyes a vile person is despised but (viii) honors those who fear the Lord. (ix) He swears to his own hurt and changes not. (x) He does not lend on interest. (xi) He does not take a bribe against the innocent' (Psalm 15)."

"Isaiah came and reduced them to six: '(i) He who walks righteously and (ii) speaks uprightly, (iii) he who despises the gain of oppressions, (iv) shakes his hand from holding bribes, (v) stops his ear from hearing of blood (vi) and shuts his eyes from looking upon evil, he shall dwell on high' (Isaiah 33:25–26)."

"Micah came and reduced them to three: 'It has been told you, man, what is good, and what the Lord demands from you, (i) only to do justly and (ii) to love mercy, and (iii) to walk humbly before God' (Micah 6:8)."

"only to do justly:" this refers to justice.

"to love mercy:" this refers to doing acts of loving kindness.

"to walk humbly before God:" this refers to accompanying a corpse to the grave and welcoming the bread.

"And does this not yield a conclusion a fortiori: if matters that are not ordinarily done in private are referred to by the Torah as 'walking humbly before God,' all the more so matters that ordinarily are done in private.

"Isaiah again came and reduced them to two : 'Thus says the Lord, (i) Keep justice and (ii) do righteousness' (Isaiah 56:1).

"Amos came and reduced them to a single one, as it is said, 'For thus says the Lord to the house of Israel. Seek Me and live.'"

"Habakkuk further came and based them on one, as it is said, 'But the righteous shall live by his faith' (Habakkuk 2:4)."

Bavli *Makkot* 23b–24a 3:16 II.1B, D, V, FF–NN

If we can reduce "the whole Torah" to a handful of teachings, then clearly, the meaning of the word "Torah" has shifted. The word no longer refers to a particular body of writings. Nor does it speak mainly of God's revelation to Moses at Mount Sinai. A variety of meanings now gather around a single word, and it is time systematically to review them.

How does the Golden Rule appear in rabbinic Judaism?

Simlai's is only one such effort at summarizing the whole Torah in a few encompassing rules. The single most famous such statement of "the whole Torah" drives from Hillel, the first-century C.E. Pharisaic authority, whom we have met before:

> There was another case of a gentile who came before Shammai. He said to him, "Convert me on the stipulation that you teach me the entire Torah while I am standing on one foot." He drove him off with the building cubit that he had in his hand.
>
> He came before Hillel: "Convert me."
>
> He said to him, " 'What is hateful to you, to your fellow don't do.' That's the entirety of the Torah; everything else is elaboration. *So go, study.*"
>
> Bavli *Shabbat* 30b–31a/2:5 I.12

This famous saying frequently is cited only in part, the part about elaboration and Torah-study is left out. But, we see, Torah-study is integral to life under the law of the Torah, and ignorance is the enemy of piety. So we have to ask whether the rabbinic sages address the question of which takes priority, study or action?

What is the role of Torah-study in the Halakah?

Everything else is elaboration; the work is to go, study. Then which is more important, doing the deed or studying about it in the Torah? That question is answered in so many words:

> Once R. Tarfon and the elders were reclining at a banquet in the upper room of the house of Nitseh in Lud. This question was raised for them: "Is study greater or is action greater?"
>
> R. Tarfon responded: "Action is greater."
>
> R. Aqiba responded: "Study is greater."
>
> All responded, saying, "Study is greater, for study brings about action."
>
> Bavli *Qiddushin* 22a 1:10E–G I.2

So the point of the way of life set forth by the law of the Torah is studying the Torah so as to keep the commandments. The value of study depends on the doing of the deed. The matter is resolved by Eleazar b. Azariah in this language:

R. Eleazar b. Azariah says, "If there is no learning of Torah, there is no proper conduct.

If there is no proper conduct, there is no learning in Torah. . . ."

He would say, "Anyone whose wisdom is greater than his deeds—to what is he to be likened? To a tree with abundant foliage, but few roots.

"When the winds come, they will uproot it and blow it down,

as it is said, *He shall be like a tamarisk in the desert and shall not see when good comes but shall inhabit the parched places in the wilderness* (Jer. 17:6).

But anyone whose deeds are greater than his wisdom—to what is he to be likened? To a tree with little foliage but abundant roots.

For even if all the winds in the world were to come and blast at it, they will not move it from its place,

as it is said, *He shall be as a tree planted by the waters, and that spreads out its roots by the river, and shall not fear when heat comes, and his leaf shall be green, and shall not be careful in the year of drought, neither shall cease from yielding fruit* (Jer. 17 :8)."

Mishnah *Avot* 3:17

The picture we gain of life under the law of the Torah is a life focused on God's concerns, a life meant to respond to the expression of God's love for Israel that is embodied in the Torah. Above all, we see an insistent effort on classifying religious requirements as less or as more important, depending on the sense of proportion and purpose that animates the law as a whole.

But that is not the view of Judaism that its critics have formed. A cultural bias comes into play as a result of millennia of criticism of people who supposedly care more for what goes into their mouths—kosher food—than for what comes out—gossip and slander. As we have seen, the rabbinic sages understood full well that some commandments are more important than others, for example, that the religious duty of saving a life takes priority even over the observance of the Sabbath. But one cannot desecrate the Sabbath to save one's property.

Still, when people think of law, they ordinarily imagine a religion for bookkeepers, who tote up the good deeds and debit the bad and call the result salvation or damnation, depending on the outcome. But life under the law of the Torah—covenantal nomism—brings the joy of expressing love of God through the covenant between Israel and God.

PART 7

SOCIAL DOCTRINES OF RABBINIC JUDAISM: FAMILY, GENDER, VIRTUE, AND WORK

37. FAMILY AND LIFE ROLES

What was the role of the family in rabbinic Judaism?

The household—an extended family—formed the building block of the Israelite social order envisaged by rabbinic Judaism. The governing language is theological, with the key word being "holiness." The family is formed when a man betroths a woman and consummates the betrothal, and the Hebrew word for "betroth" is "sanctify." The relationship of that woman to that man is one of sanctification; she is uniquely his, having consented to consecrate herself to him. God has a heavy stake in what is set apart as sanctified, whether the offering in the Temple on his altar, or the wife in the household in bed.

What was the policy of the Halakah toward women? Could a woman be a householder?

Can the householder be the mother, not the father? In the law of the Torah, women can own land and engage in the economic activities of a household. The system theoretically could accommodate a female householder. In Halakic practice, however, a woman is always taken to relate to a man, first as her father, then as her husband, when he is alive, and, when he is deceased, to her male sons or stepsons by her deceased husband. These support her as a widow. It is further taken for granted that when a woman is divorced or widowed, she will remarry within a brief spell, so that the alimony provided in the marriage settlement is meant to tide her over until she does so. Or she reverts to her "father's house," which means that she rejoins the household of her father, if he is alive, and if he is dead, of her brothers.

What does the wife owe the husband?

The laws of the Torah set forth in the Mishnah define what the wife owes the husband and the husband the wife. The law focuses, for the wife, on the labor that she owes, and, for the husband, on the restraint he must exercise, the respect for the wife's autonomy he must display. Stated simply: the wife or wives (we deal, in ancient times, with a polygamous society) represent participants in the household, and the wife owes the husband the fruit of her labor. The husband reciprocates by honoring the wife's desires and attitudes and refraining from trying to control and isolate her. The wife's domestic duties encompass these:

These are the kinds of labor which a woman performs for her husband:

she (1) grinds flour, (2) bakes bread, (3) does laundry, (4) prepares meals, (5) feeds her child, (6) makes the bed, (7) works in wool.

[If] she brought with her a single slave girl, she does not (1) grind, (2) bake bread, or (3) do laundry.

[If she brought] two, she does not (4) prepare meals and does not (5) feed her child.

[If she brought] three, she does not (6) make the bed for him and does not (7) work in wool.

If she brought four, she sits on a throne.

Mishnah *Ketubbot* 5:5A–F

The wife, further, is expected to conduct herself in a modest and pious manner, and if she does not do so, the husband may divorce her without paying the alimony that is required in the marriage agreement—a huge incentive for the wife to keep the law:

And those women go forth without the payment of the marriage contract at all:

She who transgresses against the law of Moses and Jewish law.

And what is the law of Moses [which she has transgressed]? [If] (1) she feeds him food which has not been tithed, or (2) has sexual relations with him while she is menstruating, or [if] (3) she does not cut off her dough-offering, or [if] (4) she vows and does not carry out her vow.

And what is the Jewish law? If (1) she goes out with her hair flowing loose, or (2) she spins in the marketplace, or (3) she talks with just anybody.

Abba Saul says, "Also: if she curses his parents in his presence."

R. Tarfon says, "Also: if she is a loudmouth."

What is a loudmouth? When she talks in her own house, her neighbors can hear her voice.

Mishnah Ketubbot 7:6

Clearly, considerations of modesty and propriety figure heavily.

What does the husband owe the wife?

The husband, for his part, owes his wives not only the required domestic support for which Scripture provides—food, clothing, conjugal relations—but also an allowance that she may spend as she sees fit:

> He gives her in addition a silver *maah* [a sixth of a *denar*] for her needs [per week].

> And she eats with him on the Sabbath by night {when sexual relations are owing}.

> And if he does not give her a silver *maah* for her needs, the fruit of her labor belongs to her. {She may sell what she makes, e.g., spun wool, and use the money ad lib.}

> And if she was feeding {nursing} a child, they take off {the required weight of wool which she must spin as} the fruit of her labor, and they provide more food for her.

> Under what circumstances?

> In the case of the most poverty-stricken man in Israel.

> But in the case of a weightier person, all follows the extent of his capacity [to support his wife].

Mishnah Ketubbot 5:9A–C, F–I

What we see in the requirements of husband to wife and wife to husband, then, is heavy emphasis upon shared personal and material obligations. The wife brings to the marriage her dowry, which stands for her share in the father's estate; this reverts to her (hence to her father) in the event of divorce or the husband's demise. So the marriage represents the formation of a partnership based on quite practical considerations. Matters of emotion enter in—but mainly as the husband's responsibility.

The husband may not abuse the wife, may not try to keep her away from the normal social relations that she should enjoy as an independent personality, and must accord to her all of the rights and dignities of a free woman:

> He who prohibits his wife by vow from deriving benefit from him
>
> for a period of thirty days, appoints an agent to provide for her.
>
> [If the effects of the vow are not nullified] for a longer period, he puts her away and pays off her marriage contract.
>
> Mishnah *Ketubbot* 7:1A–C

Since, in the marital negotiations, the husband receives property that, in the event of divorce, he must restore to the wife's father's household, divorce is not undertaken lightly. It involves not only a year of alimony, but also loss of considerable capital or real estate. Hence the husband has a strong incentive not to impose a vow upon the wife that denies her the right to gain benefit from him, e.g., eat at his table, share his bed, and the like.

The same considerations strongly discourage the husband from browbeating or otherwise trying to manipulate or control the wife. If he imposes on her a vow not to eat even one sort of fruit or vegetable, he must divorce her, giving her her freedom and losing the capital she has brought into his household:

> He who prohibits his wife by vow from tasting any single kind of produce whatsoever
>
> must put her away and pay off her marriage contract.
>
> Mishnah *Ketubbot* 7:2A–B

The law shows remarkably little patience for the intrusive or controlling husband who would transform his wife into his slave, lacking all freedom of will. The same protection encompasses the wife's right to adorn herself as a beautiful woman; such petty annoyances become very costly:

> He who prohibits his wife by a vow from adorning herself with any single sort of jewelry must put her away and pay off her marriage contract.
>
> Mishnah *Ketubbot* 7:3A

The husband must permit the wife to maintain a circle of friends and relationships beyond the limits of the household. The husband may not interfere in the wife's relationships with her father and family; he may not stop her from seeing her relatives. The wife has the absolute right to visit her father's household pretty much when her duties permit. Nor may the husband interfere with the wife's normal social intercourse. Here too, if he tries to keep her caged at home and cut off her ties to other people, particularly the society of women, he loses heavily. In these and other ways, the husband is given a weighty incentive to treat the wife with enormous respect. And, as we have seen, if the woman behaves improperly, not keeping the Torah of Moses, committing adultery, for example, she too loses the assets she has brought to the marriage and the household. The provisions of her marriage settlement are null; the husband keeps the dowry, and she loses everything.

What do parents owe their children?

The father owes the son a number of specific duties. He must bring him into the covenant of Abraham through circumcision. He must redeem him, if the son is a firstborn and the father is not of the priestly caste, by handing over to a priest five silver coins; he must teach him Torah; he must get him a wife; and he must teach him a trade. In these ways the father provides for the son's religious, personal, and economic future:

> [The father is responsible with respect to his son] to circumcise him, to redeem him, to teach him Torah, to teach him a trade, and to marry him off to a woman.
>
> And there are those who say, "Also: to row him across the river."
>
> R. Judah says, "Whoever does not teach his son a trade teaches him to be a mugger."
>
> Tosefta *Qiddushin* 1:11F–H

But both parents owe their children an honorable example of how to conduct themselves. And they owe the children a heritage of virtue and not of sin, because Scripture is explicit that God visits the iniquity of the fathers upon the children but shows steadfast love for a thousand generations of those who love him and keep his commandments, so Exod 20:5–6.

What do children owe their parents?

The Ten Commandments deem honor of father and mother as one of the principals of God's dominion. Paying honor to parents represents a primary act of acceptance of God's rule (Exod 20:12). Then sages take as their task to spell out what honor of parents means. They want concrete actions of respect, support, and obligation: supporting parents with food, drink, and clothing. That honoring parents is tantamount to honoring God is made explicit. The reason is not difficult to fathom. It is stated explicitly:

> Three form a partnership in the creation of a human being, the Holy One, blessed be He, one's father and one's mother. When someone honors father and mother, said the Holy One, blessed be He, "I credit it to them as though I had lived among them and they honored me."
>
> Bavli *Qiddushin* 30b–31a 1:7 II.3B/

Why should the parents be given the same honor as God? When we recall that the act of procreation recapitulates God's act of creation, making life, we realize that the parents possess the power of creation and in that aspect are like God. Since the parents compare with God, the honor owing to God extends to the parents.

Did rabbinic Judaism look down on, or subjugate, women?

The Halakah secured for Israelite women dignity, responsibility, and a critical role in the conduct of the social order. Women were not arbitrarily subjugated, and women were appreciated and honored, in no way denigrated in their position in law and equity.

38. GENDER ROLES

How did rabbinic Judaism construct gender roles? What was rabbinic Judaism's attitude towards celibacy?

Rabbinic Judaism in defining virtuous gender roles joins traits explicitly marked as male to those explicitly classified as female. It insists upon both in the formation of models of virtue. It therefore may be classified as androgynous, affirming the traits of both sexes as the religion itself defines those gender qualities. In this world holy Israel is to emulate women's virtue, the condition of the coming of the Messiah. And women's capacity for devotion, selfless faith, and loyalty defines the model of what is required of Israel for its virtue.

Within their system was no place for celibacy. Sexuality was conceived as natural, God's plan for Adam and Eve. No virtue was attached to refraining from sexual relations. The first commandment God gave to humanity was, "Be fruitful and multiply" (Gen 1:28 RSV).

How were God and Israel rendered in the metaphor of husband and wife?

Since the Song of Songs ("Song of Solomon") portrays God's love for Israel and Israel's love for God, we anticipate finding the rabbinic doctrine of gender roles in the exposition of that holy poetry. There we find the patterns of virtue assigned to the respective genders. The relationship of Israel to God is the same as the relationship of a wife to the husband, and this is explicit in the following:

"I am my beloved's, and his desire is for me" (Song 7:10 RSV):

There are three yearnings:

The yearning of Israel is only for their Father who is in heaven, as it is said, "I am my beloved's, and his desire is for me."

The yearning of a woman is only for her husband: "And your desire shall be for your husband" (Gen. 3:16).

The yearning of the Evil Impulse is only for Cain and his ilk: "To you is its desire" (Gen. 4:7).

Song of Songs Rabbah XCIX:i.1B–E

Here, therefore, we find that gender relationships are explicitly characterized, and, with them, the traits associated with the genders as well.

The rabbinic sages turn to everyday experience—the love of husband and wife—for a metaphor for God's love for Israel and Israel's love for God. And Israel is assigned the feminine role and the feminine virtues. It is difficult to identify a more extravagant form of praise for women's virtue, her capacity to love generously and in an act of unearned grace.

What were masculine virtues?

No account of feminine virtue can accomplish its goals without cataloguing masculine virtue as well. Our survey of the feminine and the masculine begins with the clear characterization of God as masculine, Israel as feminine:

"My beloved has gone down to his garden, to the beds of spices, [to pasture his flock in the gardens, and to gather lilies]" (Song 6:2):

Said R. Yosé b. R. Hanina, "As to this verse, the beginning of it is not the same as the end, and the end not the same as the beginning.

"The verse had only to say, 'My beloved has gone down to pasture in his garden,' but you say, 'in the gardens'!

"But 'my beloved' is the Holy One, blessed be he;

" 'to his garden' refers to the world.

" 'to the beds of spices' refers to Israel.

" 'to pasture his flock in the gardens' refers to synagogues and schoolhouses.

" 'and to gather lilies' speaks of picking [taking away in death] the righteous that are in Israel."

Song of Songs Rabbah LXXVIII:i.1A–H

"My beloved" is God; the choice part of the garden, which is the world, is Israel, its synagogues and houses of study. Torah-study embodied masculine virtues.

How was Israel represented as feminine?

The virtues of wives, portrayed as feminine, are those of loyalty and submission. This metaphor is exploited through the invocation of the wife's trust in the husband, the mark of the perfect wife. Israel follows wherever Moses, in behalf of God, leads; Israel trusts in God the way a woman who has accepted marriage trusts her husband:

R. Berekhiah in the name of R. Judah b. R. Ilai: "It is written, 'And Moses led Israel onward from the Red Sea' (Ex. 15:22):

"He led them on from the sin committed at the sea.

"They said to him, 'Moses, our lord, where are you leading us?'

"He said to them, 'To Elim, from Elim to Alush, from Alush to Marah, from Marah to Rephidim, from Rephidim to Sinai.'

"They said to him, 'Indeed, wherever you go and lead us, we are with you.'

"The matter is comparable to the case of one who went and married a woman from a village. He said to her, 'Arise and come with me.'

"She said to him, 'From here to where?'

"He said to her, 'From here to Tiberias, from Tiberias to the Tannery, from the Tannery to the Upper Market, from the Upper Market to the Lower Market.'

"She said to him, 'Wherever you go and take me, I shall go with you.'

"So said the Israelites, 'My soul cleaves to you' (Ps. 63:9)."

Song of Songs Rabbah IV.iii.10

Israel's feminine virtue must exceed even the wife's trust in the husband's protection. In the model of Hosea's prophecy, Israel also must care only for God, the way a wife's entire desire is solely for her husband.

The point is unmistakable and critical. Israel is subject to an oath to wait patiently for God's redemption, not to rebel against the nations on its own; that is the concrete social politics meant to derive from the analogy of Israel's relationship to God to the wife's relationship to the husband: perfect submission, and also perfect trust. Rebellion against the nations stands for arrogance on Israel's part, an act of lack of trust and therefore lack of faithfulness. Implicit in this representation of the right relationship, of course, is the promise that feminine Israel will evoke from the masculine God the response of commitment and intervention: God will intervene to save Israel, when Israel makes herself into the perfect wife of God.

The upshot is, Israel must fulfill the vocation of a woman, turn into a woman, serve God as a wife serves a husband. Does rabbinic Judaism ask men to turn themselves into women? Indeed so, that demand is stated in so many words. Here we find a full statement of the feminization of the masculine. The two brothers, Moses and Aaron, are compared to Israel's breasts, a reversal of gender classifications that can hardly be more extreme or dramatic:

> "Your two breasts are like two fawns, twins of a gazelle, that feed among the lilies" (Song 4:5):

> "Your two breasts are like two fawns:"

> this refers to Moses and Aaron.

> Just as a woman's breasts are her glory and her ornament,

> so Moses and Aaron are the glory and the ornament of Israel.

> Just as a woman's breasts are her charm, so Moses and Aaron are the charm of Israel.

> Just as a woman's breasts are her honor and her praise, so Moses and Aaron are the honor and praise of Israel.

> Just as a woman's breasts are full of milk, so Moses and Aaron are full of Torah.

> Just as whatever a woman eats the infant eats and sucks, so all the Torah that our lord, Moses, learned he taught to Aaron: "And Moses told Aaron all the words of the Lord" (Ex. 4:28).

> And rabbis say, "He actually revealed the Ineffable Name of God to him."

> Just as one breast is not larger than the other, so Moses and Aaron were the same: "These are Moses and Aaron" (Ex. 6:27), "These are Aaron and Moses" (Ex. 6:26), so that in knowledge of the Torah Moses was not greater than Aaron, and Aaron was not greater than Moses.

Happy are these two brothers, who were created only for the glory of Israel.

That is what Samuel said, "It is the Lord that made Moses and Aaron and brought your fathers up" (1 Sam. 12:6).

Thus "Your two breasts are like two fawns:"

this refers to Moses and Aaron.

Song of Songs Rabbah XLIX:i.1, 6–7

Not only are Moses and Aaron represented through feminine metaphors, so too are Abraham, Isaac, and Jacob, as well as the tribal progenitors, Jacob's sons.

What is the meaning of serial androgyneity?

Israel is serially androgynous: now feminine, later on, when the Messiah comes, masculine. The following makes this point in respect to God as well, who responds to Israel's character:

"What is your beloved more than another beloved, O fairest among women! [What is your beloved more than another beloved, that you thus adjure us?] My beloved is all radiant and ruddy, distinguished among ten thousand" (Song 5:9–10):

The Israelites answer them, "My beloved is all radiant and ruddy."

"radiant:" to me in the land of Egypt,

"and ruddy:" to the Egyptians.

"radiant:" in the land of Egypt, "For I will go through the land of Egypt" (Ex. 12:13).

"and ruddy:" "And the Lord overthrew the Egyptians" (Ex. 14:27).

"radiant:" at the Sea: "The children of Israel walked upon dry land in the midst of the sea" (Ex. 14:29).

"and ruddy:" to the Egyptians at the Sea: "And the Lord overthrew the Egyptians in the midst of the sea" (Ex. 14:27).

"radiant:" in the world to come.

"and ruddy:" in this world.

> R. Levi b. R. Hayyata made three statements concerning the matter:
>
> " 'radiant:' on the Sabbath.
>
> " 'and ruddy:' on the other days of the week.
>
> " 'radiant:' on the New Year.
>
> " 'and ruddy:' on the other days of the year.
>
> " 'radiant:' in this world.
>
> " 'and ruddy:' in the world to come."
>
> Song of Songs Rabbah LXX:i.1–2G

So much for the contrast between Israel now and Israel in the world to come.

What was at stake in the feminization of Israel?

The repertoire of virtues inculcated by the Torah for this age—as distinct from the world to come—is characterized by the rabbinic sages as feminine. Rabbinic Judaism taught that the Israelite was to exhibit the moral virtues of subservience, patience, endurance, and hope. These would translate into the emotional traits of humility and forbearance. And they would yield to social virtues of passivity and conciliation. The hero was one who overcame impulses, and the truly virtuous person, the one who reconciled others by giving way before the opinions of others. All of these acts of self-abnegation and self-denial, accommodation rather than rebellion, required to begin with the right attitudes, sentiments, emotions, and impulses.

The single dominant motif of the rabbinic writings, start to finish, is its stress on the right attitude's leading to the right action, the correct intentionality's producing the besought decision, above all, accommodating in one's heart to what could not be changed by one's action. And that meant the world as it was. Sages prepared Israel for the long centuries of subordination and alienation by inculcating attitudes that best suited a subordinated people, who could govern little more than how they felt about things. The rabbinic sages themselves classified the besought virtues as feminine, and they proposed to feminize Israel, the holy people.

39. VIRTUE

<hr>

What was the doctrine of virtue in rabbinic Judaism?

In line with the Creation narrative, virtue is humility, and vice is arrogance. The emotions encouraged by rabbinic Judaism are humility, forbearance, accommodation, a spirit of conciliation. What disrupts the perfection of creation is the sole power capable of standing on its own against God's power, and that is humanity's will. What humanity controls and God cannot coerce is humanity's capacity to form intention and therefore choose either arrogantly to defy, or humbly to love, God. So the Shema bears the message: "You will love the Lord your God with all your heart, soul, and might"—the commandment to love. But love cannot be commanded, only yearned for.

What kind of actions does God really admire?

What God really admires is acts of selflessness, and the highest virtue of all, so far as the Torah is concerned, is the act that God cannot coerce but very much yearns for, that act of love that transcends the self. Virtue begins in obedience to the Torah, but reaches its pinnacle through deeds beyond the strict requirements of the Torah, and even the limits of the law altogether, that transform the hero into a holy man, whose holiness served just like that of a sage marked as holy by knowledge of the Torah.

To understand how the rabbinic sages make their statement, we have to keep in mind two facts. First, they believed that God hears and answers prayer, and that if God answers prayer, it is a mark of Heaven's favorable recognition of the one who says it. Therefore if someone has the reputation of saying prayers that are answered, the rabbinic sages want to know why. Second, the sages believed that Torah-study defined the highest ideal that a man could attain, and they maintained that God wanted them to live a life of Torah-study. But in these stories, they discover people who could pray with effect in ways that they, the sages themselves could not. And they further discovered that some people won Heaven's favor not by a lifelong devote to the divine service but by doing a single remarkable action. So the rabbinic sages themselves are going to tell us stories about how one enormous deed outweighed a life of Torah-study.

These stories speak of God's bestowing grace in response to uncoerced acts of supreme self-sacrifice. They refer to, or use, the word *zekhut*, which means, "the heritage of virtue and its consequent entitlements." *Zekhut* pertains to deeds of a supererogatory character to which Heaven responds by deeds of a supererogatory character. It produces supernatural favor to one who through deeds of self-abnegation or restraint exhibits the attitude that in Heaven precipitates a counterpart attitude, hence generating *zekhut*. The simple fact that, as we shall see, rabbis cannot pray and bring rain, but a simple ass-driver can, tells the whole story.

To what virtues does God respond by bestowing uncoerced favor or zekhut?

An act that produces in Heaven the response of grace done even once not only makes up for a dissolute life but in that single moment wins Heaven's perpetual favor:

> A certain ass driver appeared before the rabbis [the context requires: in a dream] and prayed, and rain came. The rabbis sent and brought him and said to him, "What is your trade?"
>
> He said to them, "I am an ass driver."
>
> They said to him, "And how do you conduct your business?"
>
> He said to them, "One time I rented my ass to a certain woman, and she was weeping on the way, and I said to her, 'What's with you?' and she said to me, 'The husband of that woman [me] is in prison [for debt], and I wanted to see what I can do to free him.' So I sold my ass and I gave her the proceeds, and I said to her, 'Here is your money, free your husband, but do not sin [by becoming a prostitute to raise the necessary funds].'"
>
> They said to him, "You are worthy of praying and having your prayers answered."

Yerushalmi *Ta'anit* 1:4 I:2G–J

The ass-driver clearly has a powerful lien on Heaven, so that his prayers are answered, even while those of others are not. What did he do to get that entitlement? He did what no law could demand: impoverished himself to save the woman from a "fate worse than death."

> In a dream of R. Abbahu, Mr. Pentakaka ["Five sins"] appeared, who prayed that rain would come, and it rained. R. Abbahu sent and summoned him. He said to him, "What is your trade?"

> He said to him, "Five sins does that man [I] do every day, [for I am a pimp:] hiring whores, cleaning up the theater, bringing home their garments for washing, dancing, and performing before them."

> He said to him, "And what sort of decent thing have you ever done?"

> He said to him, "One day that man [I] was cleaning the theater, and a woman came and stood behind a pillar and cried. I said to her, 'What's with you?' And she said to me, 'That woman's [my] husband is in prison, and I wanted to see what I can do to free him,' so I sold my bed and cover, and I gave the proceeds to her. I said to her, 'Here is your money, free your husband, but do not sin.'"

> He said to him, "You are worthy of praying and having your prayers answered."

> Yerushalmi *Ta'anit* 1:4 I:3A–E

Mr. Five Sins has done everything sinful that (within the rabbinic sages' imagination) one can do, and, more to the point, he does it every day. What he should do is carry out the commandments, and he should study the Torah every day. So what he has done is what he should not have done, and what he has not done is what he should have done—every day. And yet in a single action, in a moment, everything changes. So the singularity of the act of *zekhut*, which suffices if done only one time, encompasses its power to outweigh a life of sin—again, an act of *zekhut* as the mirror image and opposite of sin. Here again, the single act of saving a woman from a "fate worse than death" has sufficed. Mr. Five Sins has carried out an act of grace, to which Heaven, uncoerced and uncompelled, responds with that love in which God so richly abounds for humanity. The extraordinary person is the one who sacrifices for the other in an act of selfless love—and that can be anybody, at any time, anywhere. That is why, for rabbinic Judaism, the great commandment is one of love: "You shall love the Lord your God with all your heart, with all your soul, and with all your might," as the creed of Judaism maintains. The one thing one person cannot command of another person is love. That, by definition, is freely given, or not given at all. It cannot be coerced or commanded. Then virtue consists in doing on one's own what God yearns for but cannot impose, which is, to love God.

But *zekhut* derives from other acts of uncoerced merit as well, and going beyond the measure of the law is the source:

A pious man from Kefar Immi appeared [in a dream] to the rabbis. He prayed for rain and it rained. The rabbis went up to him. His householders told them that he was sitting on a hill. They went out to him, saying to him, "Greetings," but he did not answer them.

He was sitting and eating, and he did not say to them, "You break bread too."

When he went back home, he made a bundle of faggots and put his cloak on top of the bundle [instead of on his shoulder].

When he came home, he said to his household [wife], "These rabbis are here [because] they want me to pray for rain. If I pray and it rains, it is a disgrace for them, and if not, it is a profanation of the Name of Heaven. But come, you and I will go up [to the roof] and pray. If it rains, we shall tell them, 'We are not worthy to pray and have our prayers answered.'"

They went up and prayed and it rained.

They came down to them [and asked], "Why have the rabbis troubled themselves to come here today?"

They said to him, "We wanted you to pray so that it would rain."

He said to them, "Now do you really need my prayers? Heaven already has done its miracle."

They said to him, "Why, when you were on the hill, did we say hello to you, and you did not reply?"

He said to them, "I was then doing my job. Should I then interrupt my concentration [on my work]?"

They said to him, "And why, when you sat down to eat, did you not say to us 'You break bread too'?"

He said to them, "Because I had only my small ration of bread. Why would I have invited you to eat by way of mere flattery [when I knew I could not give you anything at all]?"

They said to him, "And why when you came to go down, did you put your cloak on top of the bundle?"

He said to them, "Because the cloak was not mine. It was borrowed for use at prayer. I did not want to tear it."

They said to him, "And why, when you were on the hill, did your wife wear dirty clothes, but when you came down from the mountain, did she put on clean clothes?"

He said to them, "When I was on the hill, she put on dirty clothes, so that no one would gaze at her. But when I came home from the hill, she put on clean clothes, so that I would not gaze on any other woman."

They said to him, "It is well that you pray and have your prayers answered."

Yerushalmi *Ta'anit* 1:4 I:3F–V

Here the woman is at least an equal player; her actions, as much as her husband's, prove exemplary and illustrate the ultimate wisdom. The pious man finally enjoys the recognition of the rabbinic sages by reason of his lien upon Heaven, able as he is to pray and bring rain. What has so endowed him with *zekhut*? Acts of punctiliousness of a moral order: concentrating on his work, avoiding an act of dissimulation, integrity in the disposition of a borrowed object, his wife's concern not to attract other men, and her equal concern to make herself attractive to her husband. The law of the Torah cannot define acts of virtue, which transcend its capacities to speak of specific deeds of commission or omission. Only right attitude can lead people to live fully virtuous lives of humility and self-abnegation.

The relationship measured by *zekhut*—Heaven's response by an act of uncoerced favor to a person's uncoerced gift, e.g., act of gentility, restraint, or self-abnegation—contains an element of unpredictability for which appeal to the *zekhut* inherited from ancestors accounts. So while one cannot coerce heaven, one can through *zekhut* gain acts of favor from Heaven, and that is by doing what Heaven cannot require but only admire. Heaven then responds to one's attitude in carrying out one's duties—and more than those duties. That act of pure disinterest—giving the woman one's means of livelihood—is the one that gains for the humble man Heaven's deepest interest. The ultimate act of virtue turns out to be an act of pure grace, to which God responds with pure grace.

40. WORK

What did rabbinic Judaism say about work? Why must we work?

Work is natural to the human condition after Eden, before the restoration: "In the sweat of your face you shall eat bread" (Gen 3:19), in consequence of humanity's rebellion against God. The natural world ought to maintain man without his having to work. That is shown by the fact that nature sustains itself without menial labor. But with sin man has found it necessary to work, nature having lost its abundance:

> R. Simeon b. Eleazar says, "In your whole life, did you ever see a lion working as a porter, a deer working as a fruitpicker, a fox working as a storekeeper, a wolf selling pots, a domestic beast or a wild beast or a bird who had a trade?
>
> "Now these are created only to work for me, and I was made only to work for my Master.
>
> "Now is there not an argument *a fortiori:* Now if these, who were created only to work for me, lo, they make a living without anguish, I who have been created to work for my Master, is it not reasonable that I too should make a living without anguish!
>
> "But my deeds have ruined things, and I have spoiled my living."
>
> Tosefta *Qiddushin* 5:15E–H

It is the natural order that has each species doing what it is created to do. Man is created to live without much trouble, but because of sin (Adam in Eden), he is condemned to hard labor.

How does Sabbath repose remit the tedium of work?

Now if we examine work in the required context, namely, the workweek ending with the Sabbath of rest and repose, matters take on a different appearance. When we work, it is with the knowledge that we are destined to the Sabbath rest, so while we must work, we are not imprisoned by that obligation:

"Six days you shall labor and do all your work:"

But can a mortal carry out all of one's work in only six days?

But the nature of Sabbath rest is such that it should be as though all of your labor has been carried out.

Mekilta Attributed to R. Ishmael LIII:ii.9

Man and woman have left Eden and entered the world of work. But the Sabbath, every seventh day, restores them for the moment to that world of Eden that they have lost. It gives them a foretaste of the age to come, when, the dead having been raised and life eternal having come, humanity will recover Eden.

But how to do so? Adam's sin finds its antidote in the Torah, which, the rabbinic sages maintain, is given to purify the heart of humanity. The most important work a person can do is study the Torah, in which the religion, Judaism, is practiced in its classical forms. Israelites were created to study the Torah. That fundamental conviction explains why, from the rabbinic sages' perspective, the kind of work that Israelites were made to carry out is labor in Torah-study. That position is expressed in so many words by a principal figure in the formation of the oral part of the Torah, Yohanan ben Zakkai, who flourished in the first century, at about the time of the destruction of the Jerusalem Temple in 70 C.E.:

Rabban Yohanan b. Zakkai received {the tradition of the Oral Torah} from Hillel and Shammai.

He would say, "If you have learned much Torah, do not puff yourself up on that account, for it was for that purpose that you were created."

Mishnah Avot 2:8A–B

So one must work for three reasons, each quite distinct from the others. First, one must work to be like God, who created the world in six days of labor and rested on the seventh. Second, one must do servile labor because humanity is party to the human condition, cast from

Eden by reason of rebellion against God. Third, one ought to conduct the labor of divine service, particularly Torah-study, because that is how one may regain Eden. So work finds its place within a restorationist-theology that aims at bringing Adam and Eve back to Eden.

Why must one help others: private gain and public benefit?

When people help others, it is because they are using what God owns and has given to them in such a way as to carry out the will of the One who owns it all.

How does the Torah situate charity in the hierarchy of virtues and meritorious deeds? As in Islam, charity (called by the same Hebrew word that is used for "righteousness," *sedaqah*) forms a principal religious obligation. But when it comes to hierarchizing the virtues of charity, loving-kindness, and justice, when they are to be compared with one another, they are shown in the end to be equivalent in God's eyes:

> Said R. Eleazar, "Greater is the one who carries out an act of charity than one who offers all the sacrifices.
>
> "For it is said, 'To do charity and justice is more desired by the Lord than sacrifice' (Prov. 21:3)."
>
> Bavli *Sukkah* 49b 4:10 V.8J–K

So far the sages have set the world on its head by declaring charity for the poor a greater act of service to God than the offering of sacrifices to God in Heaven. But an act of loving-kindness takes priority over an act of charity:

> And R. Eleazar said, "An act of loving kindness is greater than an act of charity.
>
> "For it is said, 'Sow to yourselves according to your charity, but reap according to your loving kindness' (Hos. 10:12).
>
> "If a man sows seed, it is a matter of doubt whether he will eat a crop or not. But if a man harvests the crop, he most certainly will eat it."
>
> And R. Eleazar said, "An act of charity is rewarded only in accord with the loving kindness that is connected with it.
>
> "For it is said, 'Sow to yourselves according to your charity, but reap according to your loving kindness' (Hos. 10:12)."
>
> Bavli *Sukkah* 49b 4:10 V.8L–P

The point is, if an act of charity is done out of a sense of obligation and devotion to the other, then it has value, but if it is done in a spirit of arrogance and condescension, then it does not. Not only so, but an act of personal service takes priority over an act of charity in the form of mere money:

> In three aspects are acts of loving kindness greater than an act of charity.
>
> An act of charity is done only with money, but an act of loving kindness someone carries out either with his own person or with his money.
>
> An act of charity is done only for the poor, while an act of loving kindness may be done either for the poor or for the rich.
>
> An act of charity is done only for the living. An act of loving kindness may be done either for the living or for the dead.
>
> Bavli *Sukkah* 49b 4:10 V.9B–E

Charity and justice are the same thing. We give to the poor because it is an act of righteousness, it is owing from us, not a matter of volition but of obligation:

> And R. Eleazar has said, "Whoever does an act of charity and justice is as if he has filled the entire world with mercy.
>
> "For it is said, 'He loves charity and justice, the earth is full of the loving kindness of the Lord' (Ps. 33:5).
>
> "Now you might wish to say that whoever comes to jump may take a leap [whoever wishes to do good succeeds without difficulty].
>
> "Scripture accordingly states, 'How precious is your loving kindness, O God' (Ps. 36:8). [The opportunity of doing real, well deserved charity and dispensing it in a judicious manner is rare].
>
> "Now you might wish to say that the same is the case for fear of Heaven [so that one who fears Heaven nonetheless has trouble in carrying out charity and justice].
>
> "Scripture accordingly states, 'But the loving kindness of the Lord is from everlasting to everlasting upon them that fear him' (Ps. 103:17)."
>
> Bavli *Sukkah* 49b 4:10 V.10A–F

The hierarchizing of loving-kindness and charity produces the result that the former takes priority, for specified reasons, deriving from Scripture.

PART 8

RABBINIC JUDAISM AND CHRISTIANITY: POINTS OF INTERSECTION OF TWO COORDINATE SCRIPTURAL SYSTEMS

41. THE DEVELOPMENT OF RABBINIC JUDAISM'S THEOLOGY

What was the documentary history of rabbinic Judaism? How did it unfold from philosophy to religion to theology?

Our knowledge of rabbinic Judaism in the first six Christian centuries comes to us from its documents, which reached closure at that time. These fall into three successive divisions, (1) philosophical (to 300 C.E.), (2) religious (300–500 C.E.), (3) theological (500–600 C.E.)—each with its own traits, and each representing a phase in the history of rabbinic Judaism in its formative age, the first six centuries C.E.

First comes the Mishnah and Tosefta and associated Midrash-compilations, *Sifra, Sifré to Numbers,* and *Sifré to Deuteronomy,* covering the first three centuries C.E. They produced a philosophical structure comprising of politics, philosophy, economics. These categories were defined as philosophers in general understood them: a theory of legitimate violence (politics), an account of knowledge gained through the methods of natural history (natural philosophy), and a theory of the rational disposition (and increase) of scarce resources (economics). A philosophical system forms its learning inductively and syllogistically by appeal to the neutral evidence of the rules shown by the observation of the order of universally accessible nature and society. That is how the Mishnah conducts its work.

Second are the Talmud of the Land of Israel and its companion Midrash-compilations, *Genesis Rabbah* and *Leviticus Rabbah,* deriving from the fourth and fifth centuries. They attest to a Judaic system that was religious. A religious system frames its propositions deductively and exegetically by appeal to the privileged evidence of a corpus of writing deemed revealed by God. That characterizes the rabbinic documents of the Land of Israel that came to closure in fourth and fifth centuries.

Finally there are the Talmud of Babylonia and its related Midrash-compilations, *Lamentations Rabbah, Ruth Rabbah, Esther Rabbah I,* and *Song of Songs Rabbah,* coming to closure in the sixth and seventh centuries. They represent a system that was theological. This theological re-presentation of the religious system was effected through the recovery of philosophical method for the formulation of religious conceptions. Theology is the science of the reasoned knowledge of God, in the case of a Judaism made possible by God's self-manifestation in the Torah. Seen in its whole re-presentation in the Talmud of Babylonia, the theology of Judaism sets forth knowledge of God.

A theological system imposes upon a religious one systematic modes of thought of philosophy, so in its message regularizing and ordering in a cogent and intellectually rigorous way the materials received from a religious system. That characterizes the documents of the sixth and seventh centuries, particularly the Talmud of Babylonia.

The historical formation of rabbinic Judaism reached completion when

(1) a philosophical system having been transformed into

(2) a religious one was then systematized in its own terms through the disciplines of philosophy and re-presented as

(3) theology.

So Judaism progressed in its formation from philosophy through religion to theology. For that Judaism in its fullness, (1) philosophy provided the method and mode of thought, (2) religion, the message, and (3) theology, the medium of persuasive re-presentation.

From the Mishnah to the Yerushalmi: how does a philosophical statement of a religious system differ from a religious statement of the same system?

A philosophical system of the social order, whether of a religious or secular character in its premises and conclusions, forms its learning inductively and syllogistically, by appeal to the neutral evidence of the rules shown to apply to all things by the observation of the order of universally accessible nature and society. A distinctively religious system of the social order frames its propositions deductively and exegetically by appeal to the privileged evidence of a corpus of truths deemed revealed by God. The difference pertains not to detail but to the fundamental facts deemed to matter. Some of those facts lie at the very surface, in the nature of the writings that express the system. A philosophical system will state its propositions through syllogistic writings, a distinctively religious system

will prefer the literary form of commentary. The former appeals to reasoning about established facts, the latter, interpretation of revealed truths.
How do they differ? The one begins in this world and its facts,
which are analyzed and categorized through the traits inherent in them,
and the other commences in the world above and its truths, which are
analyzed and categorized by the categories of revelation. The one yields
philosophy of religion, the other, religious statements, attitudes, convictions, rules of life; the one represents one way of knowing God, specifically, the way through the data of this world, the other, a different way
to God, the way opened by God's revelation and self-manifestation,
whether through nature or beyond.

The Mishnah set forth in the form of a law code a highly philosophical system. We have no difficulty in calling its account of a way of
life an economics, that is, a theory of the rational disposition of scarce
resources, because the account of material reality provided by the Mishnah corresponds, point for point, with that given in Aristotle's counterpart. The Mishnah moreover sets forth a politics, a theory of the
legitimate and ongoing (institutional) exercise of violence, by dealing
with the same questions, about the permanent and legitimate institutions that inflict sanctions, that occupy Greek and Roman political
thinkers. There is no economics of another-than-this-worldly character,
no supernatural politics. All is straightforward, worldly, material, and
consequential for the everyday world.

The Yerushalmi and associated Midrash-compilations attest to a
system that did more than merely extend and recast the categorical
structure of the system for which the Mishnah stands. They took over
the way of life, worldview, and social entity, defined in the Mishnah's
system. And while they rather systematically amplified details, at the
same time they formed categories corresponding to those of the Mishnah: a politics, a philosophy, an economics. But these categories proved
so utterly contrary in their structure and definition to those of the Mishnah that they presented mirror images of the received categories: truth
revealed, not discovered, for an anti-philosophy; abundant resources of
Torah learning in place of scarce resources of real estate, for economics;
and an anti-politics that substituted weakness for legitimate violence.

The God of the Mishnah's philosophers as against the God of the Yerushalmi's religious thinkers: what is the difference?

The Mishnah's God—the God of the philosophers, the apex of the
hierarchy of all being as the framers of the Mishnah have positioned

God—has made the rules and is shown by them to form the foundation of cosmic order. All things reach up to one thing, one thing contains within itself many things. These form twin propositions of (philosophical) monotheism. That is the philosophical system of Judaism to which the Mishnah attests. The Mishnah and the Halakic category-formations framed thereby define a God who in an orderly way governs all the palpable relationships of nature as of supernature. The God of the philosophers assures, sustains, supports, nourishes, guarantees, and governs. But the way that God responds to what we do is all according to the rule. That is, after all, what natural philosophy proposes to uncover and discern, and what more elevated task can God perform than the nomothetic one accomplished in the daily creation of the world?

But God in the religious system of the Yerushalmi gains what the philosophical God lacks, which is personality, active presence, pathos, and empathy. The God of the religious system breaks the rules, accords an entitlement (*zekhut*) to this one, who has done some one remarkable deed, but not to that one, who has done nothing wrong and everything right. So a life in accord with the rules—even a life spent in the study of the Torah—in Heaven's view is outweighed by a single moment, a gesture that violates the norm, extending the outer limits of the rule, for instance, of virtue. If the God of the philosophers' Judaism makes the rules, the God of the religious Judaism breaks them.

The systemic difference is readily extended outward from the personality of God: the philosophers' God thinks, the God of the religious feels. He responds, and we are in God's image, after God's likeness, not only because we through right thinking penetrate the principles of creation, but through right attitude replicate the heart of the Creator. Humanity on earth incarnates God on high, the Israelite family in particular, and, in consequence, earth and Heaven join—within.

How did rabbinic Judaism at the end restate its religious message theologically?

What distinguishes religious from theological writing? When we find reflective labor on the rationality of statements of religious truth, e.g., truth revealed by God, then we have identified a theological writing. By "rationality" in context are meant cogency, harmony, proposition, coherence, balance, order, and proper composition.

The second Talmud forms the sustained, rigorous, open-ended activity of rational reflection on the sense and near-at-hand significance of the Torah. Concern with argument, the attempt to solve conceptual problems—these characterize that writing. Argument concerning conceptual problems yields theology when the argument deals with religion, and the conceptual problems derive from revelation. Only the source of the givens of the writing—revelation, not merely reasoned analysis of this world's givens—distinguishes theology from philosophy, including philosophy of religion. But that suffices.

Take for example the Mishnah's formulation of religion as philosophy. The Mishnah states its principles through method of natural history, sifting the traits of this-worldly things, demonstrating philosophical truth—the unity of the one and unique God at the apex of the natural world—by showing on the basis of the evidence of this world, universally accessible, the hierarchical classification of being. That is a philosophical demonstration of religious truth. The Talmud of Babylonia states its principles through right reasoning about *revealed* truth, the Torah. The Torah (written, or oral) properly read teaches the theological truth that God is one, at the apex of the hierarchy of all being. That is a theological re-presentation of (the same) religious truth. But that re-presentation in the two Talmuds (and in the Midrash-compilations, not treated here) also exhibits the traits of philosophical thinking: rigor, concern for harmonies, unities, consistencies, points of cogency, sustained argument and counterargument, appeal to persuasion through reason, not coercion through revelation. Thus the methods of philosophy applied to the data of religious belief and behavior produced theology.

With the first of the two Talmuds (and its associated Midrash-compilations), the received Torah, oral and written, was ordered: the components were brought into relationship, on the one side, the details made to form propositions, on the other. With the second of the two Talmuds (and its companions of Midrash-collection), these propositions were cast into a few large and simple statements. These statements were expressed by the quest of the Bavli for the law behind the laws. They were shown through sustained argument to be reasonable and rigorously demonstrable. While the received religious categories and convictions (merely) came to restatement, in the theological formulation of the religion, the whole changed in character, focus, and effect.

42. RABBINIC JUDAISM'S RESPONSES TO THE CHALLENGE OF CHRISTIANITY

———◆———

How are we to identify the response of rabbinic Judaism to the advent of Christianity?

The response of rabbinic Judaism to the competing system represented by Christianity in its orthodox, catholic formulation culminating in Scripture and tradition sometimes manifests itself in articulate, but somewhat trivial ways, and often it appears in implicit, but fundamental ways.

The trivial ways involve episodic allusions to teachings of "Jesus b. Pantera," e.g., attributed to Eliezer b. Hyrcanus at Tosefta *Hullin* 2:22ff. and to the Evangelists' writings attributed to Tarfon at Tosefta *Shabbat* 13:5E–F,

> ". . . if someone was running after me, I should go into a temple of idolatry, but I should not go into their houses [of worship]. For idolators do not recognize the Divinity in denying him, but these recognize the Divinity and deny him."

These show that a document assumed to have come to closure by ca. 300 C.E. included sayings, attributed to first century authorities, that were hostile to Jesus and to the Gospels. But we did not require such sayings to tell us about conflict between the two heirs of Scripture. And the response they reveal is superficial.

A fundamental, systemic response, by contrast, should show how the rabbinic system as a whole addressed orthodox, catholic Christianity as a whole. Can we show that rabbinic Judaism recast its principal categories to respond to the challenge of the competing Christian reading of Scripture? For evidence of a systemic reconfiguration, we have to find reason to account for a shift in the basic character of the rabbinic system that can be explained by appeal to the axial event represented by the advent of Christianity. And that requires that we correlate the documentary history of rabbinic Judaism with the political and doctrinal challenge of Christianity: at what point do the two histories intersect?

With what period in the documentary unfolding of rabbinic Judaism did the conversion of Constantine to Christianity coincide?

We have seen three periods in the unfolding of the rabbinic structure, the philosophical one focused on the Mishnah, the religious one centered on the Talmud of the Land of Israel, and the theological one realized in the Talmud of Babylonia. The second, the shift from a philosophical to a religious approach, is exposed by documents of the late fourth and fifth centuries of the Common Era. So we ask ourselves, what happened from ca. 300 to ca. 400 C.E. that can have made so profound an impact on rabbinic Judaism as to lead to a reformation of its modes of thought and consequent category-formations? Specifically, can we correlate changes in rabbinic Judaism with challenges set forth by Christianity? The answer is, what happened between 300 and 400 was the political triumph of Christianity, and we can correlate changes in rabbinic doctrine at three critical points with the challenges set forth by Christian theologians of that period.

The conversion of Constantine to Christianity, the single most influential event in the history of Christianity from the first century forward, coincided with the transformation of a philosophical into a religious system for rabbinic Judaism. We have reason to consider that it was to the Christian triumph of the early fourth century C.E. that rabbinic Judaism responded in the Talmud of the Land of Israel and related documents. Specifically, Constantine had legitimated, then himself adopted Christianity, which in the fourth century became the state religion of the Roman Empire. Political history proved the truth of the Christian claim. Christians fairly pointed out to Jews that their claim that Christ was King had now been validated by events. Then what of the awaited Messiah of Judaism? And what of the fate of "Israel after the flesh" celebrated by rabbinic Judaism?

How did Christianity challenge Judaism?

What challenge emerged because the emperor of Rome adopted Christianity? To begin with, Jews had not anticipated that the new religion, Christianity, would amount to much. Christians now maintained that their faith in Jesus as Christ, Messiah and God incarnate, found full vindication. They pointed to passages in the Hebrew Scriptures that, in their view, had now come to fulfillment. They declared themselves heirs of ancient Israel and denied to the Jews the long-standing position of God's first and chosen love. So at issue in the Christians' success in imperial politics we find profoundly theological questions: (1) Does history now vindicate Christianity? (2) Was and is Jesus the Messiah? (3) Who, in light of events, is "Israel" and who is not? The foundations of the Judaic system and structure were shaken.

Why, specifically, did the advent of Christian rule in the Roman Empire make so profound an impact as to produce a Judaism? A move of the empire from reverence for Zeus to adoration of Mithra meant nothing. To Jews paganism was what it was, lacking all differentiation. Christianity was something else. Why? Because it was like Judaism. Christians claimed that theirs was Judaism now fulfilled in Christ. Christians read the Torah and claimed to declare its meaning. They furthermore alleged, like Israel, that they alone worshipped the one true God. And they challenged Israel's claim to know that God—and even to be Israel, continuator of the Israel of the promises and grace of ancient Scripture.

How did rabbinic Judaism respond to the Christian challenge concerning history?

In the age of Constantine important Judaic documents undertook to deal with agenda defined, for both Judaism and Christianity, by the political triumph of Christianity. Christian thinkers, represented here by Eusebius and Chrysostom on the Roman side of the international frontier and Aphrahat on the Iranian, reflected on issues presented by the fourth century revolution in the political status of Christianity. Issues of the interpretation of history, the restatement of the challenge and claim of Christ as Messiah against the continuing expectation of Israel that the Messiah is yet to come, and the definition of who is Israel made their appearance in Christian writings of the day as well as in documents of Judaism brought to closure at the end of the century.

A shared program brought the two religions into protracted confrontation on an intersecting set of questions, a struggle that has continued until our own time—originated in the fact that, to begin with, both religions agreed on almost everything that mattered. They differed on little, so made much of that little. Scripture taught them both that vast changes in the affairs of empires came about because of God's will. History proved principles of theology. In that same Torah prophets promised the coming of the Messiah, who would bring salvation. Who was, and is, that Messiah, and how shall we know? And that same Torah addressed a particular people, Israel, promising that people the expression of God's favor and love. But who is Israel, and who is not Israel? In this way Scripture defined the categories shared in common, enabling Judaism and Christianity to engage, if not in dialogue, then in two monologues on the same topics.

The Judaic sages, for their part, constructed their own position, which implicitly denied the Christian one. They worked out a view of history consisting in a rereading of the book of Genesis in light of the entire history of Israel, read under the aspect of eternity. The book of Genesis then provided a complete, profoundly typological interpretation of everything that had happened as well as a reliable picture of what, following the rules of history laid down in Genesis, was going to happen in the future. Typological in what sense? The events of Genesis served as types, prefiguring what would happen to Israel in its future history. Just as the Christians read stories of the (to them) Old Testament as types of the life of Christ, so the sages understood the tales of Genesis in a similarly typological manner. For neither party can history have retained that singular and one-dimensional, linear quality that it had had in Scripture itself.

How did rabbinic Judaism respond to the Christian challenge concerning the Messiah?

The Christian challenge is what stimulated sages' thought to focus upon the Messiah-theme. The Mishnaic system had come to full expression without an elaborated doctrine of the Messiah, or even an eschatological theory of the purpose and goal of matters. The Mishnah had put forth a teleology without an eschatological dimension at all. By the closing of the Talmud of the Land of Israel, by contrast, the purpose and end of everything centered upon the coming of the Messiah, in sages' terms and definition, to be sure. In the Talmud of the Land of Israel (cf. Section 28), we find a fully exposed doctrine of not only a Messiah, but *the* Messiah: who he is, how we will know him, what we must do to bring him. The disposition of the issue proves distinctive to sages: the Messiah will be a sage, the Messiah will come when Israel has attained that condition of sanctification, marked also by profound humility and complete acceptance of God's will that signify sanctification.

How did rabbinic Judaism respond to the Christian challenge concerning Israel?

Both parties concurred that God did favor and therefore make use of one group and not another. Both concurred that the group chosen by God will bear the name Israel. God's choice among human societies would settle the question, Which nation does God love and favor? Jews saw themselves as the Israel today joined in the flesh to the Israel of the scriptural record. Christians explained themselves as the Israel formed just now, in recent memory, even in the personal experience of the living, among those saved by faith in God's salvation afforded by the resurrection of Jesus Christ.

The powerful stress of *Genesis Rabbah* and *Leviticus Rabbah*, fifth-century compilations, on the enduring merit of the patriarchs and matriarchs, the social theory that treated Israel as one large, extended family, the actual children of Abraham, Isaac, and Jacob—these metaphors for the fleshly continuity surely met head on the contrary position framed by Paul and restated by Christian theologians from his time onward. Israel remains Israel, the Jewish people, after the flesh, because Israel today continues the family begun by Abraham, Isaac, Jacob, Joseph and the other tribal founders, and bears the heritage bequeathed by them.

43. THE PHARISEES

How did rabbinic Judaism regard the Pharisees?

Rabbinic Judaism in its normative writings contains conflicting evidence on the Pharisees, some negative, some implicitly positive.

First, the condemnation of hypocrisy and self-serving external ritualism that Jesus set forth in Matthew's and Mark's "Woe unto you, scribes, Pharisees, hypocrites"-sayings proves mild compared to a counterpart indictment in rabbinic writings. Here sages castigate a variety of Pharisees, who serve God in an ostentatious way, displaying their piety in public:

> There are seven types of [improper, wrong-headed] Pharisees: the shoulder-Pharisee; the wait-a-while Pharisee; the bookkeeping Pharisee; the niggardly Pharisee; the show-me-what-I-did-wrong Pharisee; the Pharisee-out-of-fear; and the Pharisee-out-of-love.
>
> "The shoulder-Pharisee" carries the religious deeds he has done on his shoulder [for all to see].
>
> "The wait-a-while Pharisee"—"Wait a minute, so I can go off and do a religious deed."
>
> "The bookkeeping Pharisee"—He does one deed for which he is liable to punishment and one deed which is a religious duty, and then he balances one off against the other.
>
> "The niggardly Pharisee"—"Who will show me how I can save so that I can do a religious deed."
>
> "The show-me-what-I-did-wrong Pharisee"—"Show me what sin I have done, and I will do an equivalent religious duty."
>
> "A Pharisee-out-of-fear," like Job.
>
> "A Pharisee-out-of-love," like Abraham.

And the only one of them all who is truly beloved is the Pharisee-out-of-love, like Abraham.

Yerushalmi *Sotah* 5:5 I:3:

Clearly, rabbinic circles included critics of Pharisaism for the very traits to which Jesus objected.

But, second, principal rabbinic authorities of the first century, Simeon b. Gamaliel and Gamaliel, listed on the chain of tradition that extends back to Sinai, are identified as Pharisees by Josephus (for Simeon b. Gamaliel) and Acts (for Gamaliel). And Hillel, famous for the Golden Rule (cf. Section 36) was their principal teacher. Hence the Pharisees formed a component of rabbinic Judaism as it took shape at the end of the first century. And those that identify the starting point of rabbinic Judaism with the Pharisees certainly stand on solid ground.

Third, the Halakic focus of the Mishnah on tithes, purity laws, and observance of the Sabbath corresponds to the Halakic focus of the Pharisaic sayings of the Gospels. As to subject matter covered by the rabbinic traditions that allude to persons or groups we assume to have been Pharisees, approximately 67% of all legal pericopae deal with dietary laws. These laws concern (1) ritual purity for meals and (2) agricultural rules governing the fitness of food for Pharisaic consumption. Observance of Sabbaths and festivals is a distant third. So rabbinic Judaism encompasses a corpus of law that in topic and in some details derives from Pharisaic tradition.

What are the sources of knowledge concerning the Pharisees?

Three discrete sources that refer to Pharisees, in order of closure: (1) the Gospels (70–90 C.E.), (2) the writings of Josephus (90–100 C.E.), and (3) the later rabbinic compositions, beginning with the Mishnah (200 C.E.). No writings survive that were produced by them; all we do know is what later writers said about them. The three separate bodies of information are quite different in character: first come biographical traditions about, and sayings attributed to, Jesus; second are the historical narratives of Josephus, a Jewish historian who, between 75 and ca. 100, wrote the history of the Jews from the beginnings to the destruction of Jerusalem; and third are the laws and sayings attributed to pre-70 Pharisees by their successors and heirs, the rabbis of late first- and second-century Palestine. Josephus presents a systematic, coherent historical narrative. The sayings of Jesus reach us in a well-edited collection of stories and sayings. The third consists chiefly of laws, arranged by legal categories in codes and commentaries on those codes.

The several sources concerning pre-70 C.E. Pharisees were generally shaped in the aftermath of the crisis of 70 C.E. With the Temple in ruins it was important to preserve and, especially, to interpret, the record of what had gone before. Josephus tells the story of the people and the great war. The Gospels record the climactic moment in Israel's supernatural life. The rabbis describe the party to which they traced their origin, and through which they claimed to reach back to the authority of Moses at Sinai. The issue in all three cases was, What is the meaning of the decisive history just passed?

To Josephus the answer is that Israel's welfare depends upon obedience to the laws of the Torah as expounded by the Pharisees and upon peaceful relationships with Rome. The Gospels claim that, with the coming of the Messiah, the Temple had ceased to enjoy its former importance, and those who had had charge of Israel's life—chief among them the priests, scribes, and Pharisees—were shown through their disbelief to have ignored the hour of their salvation. Their unbelief is explained in part by the Pharisees' hypocrisy and self-seeking. The rabbis contend that the continuity of the Mosaic Torah is unbroken. Destruction of the Temple, while lamentable, does not mean Israel has lost all means of service to the Creator. The way of the Pharisees leads, without break, back to Sinai and forward to the rabbinical circle reforming at Yavneh. The oral Torah revealed by Moses and handed on from prophet to scribe, sage, and rabbi remains in the hands of Israel. The legal record of pre-70 C.E. Pharisaism requires careful preservation because it remains wholly in effect.

How do the sources on the Pharisees relate?

The focus of interest of the rabbinic traditions about the Pharisees is the internal affairs of the Pharisaic party itself. The competing sects, by contrast, are ignored. Essenes and Christians make no appearance at all. The Romans never occur. The Hasmonean monarchy is reduced to a single name, "Yannai the King," for Yohanan the High Priest, so far as the rabbinic traditions about the Pharisees are concerned, was a good Pharisee. In all, the traditions give the impression of intense concentration on the inner life of the party, or sect, whose intimate affairs take precedence, in the larger scheme of history, over the affairs of state, cult, and country.

The state is a shadowy presence at best. The cult is of secondary importance. The country's life and the struggle with Rome as a whole are bypassed in silence.

What about Josephus's Pharisees? To Josephus the Pharisees were a philosophical sect, with traditions of the fathers and some distinctive views of life after death. The traits of Pharisaism emphasized by Josephus, their principal beliefs and practices, nowhere occur in the rabbinic traditions of the Pharisees. When we compare what Josephus says about the Pharisees to what the later rabbinic traditions have to say, there is scarcely a point of contact, let alone intersection. Josephus says next to nothing about the predominant issues in the rabbinic traditions about the Pharisees. Above all, we find not the slightest allusion to laws of ritual purity, agricultural taboos, Sabbath and festivals, and the like, which predominate in the traditions of the Houses.

How about Matthew and Mark? The picture drawn by Matthew and Mark and that drawn by the later rabbis are essentially congruent, and together differ from the portrait left to us by Josephus. The congruity in the themes of the laws attributed to the Pharisees by both the Gospels and the later rabbinic sources is striking.

Why did the Pharisees in the time of Jesus emphasize ritual purity, tithing, and other dietary regulations?

One primary mark of Pharisaic commitment was the observance of the laws of ritual purity outside of the Temple, where everyone kept them. Eating one's secular, that is, unconsecrated, food in a state of ritual purity as if one were a Temple priest in the cult was one of the two significations of party membership. The Pharisees were lay people pretending to be priests, householders acting out for the table at home the conditions that pertained to God's altar in the Temple in Jerusalem.

To keep cultic purity and observe the dietary rules of tithing at home then formed the heart of the matter. The manifold circumstances of everyday life required the multiplication of concrete rules. Pharisees clearly regarded keeping the agricultural rules as a primary religious duty. But whether, to what degree, and how other Jews did so is not clear. And the agricultural laws, just like the purity rules, in the end affected table fellowship, namely, what one might eat, and with whom: tithed food, with those in a state of cultic cleanness like oneself.

The early Christian traditions on both points represent the Pharisees as reproaching Jesus because his followers did not keep these two kinds of laws at all. That is, why were they not Pharisees? The answer was that the primary concern was for ethics. Both the question and the answer are disingenuous. The questioners are represented as rebuking the Christians for not being Pharisees, which begs the question, for everyone presumably knew Christians were not Pharisees. The answer takes advantage of the polemical opening: Pharisees are hypocrites and not concerned with ethics, a point repeatedly made in the anti-Pharisaic pericopae, depending upon a supposed conflict between rules of table fellowship, on the one side, and ethical behavior on the other. The obvious underlying claim is that Christian table fellowship does not depend upon the sorts of rules important in the table fellowship of other groups. The Pharisees in the time of Jesus emphasized ritual purity, tithing, and other dietary regulations because they were lay-people pretending to be priests, with their table at home comparable to the altar in the Temple.

As to the Sabbath laws, the issue was narrower. All Jews kept the Sabbath. It was part of the culture of their country. The same applies to the festivals. Here the Pharisaic materials are not so broad in interest as with regard to agricultural rules and ritual purity.

When we review the substance of the purity and tithing laws, we find they pertain either immediately or ultimately to table fellowship, involve preparation of food, ritual purity, either purity rules directly relating to food, or purity rules indirectly important on account of the need to keep food ritually clean, and agricultural rules pertaining to the proper growing, tithing, and preparation of agricultural produce for table use. All agricultural laws concern producing or preparing food for consumption, assuring either that tithes and offerings have been set aside as the Law requires or that the conditions for the nurture of the crops have conformed to the biblical taboos.

That is not to suggest that the historical Pharisees were only or principally a table fellowship commune. It is only to say that, whatever else they were, they surely identified themselves as Pharisees by the dietary rules that they observed. More than this we do not know on the basis of the rabbinic evidence, as correlated with the Gospels' accounts.

Josephus's picture of the group is asymmetrical to this picture, and a simple hypothesis is to assign his account to the period of which he speaks when he mentions the Pharisees as a political party, which is the second and first centuries B.C.E., and the rabbis' and Gospels' account to the period of which they speak, which is the first century C.E. But the matter remains open for continued inquiry, and no picture of the Pharisees has held together all the diverse bodies of evidence in a single coherent construction.

44. THE SUCCESS OF RABBINIC JUDAISM

What accounts for the success of rabbinic Judaism?

Christians commonly ask their question, which is, "Why did the Jews reject Christ?" Framed more pertinently, the question is why did, and do, most Jews practice Judaism, and that is, Judaism in its rabbinic formulation?

Most Jews through the ages and the vast majority of those today who practice any religion at all practice (a form of) rabbinic Judaism. How are we to explain the success of rabbinic Judaism? That system succeeded because a great part of the Jewish people wanted it to. Why did the Jewish people want it to succeed? Its relevance to the enduring issues of the day and its authenticity to revealed Scripture's account for the success of the rabbinic system within that very sector of humanity to which that system spoke.

What in context made that system relevant for centuries to come?

The first reason is that the rabbinic system responded to the external challenge posed by Christianity. In context Christianity (and later on, Islam) made rabbinic Judaism permanently relevant to the situation in which Jews found themselves. Judaism had successfully responded to the urgent issues raised by the Christian challenge from the fourth century onward (cf. Section 42).

Christianity continued to harp on the same points—history, Messiah, Israel—so the Judaic party to the dispute for centuries to come could refer to the generative symbols and determinative myths of the Judaism that to begin with had dealt with these very issues. The Christian challenge, delivered through instruments of state and society, demanded a Judaic response, one involving not merely manipulation of power but exercise of intellect.

The rabbinic sages produced responses to the Christian challenge in their enduring doctrines of the meaning of history, of the conditions in which the Messiah will come to Israel, and of the definition of Israel. The rabbinic Judaism's symbolic system, with its stress on Torah, the eschatological teleology of that system, with stress on the Messiah-sage coming to obedient Israel, the insistence on the equivalence of Israel and Rome, Jacob and Esau, with Esau penultimate and Israel at the end of time—these constituted in Israel powerful responses to the Christian question.

Why did Israelites find rabbinic Judaism compelling? How were they persuaded of the authenticity of the rabbinic reading of Scripture?

Rabbinic Judaism was not only relevant but, in its interior structure, *right*. The rabbinic sages claimed through the oral tradition to complement the written tradition and so to set forth for all time the one whole Torah of Moses. The rabbinic reading of Scripture proved compelling.

We know it is so, because the faithful of Judaism through the ages reach Scripture through rabbinic tradition. Moses is always *rabbenu*, "our rabbi," and Isaiah, "Rabbi Isaiah." Jacob looked into the present and described the future, and—in line with rabbinic retelling of Scripture's tales—Abraham, Moses, and the prophets met God on the afternoon of the ninth of Ab in the year we now number as 70 and rebuked him for what he had done through the Romans. These realizations do not draw upon easy sentimentality or resort to figurative conceits. People acted upon them every day, built their lives around them, met God in them. Their concrete actions, the deprivations they accepted and humiliations they turned into validation—these attest to the palpable reality, for holy Israel, of the vision of the dual Torah.

Now, to find out whether and how, in the context of Scripture, their system is compelling, we require the answer to a simple question: By the criterion of Scripture's own sense, were sages right about the written part of the Torah, meaning, is what they say the written Torah says actually what the ancient Israelite Scriptures say? Will those who put forth the books of Genesis through Kings as a sustained narrative and those who in that same context selected and organized the writings of the prophets, Isaiah, Jeremiah, Ezekiel, and the twelve, in the aggregate have concurred in sages' structure and system? Certainly others who lay claim to these same Scriptures did not concur. At the time the sages did their greatest theological work, in the fourth and fifth century C.E., their Christian counterparts, in the Latin, Greek, and Syriac speaking sectors of Christianity alike, not only read Scripture in a very different way but also accused the rabbis of falsifying the Torah. How would the rabbinic sages have responded to the charge?

They would have cited the fact that nearly every proposition the rabbinic sages set forth, the main beams of the structure of faith they construct, all sit securely and symmetrically upon the written Torah. Proof texts constantly take the measure of the structure. That is why sages speak of the one whole Torah in two media, correlative and complementary. Start to finish, creation through Sinai to the fall of Jerusalem, all perceived in the light of the prophets' rebuke, consolation, and hope for restoration, Scripture's account is rehearsed in rabbinic Judaism. All is in proportion and balance.

How did the rabbinic sages read forward from Scripture?

Rabbinic Judaism builds its structure out of a reading of the written Torah. The rabbinic sages read from the written Torah forward to the oral Torah. That is not only attested by the superficial character of proof texting, but by the profound congruence of the theology of rabbinic Judaism with the course of the Scriptural exposition. Any outline of Scripture's account begins with creation and tells about the passage from Eden via Sinai and Jerusalem to Babylon—and back. It speaks of the patriarchal founders of Israel, the Exodus, Sinai, the Torah, covenants, Israel, the people of God, the priesthood and the tabernacle, the possesion of the Land, exile and restoration. True, sages proportion matters within their own logic, laying heaviest emphasis upon perfection, imperfection, and restoration of perfection to creation, focusing upon Israel, God's stake in humanity.

The theological structure and system appeal to the perfection of creation and account for imperfection by reference to the fall of man into sin by reason of arrogant rebellion and into death in consequence. They tell the story of the formation of holy Israel as God's party in humanity, signified by access to knowledge of God through God's self-manifestation in the Torah. They then present the exile of Israel from and to the Land of Israel as the counterpart to the exile of Adam from

Eden and the return of Israel to the Land. Therefore main beams of Scripture's account of matters define the structure of rabbinic Judaism's theology. The generative tensions of the Hebrew Scripture's narrative empower the dynamics of that theology.

A few obvious facts suffice. Take the principal propositions of Scripture read in sequence and systematically, meaning, as exemplary, from Genesis through Kings. Consider the story of the exile from Eden and the counterpart exile of Israel from the Land. The rabbinic sages did not invent that paradigm. Scripture's framers did. Translate into propositional form the prophetic messages of admonition, rebuke, and consolation, the promise that as punishment follows sin, so consolation will come in consequence of repentance. The rabbinic sages did not fabricate those categories and make up the rules that govern the sequence of events. The prophets said them all. They only recapitulated the prophetic propositions with little variation except in formulation. All the sages did was to interpret within the received paradigm the exemplary events of their own day, the destruction of Jerusalem and Israel's subjugation in particular. Identify as the dynamics of human history the engagement of God with man, especially through Israel, and what do you have, if not the heart of sages' doctrine of the origins and destiny of man? Review what Scripture intimates about the meaning and end of time, and how much do you miss of sages' eschatology of restoration? Details, amplifications, clarifications, an unsuccessful effort at systematization—these do not obscure the basic confluence of sages' and Scripture's account of last things.

How did Scripture's power exert itself through proof texts?

I do not have to stress the form that sages impart to their propositions, nearly everything they say being joined to a verse of Scripture. That is not a formality. Constant citations of scriptural texts cited as authority serve merely to signal the presence of a profound identity of viewpoint. The cited verses are not solely pretexts or formal proof texts. The rabbinic sages cite and interpret verses of Scripture to show where and how the written Torah guides the oral one, supplying the specificities of the process of recapitulation. And what sages say about those verses originates not in the small details of those verses but in the large theological structure and system that sages framed.

In most of the Midrash-compilations of rabbinic Judaism it is the simple fact that sages read from the whole to the parts, from the written part of the Torah outward to the oral part. That explains why nothing arbitrary or merely occasional characterized sages reading of Scripture. They produced a theology, formed whole in response to the whole. They did not think they imputed to Scripture meanings not actually there, but claimed to paraphrase what Scripture said in so many words.

The rabbinic sages read Scripture as a letter written that morning to them in particular about the world they encountered. That is because for them the past was forever integral to the present. So they looked into the written part of the Torah to construct the picture of reality that is explained by worldview set forth in the oral part of the Torah. They found their questions in Scripture; they identified the answers to those questions in Scripture; and they then organized and interpreted the contemporary situation of holy Israel in light of those questions and answers.

That explains why we may justifiably say that on every page of the writings of rabbinic Judaism we encounter the sages' response to the heritage of ancient Israel's Scripture. There they met God, there they found God's plan for the world of perfect justice, the flawless, eternal world in stasis. There in detail they learned what became of that teaching in ancient times and in their own day. The result is spread out in the sages' account of the Torah revealed by God to Moses at Sinai and handed on in tradition through the ages. That account was found self-evidently true by many generations of Israelites, down to the present moment.

45. THE RELATIONSHIP BETWEEN RABBINIC JUDAISM AND CHRISTIANITY OVER TIME

When and how did rabbinic Judaism recognize Christianity as a separate religion?

At issue is the point at which, as a religious system and structure, rabbinic Judaism framed a theory of the competition. Rabbinic Judaism has always refrained from setting forth an *explicit* response: a Judaic theology of Christianity. In fact the rabbinic response to the Christian challenge was in three phases.

In the first, from the beginning to the advent of the Christian empire in the fourth century, Christianity was acknowledged, but conversations with Christians on theological matters was strenuously avoided.

In the second, from the fourth century to the Middle Ages (cf. Section 42), it was answered implicitly, but with theological authenticity.

And in the third phase, from the Middle Ages onward, rabbinic sages explicitly replied to the truth-claims of Christian competition. They rejected those claims when forced by church and state to confront them in formal disputations.

How was Christianity responded to in the first three centuries?

The Tosefta (ca. 300 C.E.) in the context of first century rabbinic sages' teachings and conduct sets forth laws concerning conduct with *minim.* Who are they in the setting of the story at hand? Since they are differentiated from pagans and recognized as people who know the Torah and deny it, dismissed as renegades, traitors to God, they are likely to be Jews who have followed Jesus. This is made certain in the present setting by the reference to him in so many words.

> People are not to sell anything to them {*minim*} or buy anything from them.
>
> And they do not take wives from them or give children in marriage to them.
>
> And they do not teach their sons a craft.
>
> And they do not seek assistance from them, either financial assistance or medical assistance.

Tosefta *Hullin* 2:21

Now Jesus enters the narrative. Jacob of Kefar Sama, a follower of his, healed someone of a snakebite by using his name:

> R. Eleazar b. Damah was bitten by a snake.
>
> And Jacob of Kefar Sama came to heal him in the name of Jesus son of Pantera.
>
> And R. Ishmael did not allow him [to accept the healing].
>
> They said to him, "You are not permitted [to accept healing from him], Ben Dama."
>
> He said to him, "I shall bring you proof that he may heal me."
>
> But he did not have time to bring the [promised] proof before he dropped dead.
>
> Said R. Ishmael, "Happy are you, Ben Dama. For you have expired in peace, but you did not break down the hedge erected by sages.
>
> "For whoever breaks down the hedge erected by sages eventually suffers punishment, as it is said, *He who breaks down a hedge is bitten by a snake* [Qoh. 10:8]."

Tosefta *Hullin* 2:22–23

Healing in the name of Jesus was acknowledged and prohibited. It represented competing access to supernatural power. In the next unit, Jesus's teaching is acknowledged as Torah and condemned. The context is an early persecution of Christians by the Romans, who considered Judaism, but not Christianity, to be a legitimate religion. A noted rabbi was arrested on suspicion of Christianity:

The story is told: R. Eliezer was arrested on account of *minut*. They brought him to court for judgment.

That *hegemon* {presiding judge} said to him, "Should an elder of your standing get involved in such things?"

He said to him, "The Judge is reliable in my view" [I rely upon the Judge].

That *hegemon* supposed that he referred only to him, but he referred only to his Father in heaven.

He [the *hegemon*] said to him, "Since you have deemed me reliable for yourself, so thus I have ruled: Is it possible that these grey hairs should err in such matters? [*Obviously not, therefore:*] [you are] *Dimissus* [pardoned]. Lo, you are free of liability."

And when he left court, he was distressed to have been arrested on account of matters of *minut*.

His disciples came to comfort him, but he did not accept their words of comfort.

R. 'Aqiba came and said to him, "Rabbi, May I say something to you so that you will not be distressed?"

He said to him, "Go ahead."

He said to him, "Perhaps someone of the *minim* told you something of *minut* which pleased you."

He said to him, "By Heaven! You remind me. Once I was strolling in the camp of Sepphoris. I bumped into Jacob of Kefar Sikhnin, and he told me a teaching of *minut* in the name of Jesus ben Pantiri, and it pleased me.

"So I was arrested on account of matters of *minut*, for I transgressed the teachings of Torah: *Keep your way far from her and do not go near the door of her house* (Prov. 5:8)."

For R. Eliezer did teach, "One should always flee from what is disreputable and from whatever appears to be disreputable."

Tosefta *Hullin* 2:24B–L

The story told about Eliezer b. Hyrcanus is important for our inquiry, because it defines the policy of rabbinic Judaism toward Jesus: prohibition of a competing reading of the Torah. But the kind of comprehensive, doctrinal response, dealing with issues of history, Messiah, and Torah in a systematic way, had to await the advent of the Christian empire in the fourth century.

Why did the rabbinic response of the fourth century to the advent of the Christian empire continue to serve down to modern times?

By the turn of the fifth century the state was firmly Christian and its successors in Europe would remain so for nearly fifteen hundred years. The sages' framing of a Judaic system attained the status of the norm. So far as Christianity in all of its European forms raised challenges to Judaism in its one, now normative form, answers found in the fourth century retained for Jews the standing of self-evident truth. The systematic doctrinal response to the Christian challenge served.

On the side of Judaism, Christianity demanded no articulated response, its truth-claims having been disposed of through the categorical reformation of the fourth century (cf. Section 42).

When did rabbinic Judaism explicitly articulate a response to Christianity as a separate religion?

Rabbinic Judaism never explicitly articulated a response to Christianity as a separate religion, because Judaism does not regard Christianity as the valid medium of the Torah at Sinai: only Judaism is. In the fourth century sages of Judaism could pretend to ignore the challenge of Christianity, while at the same time systematically countering that challenge. Christian theologians forthrightly could enter the encounter with Judaism as with an equal. In the twelfth, thirteenth, and fourteenth centuries circumstances in no way afforded such an encounter. Judaism recognized Christianity as a separate religion, ordinarily, but not always, when Christianity could force the issue and impose the requirement of debate. In Northern France Jews were prepared to challenge Christians to debate even when not coerced.

In the twenty-first century, in conditions of freedom, only a minority of the heirs of rabbinic Judaism have accepted the notion that the truth claims of Judaism and Christianity are not mutually exclusive in any important way. Many believing Jews regard the acceptance of this problematic proposal as indicating a lack of commitment to the theology of the Torah.

46. MODERN DIVISIONS WITHIN JUDAISM

What is the connection between rabbinic Judaism and modern Judaism(s)?

In modern times, from the nineteenth century forward, rabbinic Judaism, in both its classical form and contemporary revision, has continued to thrive. Its authoritative writings, from the Mishnah through the Bavli and beyond into medieval and modern times, retain their canonical standing in vast communities of the faithful. Religious leaders who are called rabbis and who qualify through knowledge of the Torah and its traditions continue to study and teach. The received liturgy sets the program of divine worship. The way of life and worldview embodied in rabbinic Judaism come to realization in vast communities of Judaism.

But these communities are not uniform. Rabbinic Judaism in its classical statement has also produced diverse continuator-systems. The received system had not accommodated Israelites who had other loyalties, lived out other lives, besides the life of holy Israel. To give a single concrete example: the continuator-systems explained why an Israelite in the supernatural community of Israel, in addition to studying the Torah, could and should acquire a secular education as well, even at the cost of time better spent in Torah-learning. Large communities of Judaism seek to integrate themselves into the culture and politics of the countries where they live. But all Judaisms of modern times see themselves in a direct and continuous relationship with the Torah embodied in Scripture and oral tradition that defines rabbinic Judaism.

What emerged from rabbinic Judaism in the nineteenth-century West and flourished in the twentieth century were, first, Reform Judaism, then, in response to Reform, an integrationist ("modern" or "Western") Orthodox Judaism, and finally, a mediating in-between called in Europe "Positive Historical Judaism," in the USA Conservative Judaism, and in Britain and today's State of Israel Mesorti ("traditional") Judaism. All three provide space for Israelites to participate in other stories besides the Israelite one, and that provision represented a considerable innovation, whether called Reform or Orthodox or Conservative.

What is Reform Judaism?

Reform Judaism insisted that change in response to new challenges represented a valid continuation of that religion's long-term capacity to evolve. Reform Judaism denied that any version of the Torah enjoyed eternal validity. It affirmed that Jews should adopt the politics and culture of the countries where they lived, preserving differences of only a religious character, narrowly construed. How, exactly, did Reform Judaism define itself?

For Reform Judaism in the nineteenth century the full and authoritative statement of the system came to expression in an assembly in Pittsburgh in 1885 of Reform rabbis.

> We recognize in the Mosaic legislation a system of training the Jewish people for its mission during its national life in Palestine, and today we accept as binding only its moral laws and maintain only such ceremonies as elevate and sanctify our lives, but reject all such as are not adapted to the views and habits of modern civilization. . . . We hold that all such Mosaic and rabbinical laws as regular diet, priestly purity, and dress originated in ages and under the influence of ideas entirely foreign to our present mental and spiritual state . . . Their observance in our days is apt rather to obstruct than to further modern spiritual elevation . . . We recognize in the modern era of universal culture of heart and intellect the approaching of the realization of Israel's great messianic hope for the establishment of the kingdom of truth, justice, and peace among all men. We consider ourselves no longer a nation but a religious community and therefore expect neither a return to Palestine nor a sacrificial worship under the sons of Aaron nor the restoration of any of the laws concerning the Jewish state . . .

Reform Judaism formed a Judaic system that confronted immense political change and presented a worldview and way of life to an Israel defined in those categories opened up by the change at hand.

What justified change as valid reform was the theory of the incremental history of a single, linear Judaism, of which change was characteristic and Reform Judaism the necessary outcome. The ones who made changes to begin with rested their case on an appeal to the authoritative texts of rabbinic Judaism. Change is legitimate, and these changes in particular wholly consonant with the law, or the tradition, or the inner dynamics of the faith, or the dictates of history, or whatever out of the past worked that day. We cannot find surprising, therefore, the theory that Reform Judaism stood in a direct line with the prior history of Judaism. Judaism is one. Judaism has a single, coherent, unitary history, and that history was always leading to its present outcome: Reform Judaism.

What is Orthodox Judaism?

Many people reasonably identify all "traditional" or "observant" Judaisms with a single, uniform Orthodox Judaism, and they furthermore take for granted that all Judaisms that keep the Torah as received at Sinai are pretty much the same. But a wide variety of Orthodox Judaisms affirm the Torah, oral and written, and abide by its laws, as interpreted by their masters—who differ from one another on many important points. We may call all such Judaic systems all together "the Torah-camp," meaning, the Judaic systems that concur on basic doctrinal matters concerning the origin and authority of the Torah, oral and written: verbatim God's word to our rabbi, Moses, at Sinai. The components of the Torah-camp are readily differentiated, as is now clear, into those that affirm Israel's self-segregation from the nations, and those that in some ways validate Israel's integration, though not assimilation, among the nations.

Integrationist Orthodox Judaism both affirms the divine revelation and eternal authority of the Torah, oral and written, and favors the integration of the Jews ("holy Israel") into the national life of the countries of their birth. Self-segregationist (and also Orthodox) Judaisms, and they are many and diverse among themselves, affirm the Torah but in every possible way segregate the holy Israel from other people in the countries where they live, including the state of Israel. Indicators such as clothing, language, place of residence, use of leisure time, economic calling, and above all, the legitimacy of secular education, differentiate integrationist from segregationist Judaisms.

How shall we identify integrationist Orthodoxy? When Jews who kept the law of the Torah, for example, as it dictated food choices and the Sabbath observance, sent their children to secular schools, in addition to, or instead of, solely Jewish ones, or when, in Jewish schools, they included in the curriculum subjects outside of the sciences of the Torah, they crossed the boundary that distinguished self-segregation

from integration. The notion that science or German or Latin or philosophy deserved serious study, while not alien to important exemplars of
the received system of rabbinic Judaism, in the nineteenth century
struck as wrong those for whom the received system remained self-
evidently right.

What is Conservative Judaism?

A Judaic religious system with roots in the German Judaic response to the development of Reform, then Orthodox Judaism, on the
one side, and the immigrant response to the conditions of American life
in the twentieth century, on the other, Conservative Judaism seeks a centrist position on the issues of tradition and change. The Historical
School, a group of a nineteenth century German scholars, and Conservative Judaism, a twentieth century Judaism in America, took the
middle position, each in its own context. They form a single community
of Judaism, because they share a single viewpoint. The Historical School
began among German Jewish theologians who advocated change but
found Reform extreme. They parted company with Reform on some
specific issues of practice and doctrine, observance of the dietary laws
and belief in the coming of the Messiah for example. But they also found
Orthodoxy immobile. Conservative Judaism in America in the twentieth
century carried forward this same centrist position. The Historical School
shaped the worldview, and Conservative Judaism later on brought that
view into full realization as a way of life characteristic of a large group of
Jews, nearly half of all American Jews by the middle of the twentieth
century.

The Historical School in Germany and Conservative Judaism in
America affirmed a far broader part of the received way of life than Reform, while rejecting a much larger part of the worldview of rabbinic Judaism than did Orthodoxy. The Reformers had held that change was
permissible and claimed that historical scholarship would show what
change was acceptable and what was not. But the proponents of the Historical School differed in matters of detail. The emphasis on historical
research in settling theological debates explains the name of the group.
Arguing that its positions represent matters of historical fact rather than
theological conviction, Conservative Judaism maintained that "positive
historical scholarship" will prove capable, on the basis of historical facts,
of purifying and clarifying the faith, joined to far stricter observance of
the law than the Reformers required. Rabbis of this same centrist per-

suasion organized the Jewish Theological Seminary of America in 1886–1887, and from that rabbinical school the Conservative Movement developed.

How do Reform, Orthodox, and Conservative Judaisms continue rabbinic Judaism?

Reform, integrationist Orthodox, and Conservative Judaisms all maintain that they have continued the received system of rabbinic Judaism—its symbols and stories, its laws and theological system—far more than they diverged from it. All three Judaisms enjoyed ample justification for the insistence, each in its way, that it carried forward the entire history of Judaism and took the necessary step beyond where matters had rested prior to its own formation. Reform in this regard found itself subjected to vigorous criticism, but in saying that "things have changed in the past, and we can change them too," Reform established its primary position. It too pointed to precedent, and took implicitly conceded the power of the received system to stand in judgment. All the more so did the integrationist Orthodox and Conservative theologians continue rabbinic Judaism.

What of the twentieth century and the Holocaust? The politics of exterminationist anti-Semitism would challenge the received Torah. The response of Jews who practiced Judaism yielded a massive reaffirmation of the rabbinic Judaism—whether in the received or revised form—that had sustained them for two thousand years. No Judaism comes close to competing in intellectual power and popular success with rabbinic Judaism and its continuators, and none is likely to for generations to come.

INDEX OF SUBJECTS

INDEX OF ANCIENT SOURCES